Accounting Information Systems

Thinking, Development, and Evaluation

Version 1.0

Robyn L. Raschke and John A. Schatzel

Accounting Information Systems: Thinking, Development, and Evaluation
Version 1.0

Robyn L. Raschke and John A. Schatzel

Published by:

FlatWorld
292 Newbury Street
Suite #282
Boston, MA 02115-2832

Gen: 202112151640

Brief Contents

Contents

About the Author

Robyn L. Raschke (PhD Arizona State University, CPA) is Professor and the Kenneth and Tracy Knauss Endowed Chair in Accounting in the Lee Business School at University of Nevada, Las Vegas. She is a long-term participant in the American Accounting Association's (AAA) Strategic and Emerging Technologies Section, most recently serving as Section President in 2020. From 2017–2019, Robyn also served on the AAA Finance Committee (Executive Committee).

Prior to receiving her PhD, Robyn spent over 15 years working in San Francisco and the Silicon Valley. Her business experiences include vice president/controller for several high-tech companies and corporate consulting. She has received a number of awards and honors, including most recently the Lee Business School Online Teaching Fellow (2019–2020); The UNLV Teaching Academy Fellow (2018–2019); Best Paper Award, Global Innovation and Knowledge Academy (2017); and AAA Strategic and Emerging Technologies Section Service Award (2016). Robyn is Associate Editor, *International Journal of Accounting Information Systems* and is on the editorial boards of *Journal of Information Systems*, *Journal of Business Research*, *Journal of Marketing Analytics*, and *Journal of Accounting Education* among others. Robyn is a frequent conference presenter, and her research interests focus on how information presentation impacts decision making as well as organizational and process performance measurement. Her academic work is published in *International Journal of Accounting Information Systems*, *Journal of Information Systems*, *Information and Management*, *Accounting, Organizations, and Society*, and *Journal of Business Research*.

Acknowledgments

Creating a textbook requires much work and dedication from many people who provided support and feedback along the way. I wish to express my appreciation to FlatWorld, specifically Sean Wakely who provided encouragement and advice throughout the process and KB Mello who kept me on track with production. In addition, I am grateful to the copyeditor, Sheryl Nelson as well as the following faculty who provided their time in reviewing the chapters and offered me helpful feedback.

- Daniel J. Gibbons, Accounting Professor, Waubonsee Community College
- Vicki Jobst, DBA, CPA, Benedictine University
- Michael J Klatchak, Adjunct Professor, Dept of Business and Economics
- Lois S. Mahoney, Eastern Michigan University
- Dr. Christine H. Stinson, Ferrum College

I would also like to thank the family of my coauthor, John Schatzel, who trusted me to share my vision and incorporate it with John's. While we did not know each other professionally, I feel that we had a shared vision and passion in teaching Accounting Information Systems and providing the best content possible for our students. Finally, I'd like to thank my life partner, Megan Costello for her love, support, and encouragement, I would not have made it without her by my side throughout the entire process clearing all obstacles to ensure success—this book is dedicated to you!

Preface

Accounting Information Systems: Thinking, Development, and Evaluation Version 1.0 is designed for the first course in introduction to accounting information systems (AIS). It is usually taught at the undergraduate level, but it can sometimes be found at the MBA-level.

Overview

This book's key goal is to provide students with a basic understanding of AIS terminology and topics in an approachable way. As a result, the writing style is intentionally crafted to be easy to understand for students who are new to accounting information and related decision-making responsibilities. Further, there is a strong focus throughout on emerging accounting technologies such as distributive ledgers including blockchain, smart contracts, robotic process automation, machine learning, and artificial intelligence (AI). Including these topics in more meaningful ways exposes students to new technologies' impacts on accounting. Further, such coverage encourages them to develop an inquisitive and flexible mindset based on the premise that an AIS is not static. As a result, students learn an AIS must be continuously assessed and re-evaluated in order to keep pace with constant organizational change, the introduction of new technologies, and an ever-evolving regulatory environment. Finally, the narrative is consistently organized around three key perspectives: the user, design, and control. These three organizing themes support and guide the learner's journey through understanding how accountants use information to make decisions, how an AIS works, and how to recognize and minimize the threats to an AIS.

Key Themes

The three organizing themes of the user, design, and control are based on the authors' common experiences teaching AIS to thousands of students, as well as one author's (Raschke's) many years spent using and developing AIS installations in business environments. The organizing themes were extensively class-tested by the authors, and they were finely honed to best convey foundational knowledge in AIS terminology and core topics. Seasoned instructors will likely recognize and certainly appreciate that organizing the book around these three key themes provides a natural progression of learning AIS topics as well.

The below themes provide a logical structure to the narrative. However, because this book is intended to be a basic introduction to AIS, the authors also included specific learning features to further enhance learning and encourage retention.

The User Perspective

The first major theme to appear in the book is the user perspective. These early chapters impress upon students why learning about AIS is core to how accounting is done today and how the user perspective is fundamental to subsequent understanding of AIS design and control. These initial chapters establish the strategy of using a real-life case to introduce core topics such as systems basics, how the components of an AIS vary, and how information flows (Chapter 1). This first part also includes high-interest topics on data analytics (Chapter 3), introduction of emerging technologies in accounting, and establishes the critical insight that an AIS is more than a tool for generating financial statements.

The Designer Perspective

The second major theme is the design perspective. Core AIS topics include documenting an AIS (Chapter 5), AIS strategic planning and development (Chapter 6), database design including REA modeling (Chapter 7), and ERP implementation (Chapter 8).

The Control Perspective

The third major theme is the control perspective. Core AIS topics include the internal control environment (Chapter 9), IT controls (Chapter 10), transaction cycle controls such as expenditure cycle (Chapter 11), revenue cycle (Chapter 12), conversion cycle (Chapter 13), as well as fixed assets, financing and payroll cycles (Chapter 14), and financial reporting controls (Chapter 15).

Learning Features

Each chapter contains the following learning features to help students get the most out of the content presented and remember it long after the course has ended.

- "Learning Objectives" at the beginning of every main section preview the material to come
- Embedded links with URL addresses to bring concepts to life in the book using brief and engaging videos (fewer than five minutes)
- "Key Takeaways" at the end of every chapter mirror the "Learning Objectives" to summarize the key points of the preceding chapter
- References to key accounting information systems and management research cited in the text
- "End-of-Chapter Exercises" reflect a variety of question types and include extended scenarios or cases accompanied by questions for analysis. Answers to multiple-choice questions and suggested answer guidelines for case analysis are available in the accompanying instructor's manual
- Use of real-world scenarios and applications place associated discussions and documents into real-world contexts are found in the exercises and discussions at the end of the chapter.

Supplements

Teaching AIS can be daunting—especially keeping up with new topics and terminology. Robyn Raschke, the author who primarily prepared the supplements, kept this thought firmly in mind as she wrote them.

Instructor Manual

The instructor's manual (IM) will help new as well as seasoned instructors. It provides teaching tips and resources the authors successfully used in their own courses. The IM provides an overview of the chapter, recommended teaching tips that highlight ways to engage students in the classroom or how to address difficult topics that students encounter. In addition, the IM includes recommended exercises for the classroom to engage the students and suggested answer guidelines for discussions questions/case analysis that accompany case studies in the book. Each chapter includes discussion questions, multiple choice questions, exercises, and reflective assignments.

PowerPoint Slides

PowerPoint slides cover learning objectives and key concepts of each chapter in a concise manner. Many slides are created to enhance engagement with students during the lecture. Instructors may use the slides to support their lecture or customize them as needed.

Online Quizzes

Carefully written quiz questions (true/false and multiple choice) allow the student to test their comprehension.

FlatWorld Homework

FlatWorld Homework is an easy-to-use interface that includes multiple choice, fill-in-the-blank, matching, and other question types that are all auto-gradable. Students who complete these questions with success should see their performance transfer to examinations that are given using the Test Item File questions provided to adopters.

Test Item File

Each comprehensive Test Item File (TIF) includes at least fifty questions per chapter made up of multiple-choice, fill-in-the-blank, short answer, and essay questions. Each of the thirty multiple choice questions have four possible answers and each is rated for difficulty and references the key sections of each chapter. Answers are provided for each short answer and essay question. The items have been written specifically to reinforce the major chapter topics and learning objectives.

A Note from Robyn Raschke

The authors wrote *Accounting Information Systems: Thinking, Development, and Evaluation* v1.0 because AIS textbooks that once captured well the crucial role AIS plays in the business firm have become increasingly outdated. Faculty members who want their students to learn from an AIS textbook that not only covers traditional AIS topics but also exposes their students to many emerging accounting technologies in detail will be interested to assign this book.

I would like to express a special word of thanks to John Schatzel and his family. While I never met John, I was honored to restructure, revise, and expand the initial draft of this manuscript for publication following John's passing. Many of John's most important ideas and teaching strategies are reflected in this published version and will positively influence students' learning for many years to come.

Please contact me if you'd like more information or additional perspectives on teaching with this book. In particular, I am always trying to improve the material it contains and keep it up to date. I can be reached at robyn.raschke@unlv.edu. I welcome all feedback from faculty and students.

PART 1

The User Perspective

CHAPTER 1
System Basics

The world of accounting is rapidly changing. Advances in computer and data communication technologies and new laws regulating their effectiveness are driving much of this change. These technology changes also affect accounting. View the following video from the AICPA on the effect of technology and why accounting is an exciting field for today's students.

How Is Your Organization Using Technology?

This is a video on how technology is changing accounting.

View in the online reader

Before you can understand the relevance of these new technologies and control issues, we need to understand fundamental questions underlying effective accounting systems:

- What is a system problem, and how do you know if you have one?
- What is an effective accounting system? How are such systems developed?
- How does an organization make sure that these systems continue to work effectively?

These are some of the important questions addressed in this chapter and throughout Part 1 of this book as we examine accounting information systems from a user perspective. To get started, we will begin with a business case that illustrates some real-world system problems. Then, we will examine a number of relevant questions and system issues raised by the problems in the case. Then, using a problem-based learning approach, we will explore the knowledge necessary to address these problems.

To get started, we will begin with a business case that illustrates some real-world system problems. Then, we will examine a number of relevant questions and system issues raised by the problems in the case. Then, using a problem-based learning approach, we will explore the knowledge necessary to address these problems.

1.1 Introductory Case—Joe's Ristoranté

Learning Objectives

At the end of this section, students should be able to:

1. Describe a basic system and identify what determines a system problem and how one can be resolved.
2. Describe an accounting information system.
3. Describe the four related components of an AIS.

Joe is a restaurant owner, and Jennifer is Joe's certified public accountant. A recent conversation between Joe and Jennifer went as follows:

"As you know, Jennifer, after I acquired the restaurant, sales and profits have turned around," Joe began. "Our managers have worked hard, and the one who replaced Leonardo has made a big difference. Our 'all you can eat' buffets have become a great success. They enabled us to reduce our overhead as well as let our customers see the food they might want to eat."

Joe explained, "The previous owners were deep in debt and losing $3,000 a month. The first year, I borrowed $100,000 to renovate the place and almost broke even. We had an unfortunate incident, however, when we discovered that Leonardo was letting his friends eat for free. But after he was let go, it was no longer a major concern."

"The prior owners also had a strictly cash business and didn't realize that they were in financial trouble until it was too late," Joe elaborated. "Although we changed a few things, I still do not know how you were able to prepare our first profit and loss statement. You were also a great help in preparing the footnotes our lenders were interested in and required."

Joe sighed and continued, "Nevertheless, all these issues lead up to some very important questions. So far, you have prepared our tax returns and the financial statements for the bank. However, we badly need a new accounting system to keep us up to date with what is happening in our business on a timelier basis. I prepare the checks and take the cash deposits to the bank, but I cannot get an accurate read on the restaurant's performance until the end of the year. We have a large inventory of different types of food and drinks. This makes it difficult for us to know what to purchase and when. In addition, we always have a large number of bills outstanding. I also would like to find an easier way of handling my takeout orders. My customers keep telling me that there is a simpler and more streamlined way of using their cellphones for takeout order and payment. I know that I could ask you for monthly or quarterly statements, but that still would not solve my problem. I need to be able to see how we are doing on a daily basis."

"Perhaps, installing a computer in the office, so my staff could enter the day's receipts from the cash register, would help us begin moving in the right direction. The computer might even help you because I could give you more than just an old shoebox full of check stubs and bank deposit slips."

Jennifer smiled. "Joe, I think you hit the nail on the head," she said. "CPA firms like mine are spending an increasing amount of their time helping clients develop new or modified accounting systems. I think we could connect your cash registers to a computer system. Then, your daily sales data would be entered automatically into a general ledger. This would save you the job of keying in the data and reduce mistakes. We can also explore more efficient ways for your customers who want to do takeout orders too with a new system. I am sure that we can come up with a system that will meet your needs."

Does Joe understand that he may have some accounting information system problems?

Based on Joe's comments regarding the need for inventory tracking and the problem he believes exists with the timeliness of his internal reporting, it appears so. He also mentions the need to keep up with customer demand and find a more efficient way for customers to order and pay for take-out orders.

What accounting information will be needed?

While the information needed generally varies across organizations, accounting information needs can be categorized in terms of operations, decision-making, and reporting:

- To operate in an effective and efficient manner, such as collecting and safeguarding cash receipts, paying vendors, and tracking the inventory
- To make sound decisions, such as when to order inventory, where to set prices, and whether to discontinue a product or not.
- To file necessary reports in an accurate and timely manner, such as tax returns and financial statements

So, what will be required to obtain this information?

Joe will need methods for collecting and storing the data and preparing reports.

How should Joe decide what to do?

Joe needs to consider his information needs and the trade-off of costs and benefits to acquire it.

Before we can answer all of the above questions, we need to learn some fundamentals of systems in general and specifics of an accounting information system.

What Is a System?

When talking about systems, the first thing that some people think of is a computer. Nevertheless, systems are much broader than that. According to general systems theory (meaning it applies to all systems), a **system** is a framework of interacting parts that work together to achieve an objective. Therefore, the system is effective if it achieves the objective.

system
A framework of interacting parts that work together to achieve an objective.

To illustrate a system in general, we must describe all three aspects of a simple system. Simple systems are those that have relatively few parts and interactions between them. A good example of a simple system would be a *bicycle*. In this instance, the objective would be to transport someone from point A to point B. The parts would include the frame, wheels, a seat, handlebars, pedals, chain, and brakes. Finally, the working together would be described as pedals being pushed by a user to create motion from the chain to the tires while using the handlebars to guide the bike to the destination and the brakes ensuring that the system does not get out of control.

In contrast, complex systems are those that have many parts or interactions and are too difficult to identify or explain. Complex systems do not make good examples for illustrating the definition. Some examples of complex systems include the *immune system, the Federal Reserve*, and real-world *accounting systems*. While each is too complicated to illustrate here, it is important to note that all of them have the three common aspects of general systems explained previously: (1) an objective, (2) the parts, and (3) their interactions (i.e., working together).

What Is a System Problem?

system problem

When the system objective is not being met.

A **system problem** is when the system objective is not being met. System problems may be caused when parts are missing, parts are not functioning properly or are not working together, or the objective is unclear or in dispute.

For example, if the bicycle tire is flat, it makes it inefficient and difficult to ride the bicycle from point A to point B, meaning there is a system problem. The system is not achieving the objective. In accounting, failure to pay bills on time, to make sound financial decisions, or to provide reliable financial reports to users are all examples of failures to meet system objectives. This assumes that the accounting system objectives include providing information to operate effectively and efficiently, make sound decisions, and produce reports that are accurate and timely.

The need to clearly identify the system objective in order to explain why there is a system problem is an important task for accountants. For example, if a company's payroll checks are delivered late, is it because the company did not have enough people to process payroll or because they had the wrong people? Alternatively, is it because their technology broke down unexpectedly (or something else)? What if a company reports a profit and then one month later declares bankruptcy? Was something in the accounting system missing, was someone being dishonest, or was it due to circumstances beyond their control? It is also important to understand that missing parts may not create a system problem if the parts are properly backed up.

As you can see, identifying and eliminating system problems can take a great deal of critical thinking. Therefore, developing a critical perspective when thinking about accounting systems is most important. Critical thinking for our purposes is a thought process that analyzes and evaluates evidence gathered from reliable sources in order to reach an informed judgment. It is needed to apply the knowledge acquired from this textbook and related software. It can be learned through a Socratic process of questioning your own thinking and by engaging in activities that challenge you to express your opinion based on sound reasoning.

What Is an Accounting Information System?

accounting information system (AIS)

A system that involves a framework of people, processes, technologies, and controls that work together to provide information needed to operate effectively and efficiently, make sound decisions, and file necessary reports accurately and on a timely basis.

Now that we have learned what systems are in general, let's apply this knowledge to accounting. An **accounting information system (AIS)** is simply a more specific type of system that involves a framework of people, processes, technologies, and controls that work together to provide information needed to operate effectively and efficiently, make sound decisions, and file necessary reports accurately and on a timely basis. Notice how we simply made the general system parts and objective more specific to accounting.

We can also apply the theory of system problems to accounting. For example, errors (unintentional mistakes) and irregularities (deliberate misstatements) are two of the more common system problems that accountants have to contend with in organizations. These types of problems can be very serious because they can interfere with decision-making, prevent an entity from filing accurate reports, and even prevent an entity from operating.

What Are the Components of an AIS?

Notice again that accounting systems may be viewed broadly as having a framework of four components or parts: (1) people, (2) processes, (3) technologies, and (4) controls, as depicted in Figure 1.1.

FIGURE 1.1 The Components of an AIS

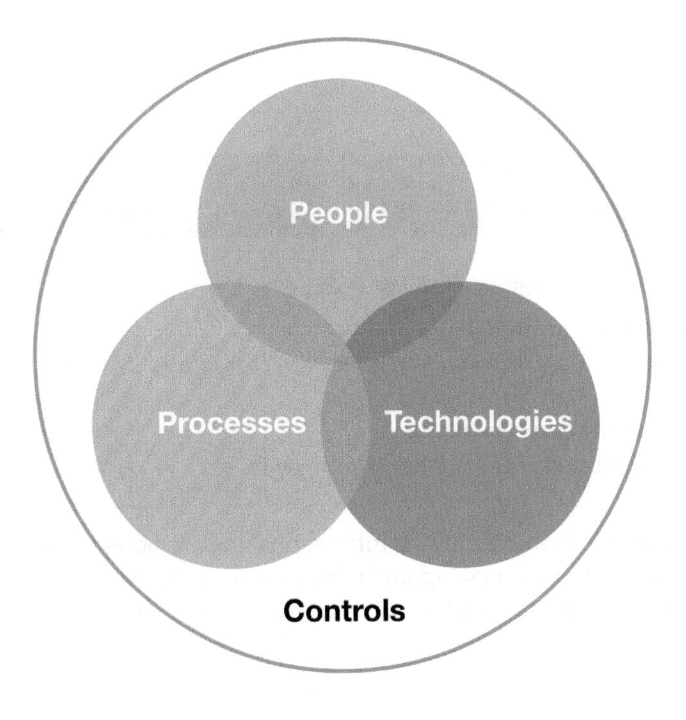

People are the human beings who perform tasks (processes) involved in collecting, processing, tracking, and reporting accounting information. These people include data entry clerks, bookkeepers, inventory clerks, and controllers as opposed to those who use the information such as executive managers. Users benefit from the system, but they are not part of it.

Processes are the tasks that people perform to get things done in an organization. These processes include transactions such as purchasing inventory, paying vendors, billing customers, paying employees, etc.

Technologies are the things (manual or electronic) used to produce accounting information. Technology includes software and hardware to produce purchase orders, journals, ledgers, income statements, checks, invoices, etc.

Controls are used to reduce the likelihood that something will go wrong. Examples include reconciling the bank accounts in a timely manner, using a cash register to protect from theft of cash, using passwords to keep unauthorized people from accessing private information, requiring a second signature on large checks, obtaining a credit check before goods are shipped, and locking the warehouse doors to prevent unauthorized people from accessing inventory. As seen in Figure 1.1, controls are important to have for people, processes, and technology!

people

Human beings who perform tasks involved in collecting, processing, tracking, and reporting accounting information.

processes

The tasks that people perform to get things done in an organization.

technologies

The things (manual or electronic) used to produce accounting information.

controls

Procedures used to reduce the likelihood that something will go wrong.

Are these the components of all systems?

No, other systems will likely have a different set of components that are applicable only to accounting.

Try locating the four components of accounting systems in Joe's Ristoranté. One of the things you should note is a lack of technology and controls in Joe's Ristoranté. Most of Joe's Ristoranté is a manual system. Even though Joe's Ristoranté is not sophisticated and is a manual accounting system, it still is considered an AIS.

1.2 The Difference Between Data and Information

Learning Objectives

At the end of this section, students should be able to:

1. Describe the difference between data and information.
2. Explain the different data types and how they are categorized from an organizational perspective.
3. Explain what makes information useful.
4. Describe who needs and uses accounting information.

data

Raw unorganized facts.

As used in this chapter, the term "accounting information" means monetary values and ratios that are useful for operations, decision-making, and filing necessary reports. This is in contrast to **data**, which represent raw unorganized facts that need to be processed. For example, the following list is considered data:

1023

January 18

Strickland's Fruit and Vegetables

100 pounds

$80.97

As seen in this list, we have data, but they are not organized in a meaningful way. Data do not become information until they are organized to provide meaning. In the previous example, if we knew that the data were in the context of a vendor invoice, such as that in Figure 1.2, from Strickland's Fruit and Vegetables for 100 pounds of tomatoes for an invoice total of $80.97, then this is meaningful information for Joe's Ristoranté.

FIGURE 1.2 Example of Information

1023

Sales Invoice

Strickland's Fruit & Vegetables
88 Happy Valley Road
Watsonville, CA 95076

Order Date: 1/18/2020

Bill To: Joe's Ristoranté
38 Harbor Way
Santa Cruz, CA 95062

Deliver To: Joe's Ristoranté
38 Harbor Way
Santa Cruz, CA 95062

Qty	Description	Cost	Subtotal
100 lbs	Tomatoes	0.69	69.00
	Delivery		11.97
		Total	80.97

Classifying Organizational Data by Source and Type

Data can be internal or external to the organization. An example of data internal to the organization is employee data needed for payroll, such as their wage rates, exemptions, etc. An example of data external to the organization would be the payroll tax percentages (federal, state, and local) needed to withhold taxes from employees' paychecks.

What data from Joe's Ristoranté are internal?

Data from sales transactions and vendor purchases found in the accounting system would be considered internal to Joe's Ristoranté.

What data for Joe's Ristoranté are external?

Tax rates for payroll, licensing fees to run a business, and tariffs for imported goods, such as cheese from Italy, would be external.

In addition, data are also classified as quantitative or qualitative. It's easy for accountants to understand **quantitative data** because it is a numerical value, such as the amount of sales revenues and the value of inventory. **Qualitative data** refers to data that have non-numerical value and are also relevant to organizations. To use Joe's Ristoranté as an example, qualitative data found on social media about customers' experiences at the restaurant or a menu item customers liked or disliked are meaningful to the organization because customer comments are considered qualitative data.

quantitative data
Data that have a numerical value.

qualitative data
Data that have a non-numerical value.

How would customer satisfaction be considered qualitative data?

If a customer is asked, "Please rate your experience at Joe's Ristoranté on a scale from 1–10, with 1 being 'not satisfied at all' and 10 being 'very satisfied,'" then the customer response value is numerical.

How would customer satisfaction be considered qualitative?

If a customer asked, "Please tell us how you liked your experience at Joe's Ristoranté today" and space is provided so that the customer can write down a response, then the response is qualitative.

What Makes Information Useful?

relevant

Characteristic of useful information that reduces uncertainty.

reliable

Characteristic of useful information that is free of error or bias.

timely

Characteristic of useful information where information is in time to affect decisions.

complete

Characteristic of useful information that includes all relevant data.

understandable

Characteristic of useful information that is intelligible to the user.

value of information

Benefits of information minus the cost of information.

For information to be useful, it must have the following characteristics: be **relevant** (reduces uncertainty), **reliable** (free of error or bias), **timely** (in time to affect decisions), **complete** (includes all relevant data), and **understandable** (intelligible to the user).

It is important to note that these characteristics are not additive, i.e., you can't keep increasing one without necessarily reducing the others. For example, trying to make an accounting report timelier can reduce its reliability and completeness. Let's look at the value of information using the transaction from Figure 1.2, where Strickland's Fruit and Vegetables (a.k.a., Strickland's) who is selling tomatoes to Joe's Ristoranté (a.k.a., Joe's). For Strickland's to even take the order from Joe's, the customer's credit is *relevant* because it helps reduce uncertainty that Strickland's will receive payment from Joe's. If Strickland's credit manager makes the decision to approve Joe's as a customer, it is considered *reliable*. We will learn more about the separation of duties in Chapter 9; however, it is fairly clear to see that the sales manager from Strickland's would not be as reliable as the credit manager in approving Joe's as a customer. Strickland's current information on Joe's payment history with other creditors from a current third-party credit report also makes the information *timely*. The order is considered complete when Strickland's has all relevant information on the invoice, such as where to deliver the tomatoes and where to send Joe's bill. Finally, if Joe's order is clear about what they want (e.g., 100 lbs. of tomatoes), then it is *understandable*.

The trade-off between the benefit produced (usually in the form of an improved decision, which may result in increased revenues, cost savings, or both) and the cost of producing it (both quantitative and qualitative) equals value: **Value of information** = Benefits–Costs.

This equation is often used as the basis for many systems-related decisions.

Should we install point-of-sale scanners and a realtime inventory system with programmed reorder points for $10 million?

Yes, if it results in a reduction in purchasing costs and an increase in customer satisfaction and related revenue of more than $10 million.

What if you are a legislator who voted for the Sarbanes-Oxley Act of 2002 and learned afterward that it cost $30 billion to implement instead of the $1 billion originally estimated. Would you vote to amend or repeal the regulation?

Quite possibly, unless there was evidence that the benefits exceeded the $30 billion. In fact, Congress did pass Section 404(b) which amends the Act and allows public companies with less than $75 million of market cap to be exempted from the internal control auditing requirement.

The concept of value is very important and should not be confused with the notion of usefulness as discussed previously. Usefulness just relates to the benefit side of the equation.

Who Needs and Uses Accounting Information?

An **information ecosystem** for an organization would be any party (internal or external) who needs to interact with the organization from an information perspective and vice versa. For example, customers and vendors are considered trading partners with the organization. Government entities such as state and federal health, employee, and tax regulations requiring compliance are also in the ecosystem. Specifically, users may include the following:

information ecosystem

Any party (internal or external) who needs to interact with the organization from an information perspective and vice versa.

- Managers—to make operating decisions and strategic plans
- Investors—to facilitate buy, hold, and sell decisions
- Creditors—to determine if a loan should be made or not and the related level of credit risk
- Auditors—to determine if a company is auditable or not and the likelihood that its financial statements are misstated
- Employees—to assess their employer's financial stability

It is important to note that while users employ the outputs from an accounting system, they are not considered to be a part of the accounting system per se. From Joe's Ristorante perspective, the information ecosystem would include, but is not limited to, the state health regulations for restaurants that require compliance as well as taxing authorities requiring compliance for the restaurant. In addition, if Joe's Ristorante imports cheese from Italy and has to pay import tariffs, this is also part of the information ecosystem. Understanding an organization's information ecosystem is an important concept of governance, compliance, and risk, which will be further explored in Part 3 of this book.

From Joe's Ristorante perspective, the information ecosystem would include, but is not limited to, the state health regulations for restaurants that require compliance as well as taxing authorities requiring compliance for the restaurant. In addition, if Joe's Ristorante imports cheese from Italy and has to pay import tariffs, this is also part of the information ecosystem. Understanding an organization's information ecosystem is an important concept of governance, compliance, and risk which will be further explored in Part 3 of this book.

1.3 The Value Proposition of an AIS

Learning Objectives

At the end of this section, students should be able to:

1. Understand how information technology can be used to create competitive advantage.
2. Explain how database technology led to modern enterprise resource planning systems.

Competitive advantage can be created with accounting technology by improving service to customers, access to data, and cutting costs, which can then lead to lower prices, improved customer satisfaction, better decisions, increased revenue, and increased profit. Consider the following example.

How do you think Walmart has been able to maintain its strategy of falling prices?

In part, by the creative use of accounting technology.

Walmart was one of the first retailers in the early 1990s to employ technology connected to real-time inventory systems with programmed reorder points. When inventory levels dropped below the reorder points, the company's computers automatically generated purchase orders, which were transmitted to one of its 1,800 vendors via a satellite-based network.

These advanced systems significantly reduced the company's purchasing, inventory, and disbursement costs, thereby giving it a major cost advantage over many of its competitors. Many of its competitors find it hard to keep up with Walmart's innovations. This video explains more on how Walmart uses technology in its business.

Walmart Information Technology

This video talks about Information Technology and innovation at Walmart.

View in the online reader

Effect of Changing Technology on AIS

At one time, accounting data were stored on paper, then processed and reported manually. Today, with the rapid development of computers, storage devices, data communications and networking, cloud-based services, and encryption algorithms, organizations can do all of the following:

- Manage larger databases.
- Access data across traditional boundaries, such as operational versus financial.
- Move data more rapidly to and from remote locations.
- Obtain immediate feedback on the effects of transactions.
- Allow customers to interact with company systems twenty-four hours a day from anywhere in the world.
- Outsource software applications, development, storage, and maintenance to a remote data center maintained completely by an outside vendor.

- Mine vast amounts of unstructured "big data" to discover information that had been previously unknown or beyond comprehension.
- Create encrypted transactions or records that are stored in a peer-to-peer fashion on computers around the world in a blockchain file that cannot be hacked.

Changing technology allows organizations to be more efficient and effective. We will learn more about data analytics, which is revolutionizing accounting, in Chapter 3. We will also explore more about the effect of emerging technologies on accounting in Chapter 4.

Integrating the AIS Throughout the Enterprise

One of the most significant developments in accounting systems over the past decade has been the integration of accounting with other functional areas of the enterprise. For example, historically, payroll was a separate transaction processing system from the human resource function. It normally stored the employee's name and pay rate and then processed the hours worked to generate a paycheck. Other potentially important information in regard to the employee, such as training, fringe benefits, hiring and seniority data, and performance appraisals were normally maintained in an independent system or not at all. In some cases, the same data might be captured and stored in more than one system, which led to redundancy, inefficiency, and conflicting data.

To overcome these problems, many organizations have developed **enterprise resource planning (ERP) systems** that integrate data from all aspects of a company's operations into one large, centralized database. These large databases are accessed in almost unlimited ways and can provide information that may not have been available. Implementing an ERP system can produce significant benefits, if designed and implemented properly, but can be time-consuming, extremely complex, and costly to develop and maintain.

enterprise resource planning (ERP) systems

Systems that integrate data from all aspects of a company's operations into one large centralized database.

1.4 Why Study AIS?

Learning Objectives

At the end of this section, students should be able to:

1. Explain why accounting systems are important and why they should be studied.
2. Understand how studying AIS provides students with many career options.

A student's knowledge of accounting is not complete without an understanding of accounting systems for several reasons. While technical accounting knowledge is required, not understanding how accounting information is collected, stored, and extracted for analysis can put you at a disadvantage. The goal of this textbook is to help you understand the nature of AIS, how to develop them, and how to make them work effectively.

Is an AIS Course about Accounting?

Introductory and intermediate accounting courses are typically concerned with how well a business is doing from a financial point of view. The class emphasis is on making journal entries and preparing reports from data provided (e.g., producing information).

In an AIS course, we ask: Where did the information come from? How was it produced? Is the system providing timely and accurate information? What can go wrong, and how can you control these risks? How can an accounting system be used to add value to a business? How are effective systems developed? The objective is to understand how a business critically assesses how well it is doing (from a strategic or physical process point of view), how effectively the current method is working, what alternatives are available, and if there is a better (more cost-effective) way of doing it. Hence, a good deal of strategic management and critical thinking is involved with using accounting information.

The accounting system—wherever its boundaries are drawn—touches most or all of an organization's activities:

- External activities through transactions with customers and vendors, through statements prepared for managers, owners, stockholders, and creditors
- Internal activities through product costing, payments to employees, budgets and payments of loans

People are also aware that they are being monitored by accounting information and may manipulate the measures or adjust their behavior. Hence, due to the pervasive influence of accounting systems, the quality of information and the related system should be of great concern to managers. The accounting system is an organization's "key to success," and most organizations will fail if the system ceases to function.

How Does Studying AIS Prepare Me for an Accounting Career?

As a student graduating with an accounting degree, you have many options. Accounting careers can be in public accounting where you may be an auditor, tax specialist, or consult with other companies in an advisory role. You may also decide to work directly for a company or with the government. The following video discusses the many options of where you can work after graduating with an accounting degree.

Accounting Career: Your First Job After Graduation (Big 4 Audit Is Not the Only Way—Alternatives)

This video is from an accounting student and considers options for a first job in accounting.

View in the online reader

Specifically, a career in public accounting requires the knowledge of fundamental AIS because you will be working with your client's information systems. This means that there will be a variety of technologies' that you will need to understand; however, the fundamentals of AIS will still be useful regardless of the accounting software your clients use. Auditors, for example, must rely on accounting systems to reduce the high cost of their audits. In addition, auditors who understand accounting systems can better protect themselves from "fraudulent management," who may manipulate information to gain unfair advantage. Hence, auditors who do not understand accounting systems may have failures in their audit process. Tax accountants will need to understand how to extract relevant transactions from their client's AIS for tax planning and preparation purposes. Consultants would be involved with how to design better systems and controls for their clients to help the clients gain competitive advantage or to solve system problems. If you have a career in public accounting, you are seen as an advisor to your clients.

While you are not strictly limited to public accounting, you may decide that you want to work for one company, be an entrepreneur, or work in the government/nonprofit sector. What do all of these varied career choices have in common? They need to understand how information is captured and flows to the financials of the organization. All managers need to know how well their organizations are doing. In fact, technology will change how we work in the future. This is an exciting time to be an accountant. This video explains more on how technology will change the accounting profession.

 Accountants, Automation, and Change

This video is about technology changing how accountants will work in the future.

View in the online reader

Key Takeaways

In this chapter, we began our journey toward understanding accounting from a systems perspective. Our first stop was an examination of a real-world case that illustrated the need for accounting information. From there, we examined a definition of systems in general. We looked at what constitutes a system problem, the possible causes, and the importance of critical thinking. We then expanded the general definition of a system to focus on accounting and identified the four main components. Next, we learned about the differences between data and information. We also learned that data are classified in an organization as internal and external and that data can be quantitative or qualitative. We examined what makes information useful and how to determine the value of this information. We explored how accounting technology has advanced and can be used to create competitive advantage. Finally, we discussed the importance of accounting systems and why we should study them. We also learned that accounting students have many career options and how technology will change how accounting is done in the future.

1.5 End-of-Chapter Exercises

Exercises

1. After reading the Joe's Ristoranté case, answer the following:
   a. Does Joe understand the need for accounting information?
   b. What information will be needed in general and in specific to the restaurant?
   c. What will be required to get it?
   d. Should the company do the accounting itself or outsource it (totally or partially) to an accounting service provider such as a CPA?
   e. What would you recommend that Joe should do?
2. Generally, what is a system? Can you provide an example of a system?

3. What is a system problem? Using this concept, what would be a good example and a possible cause?
4. What is an AIS? What is the difference between an accounting system and a system in general? What is similar and different about errors and irregularities?
5. What is critical thinking? In what context is it important?
6. What are the components of an AIS? Provide examples of each using the Joe's Ristoranté case.
7. Is an accounting systems course about accounting, per se?
8. What makes a system complex, and why is it better to illustrate a simple system when attempting to understand the basic concept?
9. What makes information useful, and how does usefulness relate to value? Can useful information not be valuable?
10. What effect has technology had on accounting systems and is it expected to continue?
11. Can information technology be used to create competitive advantage?
12. Why are advanced ERP systems that rely on transaction-based data no longer sufficient?
13. How important are accounting systems, and why should we study them?
14. Which of the following would not be part of a system according to general system theory?
    a. An objective
    b. Interacting parts
    c. Things that work together
    d. A general ledger
15. Systems problems always occur when
    a. a part is missing.
    b. the objective is clear.
    c. parts interact.
    d. the objective is not being met.
16. For information to be useful, it must be
    a. relevant.
    b. reliable.
    c. complete.
    d. timely.
    e. All of the above
17. Which of the following is not a major component of an AIS?
    a. People
    b. Education
    c. Technologies
    d. Controls
18. The value of an accounting system is generally determined by
    a. quantifying all of its benefits.
    b. ensuring that its costs are low.
    c. estimating its salvage value.
    d. subtracting its cost from its benefit.

19. Which of the following would be the best way to improve your critical thinking skills?
    a. Listening to lectures
    b. Questioning your own thinking
    c. Engaging in activities that challenge you to express your opinion based on sound reasoning
    d. Both b and c

20. **PROBLEM-SOLVING IN THE REAL WORLD**

    After graduating from college, you took a position with a public accounting firm as a staff auditor. Two and a half years later, you were up for promotion to senior, but one of your publicly held clients offered you a job for roughly $50,000 more than you were making currently plus stock options with no travel and very little overtime. Interestingly, you accepted the offer and within a few months were faced with the following situations:

    a. Although your pay is great, there seems to be a lot of complaining at the company about its software. The company has been using Windows 7 on its office computers for years and has been quite satisfied. The accounting staff has also been using Excel, Access, and Word as part of Office 2013 for a number of accounting tasks, such as budgets, cost analysis, projections, scheduling, and communication among team members. Although the software has generally met company needs, there has been concern about viruses, malware, backing up important files, and sharing files among team members. The company also does not want to spend the money to upgrade its operating system even though Microsoft announced that it will no longer support Windows 7.
    b. One of the sales managers says that she would like to know who the sales people were for certain sales made in a particular region of the country, how much each sales person sold during the year so far, and what types of sales training they had received (but said that such information was not available).
    c. A customer called and complained to customer service that she had ordered certain merchandise online (in used condition) during a sale on used items two weeks earlier but had not received the merchandise. The customer had an order number and a UPS tracking number. Upon review of the UPS tracking system, UPS showed that they had received the information from your company, but no further updates were available.
    d. Much to your surprise and disappointment, you recently learned that your company had acquired another company fourteen months ago for cash and common stock at a price significantly higher than book value only to find out that the acquired company had been inflating its sales through a revenue recognition scheme that was at variance with generally accepted accounting principles. From a preliminary investigation, you believe that the numbers may be large enough to warrant a restatement of your current quarterly and prior year's sales figures and a significant write-down of goodwill from the acquisition. In addition, you discover that the subsidiary has some nonexistent inventory and has been using month-end adjusting entries to meet your home office's budgetary and cash flow targets. If this information becomes known, it will likely have a significant negative effect on the company's stock price, precipitate a Security and Exchange Commission investigation, and wipe out the value of your stock options.

    Required: For each of the scenarios above,

    i. Analyze and indicate whether you think that there is a system problem (including your rationale).
    ii. If so, explain what you believe is the cause or if not, why not.
    iii. If so, propose a solution (including alternatives, if any).

21. Critical Thinking

    Do some research on a company that has a product you admire (e.g., Apple, Nike, Marvel) and find out the following:

    a. What kind of internal and external data do you think would be important to them?
    b. Identify if this data would be quantitative or qualitative.

22. Reflective Learning

    Boyd and Fales (1983)[1] state that reflective learning is the process of internally examining and exploring an issue of concern, triggered by an experience, which creates and clarifies meaning in terms of self, and which results in a changed conceptual perspective.

    a. Based on reading and reflecting on this chapter, what have you learned?
    b. What was the most difficult concept in the chapter? Why was it difficult?
    c. Does the material in this chapter relate to anything you have covered in another course or seen in any of your prior experiences?

23. After studying this chapter, how would you go about creating an effective accounting system for the two following organizations?
    a. You founded a company and have been running it for approximately one year.
    b. The company has been operating for 20 years, and you have just become its controller.
    c. What are the decisions one has to make with solving system problems with a company that has been operating for 20 years compared to a company operating within the first year?

Endnote

1. Boyd, Evelyn M., and Ann W. Fales. "Reflective learning: Key to learning from experience." *Journal of Humanistic Psychology 23*, no. 2 (1983): 99–117.

CHAPTER 2

AIS Structure and the Flow of Information

In the previous chapter, we learned that accounting systems have four components: people, processes, technologies, and controls. In this chapter, we illustrate how accounting system components vary in terms of their sophistication. We do this by using a unique measurement system for each component to describe that component's complexity.

2.1 AIS Component Variation

Learning Objective

At the end of this section, students should be able to:

1. Identify and describe the measurement systems used in understanding the complexity of the four components of AIS.

The measurement systems used to describe the AIS component variation include the following:

1. Bloom's Taxonomy
2. The Business Process Maturity Model
3. The System Technology Maturity Model (STMM)
4. The Control Systems Maturity Model (CSMM)

TABLE 2.1 Models Illustrating How AIS Components Vary

Component	Descriptive Measurement
People	Bloom's Taxonomy
Processes	Business Process Maturity
Technology	System Technology Maturity
Controls	Control Systems Maturity

We will also examine the general structure of accounting systems and the extent to which structure may exist in the information they produce. Next, we begin our expanded discussion of the four components and the related descriptive measurement.

The People Component

Bloom's Taxonomy[1] describes a hierarchy of learning. This taxonomy can also be used to describe the level of thinking involved in processing accounting information. It begins, as illustrated in Figure 2.1, with simple recall of information and progresses through comprehension, application, analysis, synthesis, and the evaluation of information. Notice that each level is progressive, which means the previous level is required to understand, develop, and implement the higher levels of processes, technology, and controls.

FIGURE 2.1 Bloom's Taxonomy

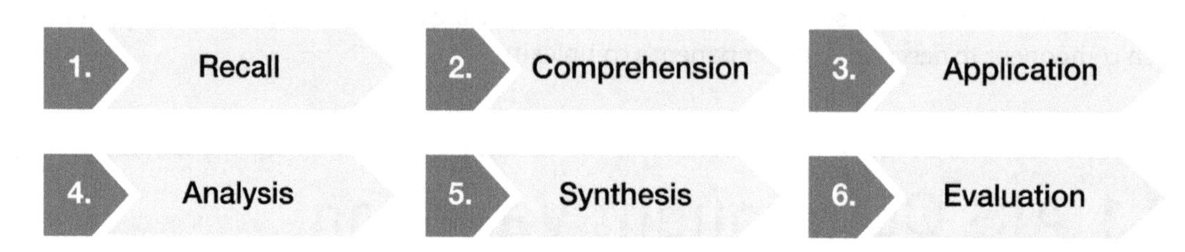

The lowest level is recall of information. Comprehension means the concept is understood and one would be able to apply examples. Application is the ability to apply the knowledge learned to solve problems. Analysis is the ability to recognize patterns and make sense of the information. Synthesis is the ability to make connections such that new ideas are created or to summarize information to make a conclusion. The highest level is evaluation, which is the ability to apply judgment relative to some criteria. Because systems involve people, it is important to understand the need to adapt or change over time in response to new technology or control requirements. As the accounting profession continues to change with emerging technology, the skill of evaluation using information from systems will be very important.

The Processes Component

Processes vary across accounting systems and are how organizations get things done. Processes also come at varying levels of maturity. According to Object Management Group (OMG.org), process maturity has five levels. Ranging from the initial level, which are ad hoc processes, to the more repeatable, standardized and finally optimized level. As illustrated in Table 2.2, the initial level is a process that is considered ad hoc. For an organization to complete a task that is considered a "one-off" type of task, an ad hoc process will suffice. However, what if the task is not a one-time deal? Then the process needs to be managed as it is repeatable. Over time, the organization may want to be more efficient in a certain process, making the process standardized as "this is how we get this task done." However, as the process matures, the organization will want to manage the process using quantifiable measures. Finally, the most mature process will be in continuous improvement, optimizing the process through feedback on the process performance. Think about Joe's Ristoranté from Chapter 1. How would the simple process of purchasing ingredients for the menu go from ad hoc to fully optimized? We will explore how to answer this question more in Chapter 3.

TABLE 2.2 Business Process Maturity Model

Level	Description
5	Optimizing: Continuously improving
4	Predictable: Quantitatively managed
3	Defined: Standardized practices
2	Managed: Repeatable practices
1	Initial: Ad hoc practice

Source: Data from OMG.org

The Controls Component

As we learned in Chapter 1, controls are the things we do to reduce the chance that something will go wrong. This part of the accounting system varies significantly from one business to the next. Some small businesses may have few, if any, controls, while large, mature enterprises will have many controls that not only minimize problems but maximize business process efficiency.

Over time, as businesses expand and adapt, their internal control evolves, as illustrated in Table 2.3; the Control Systems Maturity Model (CSMM) was adapted from the Information Systems Audit and Control Association (ISACA). What starts out as a relatively ad hoc control can mature and become well defined and effective.

TABLE 2.3 Control Systems Maturity Model

Level	Maturity of Controls
5	Optimized
4	Integrated
3	Formal and Systematic
2	Informal
1	Initial or Ad hoc
0	Nonexistent

Table 2.3 identifies levels of internal control reliability and describes what companies must do for their accounting systems to evolve from one level to the next.

Level 0 is a bit of a theoretical misnomer in the sense that most companies must have some internal control. Yet, for companies that are viewed as "incompetent" or "out-of-control," the term nonexistent is often used.

Initial controls or level 1 of the CSMM is where control policies and procedures are ad hoc and undocumented. As a result, they are generally not linked to control objectives and are inconsistent with each other. Because of this, effectiveness depends on the competence and ethical values of the people.

In level 2, informal internal control practices begin to emerge, but they may not be well documented. There is some awareness for a need to implement controls, but it is not embedded in the organizational operations. Also, the lack of formal communication together with a lack of training often prevents information about internal control from going below the managerial level.

Level 3 is when controls are formal and documentation exists. Management incorporates internal control throughout the organization.

Level 4 controls are fully integrated into the strategic and operational aspects of the business with control monitoring in place.

Level 5 means that management is in continuous improvement. Internal controls implement automation and monitoring on a real-time basis and adjustments are made as needed.

The Technology Component

The technology component of accounting systems has evolved dramatically over the last two decades. In this chapter, we only scratch the surface of this topic, but the stage is set for examining these complex technologies in more depth in later chapters. The taxonomy in Table 2.4 provides an overview of accounting systems maturity in nine levels.

TABLE 2.4 System Technology Maturity Model

Level	Description of Technology
9	Distributed file system transactions
8	Cloud computing
7	Integrated EDI, web services, and XBRL
6	Nonintegrated B2C internet systems
5	Networked computers and relational databases
4	Computer master and transaction files
3	Journals and ledgers
2	Worksheet systems
1	Shoe-box systems

electronic data interchange (EDI)

Standard format that allows companies to communicate with one another.

web services

Software applications that are distributed over the internet.

cloud-based systems

Computer model that makes IT resources such as applications and infrastructure available over the internet as on-demand services to business organizations.

Our maturity model begins as illustrated in Table 2.4 with what we call shoe-box systems and evolves up to what we present as integrated **electronic data interchange (EDI)**, **web services**, and **cloud-based systems**. Shoe-box systems were more common years ago in small businesses, but they still exist today. Traditionally, they involved placing a business's detail information, such as checks and receipts, into a box or bag and then giving them to the company's CPA at the end of the year for tax preparation and tax filing purposes.

Worksheet systems, at level 2, are used to summarize the revenue and expense transactions from deposit slips and checks, respectively. Worksheets may be done on paper or using basic software such as Excel or Quicken that tracks money going in and out of the business. Financial statements and tax returns are then prepared from these worksheet summaries.

At level 3, journals and ledgers are introduced. Journals, which serve as books of original entry, replace worksheets and are used to record an organization's journal entries. The general ledger is then organized according to a chart of accounts and is used to summarize the totals from the journals. Subsidiary ledgers are also used to keep track of the detailed customer accounts receivable and vendor accounts payable.

At level 4, journals and ledgers use computerized transaction files and master files that are normally structured using relational databases. Posting is no longer done by hand. In some cases, it occurs immediately, or the transactions are batched and posted at a later time. This raises a number of questions about how and when this is done and has implications on system costs and efficiency. Because of the time it will take to address these data processing questions, we will address them later in the chapter.

Levels 5 through 9 involve the use of advanced technologies. These technologies increase our access to information in a faster, more cost effective, and "error-free" manner. For example, enterprise resource planning (ERP) systems, to the extent that they rely on networked computers and relational databases, are considered to be a level 5 technology. However, when they include modules for business-to-consumer (B2C) e-commerce or EDI, they may be operating at levels 6 and 7. ERP systems will be discussed in more depth in Chapter 8.

At level 6, companies provide the capability for their customers to directly access their sales ordering systems from the internet. With the recent approval of using the internet for commercial purposes in the early 1990s, this type of B2C e-commerce has grown rapidly. Although B2C e-commerce appears to provide great opportunities for companies, it can also introduce substantial risks. The fundamentals and risks of doing accounting transactions on the internet are covered in Chapter 10.

EDI is essentially a set of technologies and business partnerships designed for conducting business-to-business (B2B) e-commerce. EDI allows transactions to be exchanged with business partners in a highly integrated way using a standard electronic format over proprietary, value-added, or networks of networks in a completely automated manner.

Benefits for Service-Oriented Architecture in Business Process

This is a video that describes SOA.

View in the online reader

XBRL (Extensible Business Reporting Language) uses web services as well as a specialized computer markup language over the internet to publish a company's financial statements. The Security and Exchange Commission (SEC) now requires public companies to submit their financial statements in XBRL format. XBRL, which we have classified as a level 7 technology, will be discussed in more depth in Chapter 15.

XBRL (Extensible Business Reporting Language)

A standard for financial reporting electronically, stands for extensible business reporting language.

Level 8 is cloud computing, which leverages the internet in ways similar to levels 6 and 7 technologies through the use of web services. However, because cloud computing uses a whole new set of service models and deployment methods as well as outsourcing many information technology (IT) functions, we believe it should be elevated to a whole new level. When CRN.com first introduced its annual 100 Coolest Cloud Computing Vendors[2] list in 2010, cloud computing was just an industry buzzword. Now, it is mainstream and many organizations prefer to use it to manage their information system needs.

Infrastructure as a Service (IaaS)

Provides servers, storage, or networking on a pay-per-use services model.

Software as a Service (SaaS)

Cloud-based software solution where software and infrastructure are managed entirely by a separate AIS vendor.

Platform as a Service (PaaS)

The PaaS option provides both the needed hardware (servers and storage) and software development tools to create your own AIS.

Cloud computing is a computer model that makes IT resources, such as applications and infrastructure, available over the internet as services to business organizations on demand. The American National Institute of Standards and Technology (NIST) classifies cloud computing into three service models: **Infrastructure as a Service (IaaS)**, **Software as a Service (SaaS)**, and **Platform as a Service (PaaS)**. In short, we can view IaaS as hardware, SaaS as software, and PaaS as both hardware and software. It is also important to understand that cloud technology can be deployed in different ways. NIST states that cloud computing is deployed using four methods: public, private, community, and hybrid. Public clouds are available to any company who wants to essentially rent services on it; private clouds are maintained by an entity for its own use; community clouds are maintained by a group of entities with common interests; and hybrid clouds are some combination of the first three. Here's a video that explains the differences between the three type of web service models.

IaaS versus PaaS versus SaaS

This is a video that explains the differences of the three types of web service models.

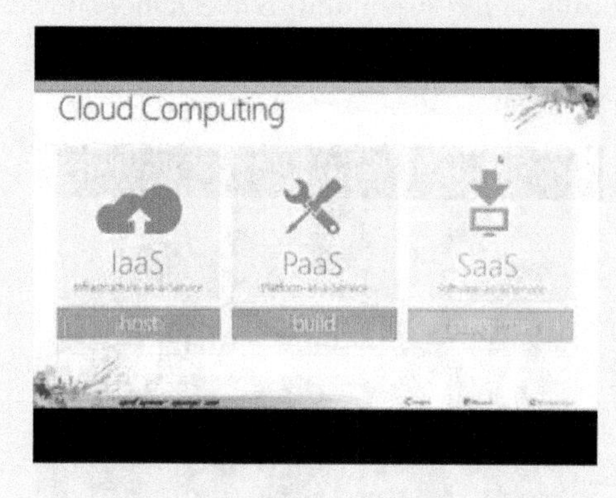

View in the online reader

For example, Roku is a fast-growing company that provides electronic devices for streaming media to TVs. In 2012, it moved its financials, inventory, and order management from an in-house implementation of QuickBooks to NetSuite's financials, inventory, and order management cloud solution. Quickbooks couldn't scale to the high transaction volumes Roku was experiencing. In addition, with NetSuite, Roku was able to reduce its monthly financial close time by 500 percent and avoid having to add personnel in accounting, order management, and IT.[3] NetSuite.com is a public cloud providing SaaS.

Outsourcing IT resources to the cloud is a complicated process. The term "cloud" is often used by many as a metaphor for the internet. True cloud computing, however, is a set of hardware, networks, storage, services, and interfaces that enable the delivery of computing as a service (generally on a subscription or pay-per-use basis). Instead of installing, maintaining, and upgrading their own software applications, middleware, and infrastructure, a company can rely on an outside vendor to provide these services.

Services can be viewed as a group of software components that automate some business process, run on a network 24/7, and are available on demand. Cloud computing is like renting an EDI value-added network or paying for minutes and data transfer on your phone as needed. This model can work exceptionally well for companies that have wide ranging demand for their automated business processes, including significant down time and major growth spurts. Cloud computing is scalable and sharable with other companies, which if managed properly can potentially save a company significant IT expenses. Chief information officers, however, will have to investigate the performance of potential cloud service providers, including the security and reliability of their services. Cloud computing will be explained in more depth in Chapter 8. In the last section of this chapter, we will discuss more advanced means of information deployment.

2.2 What Is the Overall Structure of an Accounting System?

Learning Objective

At the end of this section, students should be able to:

1. Describe and understand the two structures of accounting systems.

It is important to recall that accounting systems are not uniform and they are often complex. Because of this complexity, it is useful to decompose them into smaller parts, which can be more easily understood. This can be accomplished hierarchically (i.e., up and down) or horizontally (i.e., left to right).

Hierarchy Structure

When we decompose or breakdown an accounting system hierarchically, we see that all accounting systems have common functions or component subsystems. Hence, subsystems are nested systems within other systems. Figure 2.2 illustrates this concept using a **hierarchical block diagram**.

hierarchical block diagram

Used to represent successive levels of component subsystems; the connecting lines show inter-level associations but not information flows.

FIGURE 2.2 Hierarchical Block Diagram

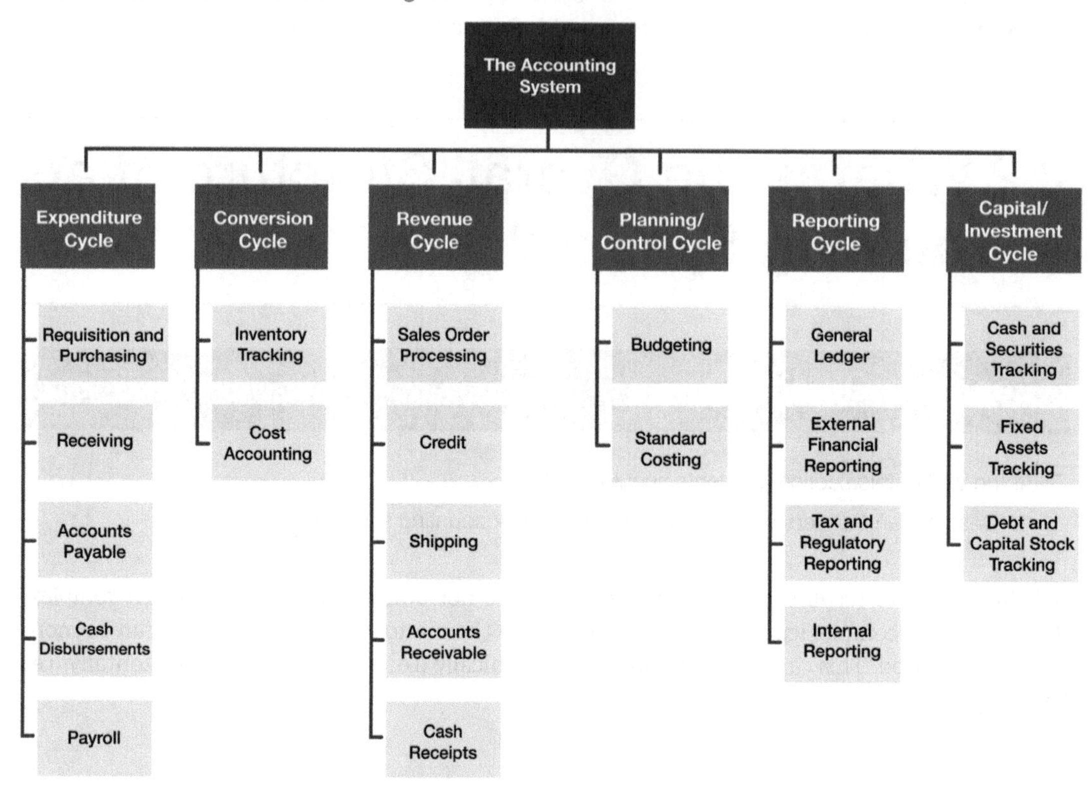

Hierarchical block diagrams are used to represent successive levels of component subsystems; the connecting lines show inter-level associations but not information flows. The top level of a hierarchical block diagram is called the overall or aggregate level with a single box representing the total or highest-level view of the system. In our illustration in Figure 2.2, the highest level is called "the accounting system."

The first level of the accounting system below the overall or aggregate view contains the major transaction cycles. These are considered subsystems because they are within and hierarchically below the overall accounting system. Every accounting system can be viewed normatively as having six subsystems or transaction cycles. Three transactions cycles relate to operations and are the expenditure cycle, revenue cycle, and conversion cycle. The other three transaction cycles are considered support cycles and include investment cycle, financial reporting cycle, and budgeting cycle. We will learn more about these cycles in detail in Part 3 of this book.

The second level below the overall or aggregate level contains the accounting applications, which for the purchasing cycle would include requisitioning, purchasing, receiving, accounts payable, cash disbursements, and payroll. Hierarchical block diagrams are very useful in gaining an overall perspective of a company's accounting system. They can help to identify what is there and what is missing. According to our definition of an effective system, if an important cycle or application is missing, there is a system problem.

Horizontal Structure

The second way of viewing an accounting system is horizontally. The **horizontal block diagram** shows the blocks representing the various activities, while the connecting lines depict information flows. This approach is generally more useful for understanding, because all accounting systems (manual or computerized) must have a fundamental way to input data, process it, and output the information. Figure 2.3 illustrates the horizontal block diagram.

horizontal block diagram
From an accounting system perspective, the blocks represent the various activities while the connecting lines depict information flows (e.g., input, process, output).

All transactions generally start with an event. This event will have inputs such as a source document and require the organization to process the information in some form. This would then create an output, such as paying a vendor with a check or billing a customer. An output can also take the form of a report that is used by management in the organization, such as the financial statements or an accounts receivable aging report. Using Joe's Ristoranté from Chapter 1 as an example, we know that Joe orders food from vendors as needed to create menu items for customers. The order from the vendor is an input. The information is processed manually by Joe as he checks the order to make sure it is correct. When Joe has a computer system, he will be able to process the order with the vendor invoice to pay the bill by check. At the end of the year, Joe may want to see how much he has ordered from certain vendors to negotiate better pricing, and he can print out a report of all the orders for the year.

FIGURE 2.3 Horizontal Block Diagram Example

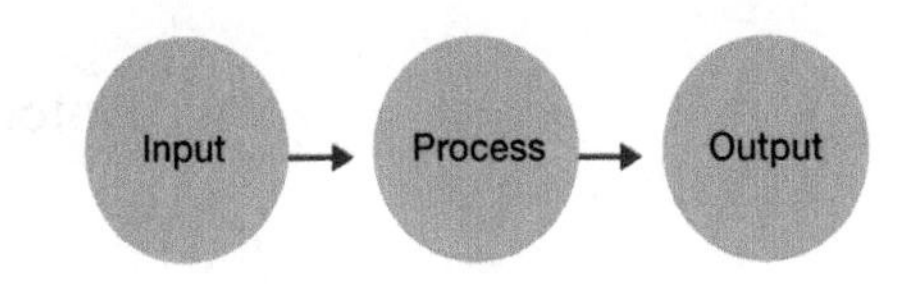

2.3 Organizing Transactions

Learning Objective

At the end of this section, students should be able to:

1. Understand how charts of accounts are constructed and how they are used to describe transactions.

Now that we have explored how the four components of an accounting information system vary, it is time to examine how they work. In doing so, it is important to understand that certain tasks are fundamental to all accounting systems. Whether the accounting system is manual or computerized, the methods for performing these tasks vary. Figure 2.4 illustrates how accounting systems work from a manual and computerized perspective.

FIGURE 2.4 How Do Accounting Systems Work?

	Manual	Computerized
Data Input	Source document	Keyed in or scanned
	Journal	Transaction file
	Coded in accordance with the chart of accounts	
Data Processing	Posted	File updated
Data Storage	General ledger	Master file
Information Output	Written reports	Printed output
		Screen view

To input data, there must be a transaction and a way of labeling and measuring it. A transaction generally results from an agreement between the organization and some outside party to exchange goods or services. Transactions result from economic events. The labeling is done with accounts, and the measuring is done in dollar amounts.

Transactions are normally recognized when the exchange is complete. For example, purchases are normally recognized as accounts payable when the goods are received, and revenues are normally recognized as sales when the goods are shipped. Unfortunately, sometimes business events are complex, and the standards for identifying and measuring them are vague.

All accounting systems must process and store accounting data once it has been input into the system. Traditionally, accounting data were posted from a journal to a book called the general ledger. With advances in computer technology, transactions are now captured, electronically transmitted, and stored in more sophisticated ways, such as computer master files or relational databases. The methods for transferring the data are numerous and raise many questions for businesses, which must decide the most cost-effective means of accomplishing the task.

Without getting into too much detail, some companies accumulate transactions and transmit them to storage at a later date in what is referred to as a batch. Others transmit their transactions to a central database as they occur. This type of update is called real-time processing. How a company accomplishes this update is ultimately a matter of critically thinking through the alternatives and analyzing the costs and benefits. Table 2.5 presents a more complete comparison of the characteristics of batch versus real-time processing.

TABLE 2.5 Comparing Batch versus Real-Time Processing

	Pure Batch	Interactive Batch	Real Time
Characteristic	Accumulates like transactions to be processed later	Accumulates like batch, but allows direct access to a master file	Posts transactions as they occur
Transaction data converted to machine-readable form	Encoded offline, punched cards, magnetic tape	Encoded online, terminals, scanners, touch screens, voice recognition devices	Encoded online, terminals, touch screens scanners, etc.
Editing and correction of data	Offline	Online	Online
Posting transaction data to master files	Periodic (e.g., monthly) posting	Periodic (e.g., monthly) posting	Immediate posting
Ability to query master files	No	Can be queried but data may not be current	Can be queried and up-to-date
Technology supported by	Magnetic tape	Magnetic disk	Magnetic disk

Every accounting system must also output necessary accounting information. The degree to which this happens in real-world companies, however, varies a great deal. Some companies collect basic transaction data but wait until the end of the year to process it and outsource report preparation to their CPA in the form of a tax return. Others generate information on a monthly or quarterly basis by hand or by computer and then make that information available to others in a form that generally must be converted to their system format before it can be analyzed and/or processed.

The process of consuming financial information around the world costs billions of dollars every year. The process requires hundreds of thousands of data entry clerks, editors, and accountants to prepare the data for use by investors, taxing authorities, auditors, financial analysts, creditors, exchange commissions, and so on. Many companies and regulatory agencies around the world are now recognizing that countless hours and millions of dollars can be saved by using a common electronic data format for financial and business reporting. This new standard, XBRL, will be adopted rapidly and will challenge every company to critically think about its costs and benefits.

What Is a Chart of Accounts?

A **chart of accounts** is a coded list of all balance sheet and income statement accounts used by a business. Charts of accounts generally use numeric codes with a combination of block coding and group coding techniques. We describe transactions by coding (labeling) them using a chart of accounts. Coding is the assignment of numbers or letters to transactions in order to organize them. Transactions are normally coded in blocks and groups.

chart of accounts
A coded list of all balance sheet and income statement accounts used by a business.

A block code reserves blocks of numbers for categories of items, such as current assets and current liabilities as shown in Table 2.6.

Group codes are used with block codes to add meaning. For example, you could add a digit to an account number for product line and one for salesperson number. If your software can accommodate it, you could also add codes for store number, regions, and anything else you want to keep track of.

For example, using the chart of accounts found in Table 2.6, we see that 610 represents the Sales Revenue account for a company. We also have two-digit product group codes (pp) and a two-digit store number code (##) that we can use to identify product sales as well as store sales. Hence, a sale recorded as 610-01-28 could represent product 01 and store number 28. This additional information can be very useful for performance reporting because the coding allows for sorting product lines and stores.

TABLE 2.6 Example Chart of Accounts

Account Code	Account Category and Name	Account Code	Account Category and Name
100–199	Current Assets	**300–399**	Current Liabilities
100	Petty Cash	300	Accounts Payable
102	Cash in Banks	310	Accrued Expenses Payable
110	Accounts Receivable	320	Other Current Liabilities
111	Allowance for Bad Debts	**400–499**	Noncurrent Liabilities
130	Inventories	410	Bonds Payable
150	Prepaid Insurance	**500–599**	Stockholders' Equity
200–299	Noncurrent Assets	510	Common Stock
200	Land	520	Retained Earnings
210	Buildings	**600–699**	Revenues
220	Equipment	610	Sales
240	Accumulated Depreciation	620	Sales Discounts
250	Patents and Trademarks	**700–799**	Expenses
260	Other Assets	701	Cost of Goods Sold
		710	Wages Expense
		720	Rent Expense
		730	Insurance Expense
		790	Income Tax Expense
Block codes are in bold			
Cost centers: pp-## where: p–product line, ##–store number			

How Does Information Flow to Financial Statements?

A chart of accounts serves as the framework for an accounting system. A chart of accounts should be designed so that needed information will be available as output (meaning contained in the necessary accounting reports). A creatively designed chart can have a significant effect on the usefulness of information. For example, as we saw in the previous section, the way transactions are coded can affect the relevance of information about product lines and stores.

As transactions get recorded, the balance in each account is aggregated to the proper line item on the financial statements. If we look at the example in Table 2.6, we can see that the balance sheet would have accounts from 100–599. The income statement would use accounts 600 and beyond. So as the balances of these accounts are sequential with balance sheet accounts first and then income statement accounts, it is simple to see how these can be arranged to create the balance sheet and income statement.

2.4 Advanced Information Deployment—The Distributed File System

Learning Objective

At the end of this section, students should be able to:

1. Describe a distributed ledger and how it is used.

Just when you think technology's stratospheric advances might be leveling off in the cloud, encrypted shared ledger technology comes along. This decentralized peer-to-peer technology, called blockchain, may be creating not only a level 9, but a whole new technology revolution. Although originally developed to facilitate the transfer of digital cryptocurrencies such as Bitcoin, blockchain technology can also be used to support the creation of smart contracts, smart property, and smart apps that can automate many business transactions in ways that could only have been imagined in a science-fiction movie.

What Is a Blockchain?

In general, a **blockchain** is simply a computer file. In reality, however, it is a complex system for storing data records using a secure encrypted procedure and then storing those records in a redundant fashion over many computers (nodes) on a computer network. To understand a blockchain, it will be helpful to identify its purpose and then to see how its parts work together to achieve the objective. In this chapter, we will provide a very gentle introduction to the topic.

A blockchain is often referred to as a **distributed ledger** (since each node on the computer network maintains a full copy of the file). This is in contrast to a centralized architecture where the computers (nodes) are connected to a centralized server as illustrated on the right side of Figure 2.5. The distributed peer-to-peer network on the left has no centralized server connected to each node. The advantage of the peer-to-peer network is that it has more computing power in total at less cost than the centralized client-server approach because the computer processing power comes from all computers on the system instead of a central server paid for by the system's owner. The main disadvantage of a pure distributed system is that no one is formally in control. On the other hand, although the centralized approach costs more for less power, the main advantage is that the centralized server and its clients are controlled by a network administrator.

blockchain

A data structure for storing transactions using a highly secure distributed approach.

distributed ledger

Blockchain.

FIGURE 2.5 A Distributed versus a Centralized Network

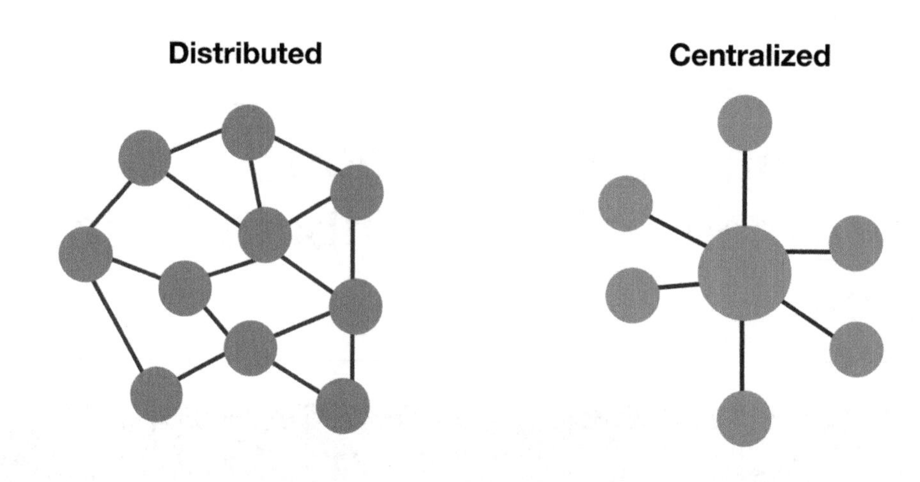

Blockchain 101 by IBM Food Trust-Part 1: What Is Blockchain?

This is a video that explains blockchain technology simply.

View in the online reader

Blockchain technology was originally developed to underpin the creation of the Bitcoin digital currency. The purpose of the original blockchain was to establish a record-keeping system for the newly created cryptocurrency. The idea was to have a digital file replace the conventional banking system (which holds the majority of the money supply in centralized digital banking records and who keep track of who owns it). What makes blockchain technology new and different is that before transactions can be added to the ledger, they must be verified. The blockchain was designed so that transactions must be confirmed for authenticity and cannot be hacked or tampered with (once added to the file).

Blockchain 101 by IBM Food Trust-Part 2: Blockchain Expanded

This is a video that explains how the blockchain technology is used and expands on the blockchain concept as a distributed ledger.

View in the online reader

Does a Blockchain Address a Particular Type of System Problem?

Ownership misrepresentation is a serious problem in the real world. Whether we are talking about paper money or digital currency, in the absence of a reliable ownership record, it can be difficult, if not impossible sometimes, to determine who owns something. If someone steals your wallet or robs a bank, it will be difficult to determine who is the rightful owner of the funds. Currency often has a serial number attached to it, but there has been no reliable way, so far, to maintain records so that rightful owners can enforce their ownership rights.

Consider the problem of verifying automobile ownership. If someone steals your car, even though each car has a vehicle identification number (VIN), it is too easy for a thief to remove the VIN and transport the vehicle to another country. Take the case of land. When buying property, we often end up paying lawyers hundreds of dollars to do title searches and then pay even more for title insurance because there is no simple procedure to establish clear title on real estate. Maintaining control over your identity can also be a problem. If someone steals your social security and credit card numbers and drains your bank account or runs up debts in your name, it can be a problem to prove who you are and to restore your funds. Managing ownership, therefore, is a multi-billion-dollar industry, and maintaining more reliable ownership records and the enforcement of ownership rights is going to be the primary use case for blockchain.

The blockchain can be thought of as another layer on the internet or on a private network for enabling secure economic transactions. These transactions can be digital currency payments or complicated financial contracts, such as derivatives, rental agreements, loan arrangements, and wills. A blockchain can also be used as a registry or inventory system for recording, tracking, and monitoring property. A blockchain could be like a giant spreadsheet for registering all assets, and an accounting system for transacting them on a global scale that can include all forms of physical and intangible property. Although Bitcoin employs the first version of the blockchain, the next versions, which will involve creating **smart contracts** and smart property as well as government, health, and identity records, are likely to be where the major expansion of the technology will take place. We will discuss these in Chapter 4.

smart contracts

Contracts that use software programming to assist with the standard process of contracts and can include verification, enforcement, and performance of the terms of the contract.

Is Blockchain Technology Appropriate for AIS?

Blockchain for AIS is feasible. Anything of value can be tracked using a blockchain, reducing risk and cutting costs for all involved. Traditional transactions can be inefficient, expensive, and vulnerable. Blockchain-based networks can arguably eliminate market frictions (such as the need for intermediaries), record transactions just once (making them available quickly to all parties), and make the ledger tamper proof (and thus reduce the possibility of fraud).

Blockchain and the Future of Audit

This is a video showing how blockchain can impact accounting and audit.

View in the online reader

Key Takeaways

In this chapter, we learned about the evolution of systems thinking, technology, and control. We learned how to evaluate the sophistication level of individual accounting systems through the use of maturity models. These models can be used by an accountant to determine how the technology and control components of individual accounting systems vary. We examined the overall structure of accounting systems through the use of hierarchical and horizontal block diagrams and discussed when it is appropriate to use each diagram to effectively communicate information to the user. We also learned more about the distributed ledger that is based on blockchain technology.

2.5 End-of-Chapter Exercises

Exercises

1. Describe the measurement systems that can be used to evaluate the complexity of the four general components of accounting systems.

2. Explain the significance of Bloom's Taxonomy to the people component of accounting systems.
3. Should all companies strive to achieve level 5 of business process maturity? How should a company decide?
4. Explain the difference between IaaS, PaaS, and SaaS. Google Gmail would be an example of which of these service models? Why?
5. What are the ways cloud computing can be deployed? Where would you classify cloud computing on the STMM? Explain your rationale.
6. Should a company outsource any of its IT resources to the cloud?
7. What is the blockchain? Do you think that blockchain will create a revolution in financial services and other industries? What is so new and different about blockchain technology? What type of networking architecture do you think works best for blockchain and why?
8. Using the CSMM, how would you assess the internal control at Joe's Ristoranté? What level do you think they should be?
9. How can the concepts of decomposition, hierarchy, and flow be used to understand the structure of an accounting system? What is the purpose and benefit of doing so?
10. Compare and contrast a hierarchical block diagram to a horizontal block diagram. Which one is better?
11. How many cycles are generally found in an accounting system? What are they? How are they grouped?
12. What is an accounting transaction cycle?
13. Which of the transaction cycles are present in Joe's Ristoranté? What are the implications of your findings?
14. Which of the possible accounting applications (i.e., modules or subsystems below the cycle level) are present or missing in Joe's system? Again, what are the implications?
15. What does evaluation mean, and why is it important to the systems field?
16. How do accounting systems work? What are the tasks that are fundamental to all accounting systems regardless of the technology?
17. What is the value of cloud-based computing?
18. What is a chart of accounts? What is its purpose? How can its design affect the quality of an accounting system?
19. What is the purpose of block codes and group codes? How do group codes play a role in providing useful accounting information?
20. What is the difference between batch and real-time accounting systems? Which one is better or better suited to keeping track of (a) payroll and (b) airline reservations? Explain how a mismatch between the processing method and the environment can be costly.
21. Bloom's taxonomy can be used to describe the level of thinking required in processing accounting information. Which of the following levels would best describe when an accountant can understand the various categories of cloud computing and can give examples of the categories?
    a. analysis
    b. comprehension
    c. application
    d. synthesis
22. The technology component of accounting systems has evolved dramatically over the last two decades. Nevertheless, many "mom-and-pop" type businesses have no bookkeepers and simply collect their transactions and turn them over to a CPA at the end of the year. Which of the following best describes this type of accounting system?
    a. worksheet
    b. journals and ledgers
    c. shoe-box
    d. transaction files

23. Which of the following would best describe the level of control maturity at a company where control practices are known but not written down and where training does not exist?
    a. nonexistent
    b. initial
    c. informal
    d. formal and systematic
24. Which of the following diagrams shows inter-level associations of data, but not information flows?
    a. horizontal block diagram
    b. hierarchical block diagram
    c. Both a and b
    d. None of the above
25. Which of the following cycles involved the transformation of raw materials, labor, and overhead into finished goods as well as nonmanufactured goods into cash?
    a. purchasing
    b. reporting
    c. planning/control
    d. conversion
26. Which of the following applications is not included within the planning/control cycle?
    a. cost estimating
    b. inventory tracking
    c. budgeting
    d. standard costing
27. When comparing how a manual accounting system works in relation to a computerized system, which of the following pairs would not be equivalent?
    a. a journal and a transaction file
    b. general ledger and a master file
    c. posting and coding the transaction
    d. written report and a screen view
28. Which of the following about new accounting technologies is false?
    a. cloud computing always uses the internet.
    b. XBRL always uses the internet.
    c. ERP systems always use an enterprise-wide database and may provide internet access.
    d. EDI always uses the internet.
29. Which type of file corresponds to the general ledger and subsidiary ledgers in a manual system?
    a. transaction
    b. open
    c. online
    d. master
30. Which utilizes periodic posting of transaction data to master files?
    a. pure batch
    b. real time
    c. interactive batch
    d. Both a and b
    e. Both a and c

31. **60000-pss## Sales** represents a possible coding scheme for describing sales at a company where the **p** is for product line, **ss** is for salesperson number, and **##** is for store number. This additional code would be an example of
    a. block coding.
    b. group coding.
    c. open coding.
    d. batch coding.
32. Using the coding scheme from the previous question, if a sale were recorded as 5000-23419, it would most likely be for
    a. product 23 accessories, salesperson number 34, at store number #19.
    b. product 2 accessories, salesperson number 34, at store number #9.
    c. product 23 accessories, salesperson number 41, at store number #9.
    d. product 2 accessories, salesperson number 34, at store number #19.
33. Which of the following would not be a good reason to outsource IT services to the cloud?
    a. It allows some business processes to be automated.
    b. It reduces the need to maintain hardware and software.
    c. It can potentially save a company significant IT expenditure.
    d. It may not be easily scalable or sharable with other companies.
34. Tracing transaction flow from creation to disposition is referred to as
    a. a test of understanding.
    b. a walkthrough.
    c. a transaction cycle.
    d. Both a and b
35. **PROBLEM-BASED LEARNING: Thinking about Blockchain and Putting the Technology into Perspective**

    After graduating from college, you accept a position in the accounting department of a large corporation in the financial services industry. Upon arrival, you immediately began to hear a lot of talk about the blockchain. Some individuals talked about it as though it were a threat, and others seemed to frame it as an opportunity. One thing was clear: Most people did not understand how a blockchain would be used in an organization.

    Required:

    a. What is the general system problem that blockchain technology is most suited to address? Explain.
    b. What type of specific applications would a blockchain be appropriate for? Provide some examples.
    c. Under what circumstances would using a blockchain in the accounting system not have value? Be specific and also comment in general.
    d. When implementing a blockchain, would you use a distributed peer-to-peer network or a centralized network approach? Explain.
    e. Can you think of some blockchain applications that would work better on the public internet versus a private permissioned network and vice versa?
    f. Is blockchain a system? If so, what is the objective, what are its parts, and how do they work together?
    g. Explaining how blockchain works requires what level of thinking on Bloom's Taxonomy?
    h. Where is blockchain on the STMM?
    i. The controls in a blockchain are operating at what level of the CSMM?
36. **A CAMPUS INTERVIEW: Bloom's Taxonomy and Critical Thinking**

    Kym is a partner at one of the public accounting firms in the Boston area. She has come to conduct interviews at your college and is hoping to extend an offer for a full-time staff position for the upcoming fall. Kym's last interview is with Ryan, a senior accounting major with a psychology minor. So far, Kym has been impressed with Ryan's eye contact and his responses to her routine questions. So, Kym asks Ryan to define critical thinking and the purpose of it from an accounting perspective. She then asks Ryan to give his opinion on the importance of critical thinking in decision-making. Kym then asks Ryan: "Assume that you are giving advice to a small business owner of a fishing and tackle shop on Cape Cod who hears that Walmart will be opening a store about 10 miles away. What recommendations would you give to the business owner in order to stay competitive?" Kym is interested in observing Ryan's business knowledge, but more importantly, she is interested in how he will take the issue and structure his response.

Required:

a. How would you answer Kym's questions?
b. Think about Bloom's Taxonomy. Based upon your answers to Kym's questions, what level would you rank yourself? What level(s) would you say is required to provide the best answers?
c. How do Kym's questions relate to critical thinking? How can this mode of thinking be important in public or private accounting?

37. Your parents own a small seafood restaurant in New England with a spectacular waterfront view. The restaurant is popular for its atmosphere and delicious food. Due to its popularity, it has "regular" customers who are loyal to the restaurant and who live in the surrounding area. You have come home for the summer to earn some money waiting on tables. The restaurant has one computer terminal into which serving staff enter the food orders. This computer is connected to a receipt printer in the kitchen. When the orders are submitted, the printer prints out the order, and the head chef rips it off the printer reel and adds it to the food preparation queue. Once the customers have finished their meals, the servers ring up the bills on the cash register in the front of the restaurant.

The restaurant does not accept any checks or credit or debit cards, just cash. At the end of the month, your parents ask you to help them calculate the end of the month sales and expenses. In the small office outside of the kitchen, your father opens up a filing cabinet with folders containing receipts and invoices. Your mom and dad take turns bringing the money from the cash register to the bank at the end of each week and depositing the funds into their checking account.

Required:

a. Read and analyze the case above and identify any risks and likely systems problems.
b. Using the STMM, explain where the restaurant functions in relation to the model. Are their operating practices sound? What level of the STMM model do you think they should be on considering the relevant costs and benefits?
c. What level would you rank the restaurant on using the control systems maturity model? Explain. What level do you think they should be on?

38. **TRANSACTION CYCLES: Identification from Examples**

Accounting systems generally contain six transaction cycles. Three are operating and three are supporting.

Required:

Given the descriptions below, please identify which transaction cycle is being described and whether that cycle is an operating cycle or a supporting cycle:

a. Involves the transformation of merchandise inventory into cash
b. Includes the credit and collection function
c. Deals with maintenance of the general ledger
d. Includes the purchase requisitioning function
e. Involves the tracking of capital stock
f. Used to determine what transactions will take place in the other cycles and how they will be controlled
g. Includes the cost accounting function
h. Includes the cash disbursements function

39. **TRANSACTION CYCLES: Identification from Examples**

Accounting systems generally contain six transaction cycles. Three are operating and three are supporting.

Required:

Given the descriptions below, please identify which transaction cycle is being described and whether that cycle is an operating cycle or a supporting cycle:

a. Pertains to processing accounts payable
b. Includes the cash receipts function
c. Includes the filing of tax and regulatory reports
d. Includes the payroll function
e. Involves the tracking of borrowed fund
f. Includes budgeting
g. Includes the shipping function
h. Includes the receiving function

Endnotes

1. For the purposes of this textbook, we are using the original version of Bloom's Taxonomy, which was published in 1953. Although a revised version, published in 1991, moves Evaluation down to level 5 and replaces it with Creativity, the authors believe that using Evaluation as the highest level of systems thinking makes more practical sense. Evaluation is also the highest level of thinking being evaluated on the CPA exam.
2. https://www.crn.com/news/storage/222600510/the-100-coolest-cloud-computing-vendors.htm
3. www.netsuite.com/portal/customer-testimonials/roku-manufacturing.shtml

CHAPTER 3

The Data Analytic Cycle—One Approach to Data-Driven Decisions

The data analytic cycle includes several stages and is a continuous process for an organization's data-driven decision strategy. This approach, as described by Raschke and Charron (2021), is seen in Figure 3.1. The first stage of the cycle is data capture and storage; the second stage is data extraction. As data are rarely extracted in a format necessary for analysis, the third stage is data preparation, which may involve restructuring the data to get it in a format readable to analyze. The fourth stage is data analysis, and finally the fifth stage is sharing and communicating data insights. You may hear the term **ETL** used by IT professionals; it is an acronym for extract, transform, and load. The data analytic cycle includes the ETL steps and adds an important step for communicating findings and insights. We will discuss the relevance of each cycle and the importance for accountants to have a good working knowledge of each stage of the data analytic cycle.

ETL
Extract, transform, and load.

FIGURE 3.1 Data Analytic Cycle

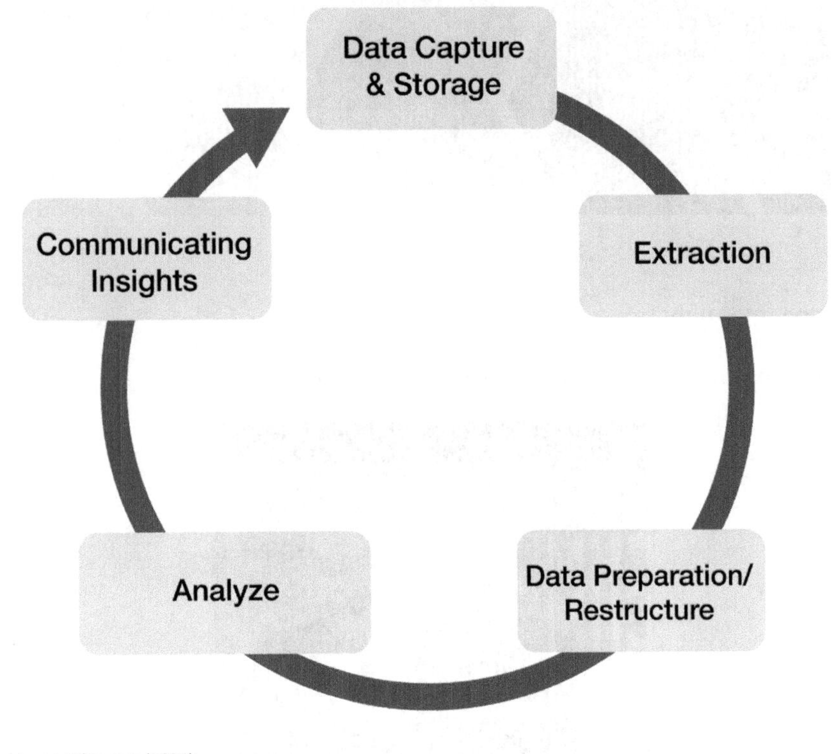

Source: Raschke and Charron (2021)

3.1 Data Capture and Storage—Stage One

Learning Objectives

At the end of this section, students should be able to:

1. Understand the steps of the data analytic cycle.
2. Understand the best way to store data in an accounting system.
3. Recognize what a flat file is and what it contains.
4. Explain the hierarchy of items in a file.
5. Understand the difference between a conventional flat-file system and a relational database.
6. Understand the logical connection of a set of related tables.

Because data storage is a fundamental building block for data analytics, it is important for accountants to understand its basics: how data are stored and where data are stored so it can be extracted and eventually analyzed. It was not that long ago when most data were stored on source documents in drawers or file cabinets. Data management has evolved over time as shown in Figure 3.2.

FIGURE 3.2 The Evolution of Data Management

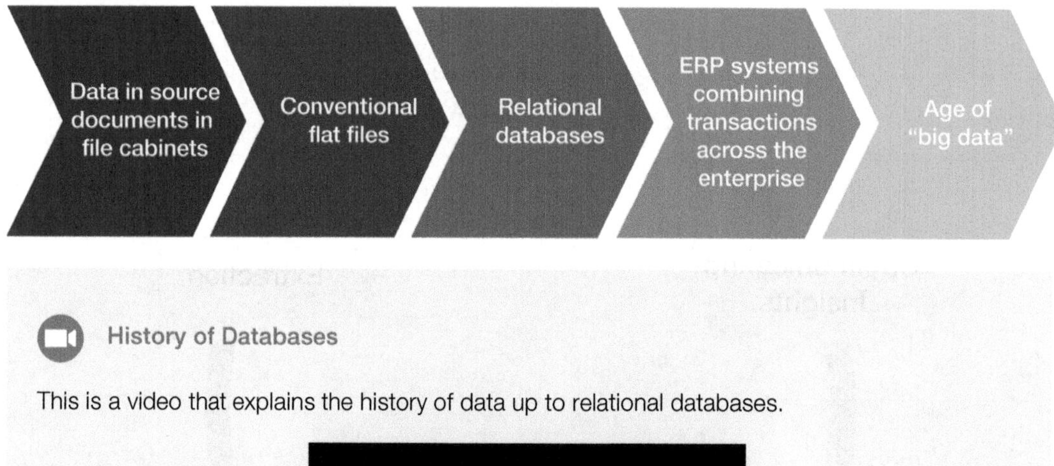

History of Databases

This is a video that explains the history of data up to relational databases.

View in the online reader

While most information is now contained in a computer-based system, data from operations can be stored in a **data file**, which stores sets of **records** such as sales transactions and inventory balances. These files are of three main types: 1) **transaction files**, 2) **master files**, and 3) **open files**, and it is important that you understand the distinctions among them.

Transaction files capture detailed transaction data, usually in chronological order, providing a diary of financial activity, e.g., sales, cash receipts. They are analogous to the paper journals in a manual system.

Master files correspond to the general ledger and subsidiary ledgers in a manual system. The general ledger master file must contain one record for each account in the organization's chart of accounts and is relatively permanent in nature. Account numbers or codes identify these accounts.

In addition to the general ledger master file, a computer-based system may have several subsidiary ledger master files, such as an inventory master file or a customer master file. The up-to-dateness and availability of these subsidiary and master file records can be significant to the successful operation of a business. For example, you cannot make effective credit and collection decisions without up-to-date information. The sum of the dollar balances in each subsidiary master file must also equal the related control account in the general ledger master file.

Open files hold data about transactions that are as yet incomplete, such as open sales order files and open purchase order files. Managers must use these computer files to ensure transactions are properly completed in a timely manner. Auditors and managers must be sure that employees do not manipulate incomplete transactions.

data file

Data stored in a data base and made up of records.

records

A group of data fields in a table (e.g., row of data in a table).

transaction files

Captures detailed transaction data in a database table.

master files

Relatively permanent data that is considered a main subject for a database table (e.g., customers, inventory, vendors).

open files

Holds data about transactions that are incomplete (e.g., open sales order files and open purchase order files).

Conventional Flat Files

Conventional flat files in an accounting information system include the following:

1. Master files, e.g., customer information, inventory
2. Open files, e.g., purchase orders

A **flat file** is a collection of records of data. They are called flat because the data do not have a hierarchical structure. The data appear similar to what you would see on a spreadsheet with column headings and list of data underneath the headings.

A record can represent a transaction in a transaction file or data, such as ledger accounts in a general ledger or inventory items along with their balances in an inventory master file. Each record consists of **fields**. Each field within a record stores data relating to the file context.

For example, think of a flat file as a pack of 3 x 5 cards where each card is a record in the file. If we create a student file, each record or card would include, for example, three data elements or fields such as (1) Student name, (2) Major, and (3) Grade Point Average (GPA). In this case, a record layout for the flat file would look like Figure 3.3.

flat file

Collection of records of data that have no hierarchical structure for the data.

field

A part of a record that stores a data element (e.g., Customer name is a field in the Customer table).

FIGURE 3.3 Example Record Layout for Student File

Student Name	Major	GPA
Sally Blair	Accounting	3.25
Joe Smith	Accounting	3.24

byte

Made up of an 8-bit (binary digit) code.

A file is made up of data records. Records, in turn, are made up of fields. Fields contain characters, such as letters, numbers, or symbols. Characters are represented in computer memory as a byte. A **byte** is made up of an 8-bit (binary digit) code. Therefore, a character and a byte are essentially the same thing hierarchically. Binary digits are essentially on-off circuits in a computer. The term bit is being increasingly used in the real world to describe the power and complexity of things such as operating systems (32 versus 64 bit), microprocessors (32 versus 64 bit), video graphics cards (32, 64, 128, versus 256 bit), data encryption (128, 256, 1024 bit), and Internet connection speeds (1.5, 3, 10, 25, 100 Mbps). The more bits a technology has, the more powerful and complex it is likely to be. Figure 3.4 shows how the data items in a file build on each other going from the bottom up.

FIGURE 3.4 Hierarchy of Data Elements Within a File

File
Record
Field1 Field2 Field3
Characters made up of bytes
Binary digits (bits)

update anomaly

Occurs when a database is not properly normalized; a multiple update operation occurs when only one update would suffice.

relational databases

Collection of inter-related files that stores information in an efficient manner.

Advantages of computer files are that large amounts of data can be stored and that data can be retrieved quickly. However, conventional flat files can have redundancy of data. For example, the same data field may be found in multiple files, and sometimes when an update is made, it is not made to all of the files (and so the data in some fields may be in conflict, which is called an **update anomaly**). Although computer-based files allowed data to be stored more efficiently so records can be searched and retrieved more easily, accountants began to discover data access, redundancy, and conflict problems with this approach. To address these file system problems, **relational databases** were developed, and many organizations still store data using this fundamental structure. Although relational databases can serve to minimize data redundancy and conflict, if not designed correctly, they can be inefficient and contain database anomalies. The concept of database design is discussed in Chapter 7.

Relational Database Concepts

A relational database is a collection of inter-related files that stores information in an efficient manner. The key feature that makes a database relational is that every file in the collection shares at least one field in common directly or indirectly with every other file. These relationships allow the database user to access all of the data in almost unlimited ways. In order to make this access possible, the database software must allow these common fields to be joined and thus act as though they are physically connected even though the relationship is only logical in nature.

Advanced accounting systems tend to use this type of data structure because it allows accounting information to be more easily accessed and reported. Relational databases are also more flexible, scalable, and easily queried. In Chapter 7 of this book, we will learn more about how relational databases are designed and organized. For now, it is important to know that all the information that you need to perform an analysis may be from many inter-related tables. To imagine the connections discussed above, let's view sales transactions that use three related tables (files), seen in Figure 3.5 joined by their common fields. We want to know what we sold and to whom we sold it. This requires one transaction file (sales transaction file) and two master files (Customer and Product master files).

FIGURE 3.5 Linkages Between Relational Tables

Sales_Transaction_File

Dates	Cust_ID	Product_ID	QTY	Amount
1/12/19	C15108	P1052599	1	2000.00
1/15/19	C15105	P1052837	1	1000.00
1/16/19	C15112	P1060001	1	2500.00
1/18/19	C15108	P1060001	1	2500.00

Customer_File (Master)

Cust_ID	Names	Address
C15105	J. Adams	15 Main St.
C15108	H. Mart	123 Washington St.
C15112	A. Smith	77 Wentworth Ave.

Product_File (Master)

Product_ID	Description	On_Hand	Cost
P1052599	Widget	8	750.00
P1052837	Gadget	21	500.00
P1060001	Smiget	15	1200.00

If we were to look at the transaction from January 12, we see that customer ID C15108 in the Sales Transaction file is related to the Customer master file information, which tells us that customer C15108 is H. Mart. If we also see that the Product ID from the January 12 transaction is 1 unit of Product P1052599, which is found in the Product master file and called a Widget. In Chapter 7, we will learn more about designing a database to meet our business process needs.

Why is this information in three separate files and not just one?

One file would make this a conventional flat file format like we previously discussed.

As the organization continues to grow and have more transactions, gets new customers, stops doing business with customers, adds new products to sell, or doesn't sell products that it used to sell, then redundancies and inefficiencies will become more problematic. That's why we have three tables that relate to each other.

entity

An item of interest about which an organization would like to collect information (also referred to a table in a database).

attributes

The data elements that define an entity such as a customer's identification code, name, and address.

Relational databases are usually organized with a data model made up of entities of interest, attributes, and occurrences. An **entity** is an item of interest about which an organization would like to collect information. Entities can be physical, like inventories and vendors, or they can be conceptual, like accounts receivable or accounts payable. **Attributes** are the data elements that define an entity, such as a customer's identification code, name, and address. Occurrences are used to describe the number of instances or records that pertain to the particular entity of interest.

Logical database files, called tables, are constructed with each entity being represented by a separate logical table (imagine that a table is one spreadsheet). Across the top of each table are the attributes, which form columns. For example, part number, description, quantity, and reorder point are the attributes of the inventory table illustrated in Table 3.1. The rows (records) of the table are then the number of occurrences of the specific entity. For example, Table 3.1 shows four occurrences or records in the inventory table.

TABLE 3.1 Inventory Table

Part #	Description	Qty.	Reorder
102345	Video Card	5	3
215001	1 TB Hard Drive	6	5
324789	Power Supply	1	1
450915	Motherboard	0	2

primary key

Attribute in a table that is the unique identifier.

A properly designed table means that at least one attribute is unique for that record. This attribute is what we will call the **primary key** of the table. The primary key is used to identify records in a table as well as to sort it efficiently. In Table 3.1, the Part# would be the best choice for the primary key because it would be unique for each record. However, Qty. would not be a good choice because several records could have the same quantity.

The difference between a conventional flat-file and a relational database is that with a conventional flat-file, the data are separated into independent files. For example, the accounts receivable application might own the customer master file and the sales transaction file, and it is independent of inventory files. In contrast, with a database system, the data are interconnected and owned by the whole system. Therefore, in an accounting system where an application needs to simultaneously access or pull data from multiple files, it is better to pool the data and use a database system. Database systems, however, bring higher software costs, increased hardware requirements, and the need for specialized technical skills.

Big Data and Storage Concepts

Big data is defined as data having one or more of the following characteristics: high volume, high velocity, veracity, or variety.[1] High volume means that a large scale of data is collected. High velocity is analysis of streaming or real-time data. Veracity is uncertainty of the data, and variety means different forms of data. What this means is that organizations that want to capture a high volume of data in real time or structured as well as unstructured data in real time may need a different type of database storage environment than a simple relational database.

big data

Data having one or more of the following characteristics: high volume, high velocity, high variability, or high variety.

The storage of big data and analysis is promising for organizations in the areas of new-product development, market targeting, and pricing. For accounting, big data is promising in the areas of risk assessment, fraud detection, and forensic investigations.

Many organizations that support single-processor relational database systems have come to a crossroads as the age of big data has emerged. As businesses find value in rapidly capturing and analyzing large amounts of variable data (such as events, documents, pictures, video, voice, and email) from devices and technologies (such as the internet and social media, credit and customer loyalty cards, surveillance cameras, Wi-Fi sensors, and electronic tags) and making immediate changes in their business based on the data they receive, organizations will find that traditional methods of data storage will no longer work. ABI Research predicts that by 2020 more than 30 billion devices will be wirelessly connected to the internet (Cisco estimates 50 billion overall).[2] To accommodate this change, NoSQL database solutions have been developed as well as software for analyzing big data, such as Apache Hadoop and Google's MapReduce.

One of the problems with "big data" is that it is not well defined. Consequently, it will not fit nicely into the data model of a relational database system. Alternatively, another data management solution might be to store the "big data" in a **data warehouse**. Data warehouses contain copies of transactions from operational transaction processing systems integrated and reformatted in a way to facilitate various types of reporting and analysis. Although this may sound redundant, it is necessary because of the performance burden and possible locking out of file records that could be caused by some of the more complex analytic queries and reporting applications contained in the reporting and business intelligence modules of enterprise resource planning systems. Many operational transaction processing systems also contain batched data stored on tape and are, therefore, incompatible with most data mining software. Data warehouses also clean and reformat the data to significantly improve the performance of these sophisticated reporting systems, creating a subset known as a **data mart**. The data models of data warehouses, however, are still based to some extent on the operational transaction-based structures and so they are not designed to accommodate "big data."

data warehouse

Contains copies of transactions from the database and are often reformatted to facilitate reporting and analysis.

data mart

Subset of a data warehouse that is specifically curated for a functional area (e.g., sales department).

Besides a data warehouse, another concept for storing "big data" is a "**data lake**." James Dixon, Chief Technology Officer (CTO) of Pentaho is credited for the term "data lake" where it first appeared in his blog. Dixon uses a simple analogy to understand the differences between a data mart and a data lake. "Think of a data mart as a store of bottled water—cleansed and packaged and structured for easy consumption."[3] A traditional lake is a large body of water with streams that flow into it. Just like a traditional lake, the data lake streams content in from a source to fill the lake, and data users of the lake can come to examine, dive in, or take samples. Therefore, a data lake can be viewed as a really large data storage that can store structured and unstructured data. Each data element in a lake is assigned a unique identifier and tagged with a set of extended metadata tags. When a business question arises, the data lake can be queried for relevant data, and that smaller set of data can then be analyzed to help answer the question. Hence, it is a way to describe any large data pool in which the data requirements are not defined until the data are queried. Here's a video that describes the differences between a data warehouse, data mart, and data lake.

data lake

A massive data repository built on inexpensive commodity computer hardware ideal for storing big data.

 Data Lake vs. Warehouse vs. Mart: What's the Difference?

This is a video that discusses the data storage differences between a data warehouse, data mart, and a data lake.

View in the online reader

distributed file system

Stores data on a network using a client/server approach to spread a very large file out over multiple file servers.

A completely different means of storing data is to spread data out over multiple file servers. This is called a **distributed file system**. The file system then uses a naming convention and mapping scheme to keep track of where the data are stored so when the system is queried and retrieved, the data will appear as a normal file on the client machine. Unlike a relational database, a distributed file system does not require a data model. When a user changes data that has been retrieved, the system will then redistribute the changed data to the file servers when the user is done.

3.2 Data Extraction—Stage 2

Learning Objectives

At the end of this section, students should be able to:

1. Describe the two types of data to be extracted.
2. Know basic structured data extraction using SQL.

query

Ask a question of the database to fetch the data.

The second stage of the data analytic cycle relates to the need to access data stored in a database, or the ability to extract the data from the database. As mentioned in Chapter 1, data are structured or unstructured. Extracting structured data is much simpler to do because the structure of the database allows us to **query**, or ask a question to the database. To accomplish this task, there must be some type of query language.

Structured Data Extraction

The most common query language available for relational databases today is called **SQL** (which stands for Structured Query Language and is pronounced "sequel"). Within this query language, there is something known as the SQL SELECT command, which allows you to fetch data from the database by specifying the field names, from the relevant file name(s), and the selection criteria.

SQL
Structured Query Language, pronounced "sequel."

For example, let's say we want to query the database in Figure 3.5 using the following SQL command:

SELECT Dates, Cust_ID, Amount

FROM Sales_Transaction_File

WHERE Amount > 2000;

Here we are simply looking for the date, customer ID, and amount for any sales made that were larger than $2,000. The result would be in Table 3.2:

TABLE 3.2 Results of SQL Select command

Dates	Cust_ID	Amount
1/16/19	C15112	2500.00
1/18/19	C15108	2500.00

Notice that the transaction dated 1/12/19 to customer C15108 is not extracted. That is because our query was "greater than" 2000. Now let's find the gross profit earned for products sold to customer C15105. To execute this query, we will need to specify fields in more than one file (the two tables must therefore be joined in SQL using a JOIN in the FROM):

SELECT Dates, Amount, Cost

FROM Sales_Transaction_File JOIN Product_File

WHERE Cust_ID = "C15105";

The above query should yield the result shown in Table 3.3, where the data are fetched from these two tables and we could calculate the gross profit:

TABLE 3.3 Results of SQL Join Command

Dates	Amount	Cost
1/15/19	1000.00	500.00

Please note that customer ID needed to be enclosed in quotes in the WHERE because the data type is text; whereas, the amount above did not because the data type is a number. If we had chosen a date data type for our criterion, we would have to enclose it with the number sign as follows: #8/19/19#.

For example, let's do a query to find out what the gross profits were on sales that occurred prior to 1/17/19. To perform this query, we would need the following SQL:

SELECT Dates, Amount, Cost

FROM Sales_Transaction_File JOIN Product_File

WHERE Dates < #1/17/19#;

The above query should yield the following results in Table 3.4:

TABLE 3.4 Results of SQL Command for sales prior to 1/17/19

Dates	Amount	Cost
1/12/19	2000.00	700.00
1/15/19	1000.00	500.00
1/16/19	2500.00	1200.00

For criteria, you can also use <= (for less than or equal to) and <> (for not equal to). Moreover, wouldn't it be cool if you could invent a fourth column for your output that actually shows the Gross Profit (a calculated field)? This can be accomplished by adding a comma and a calculated field at the end of your SELECT statement and giving it a column heading with the SQL command AS:

SELECT Dates, Amount, Cost, Amount – Cost AS Gross Profit

Unstructured Data Extraction

Unstructured data include textual data found on websites, pdf documents, social media, or emails. Unstructured data extraction is not as simple as structured data extraction. Unstructured data do not reside in a relational database but may be found in a data lake. Depending on the type and source of unstructured data, specific extraction tools could be used. Unstructured data extraction may also require the use of Python programming, depending on what you are trying to extract. Python can be used to extract specific data of interest from a specific website, commonly known as web-scraping or parsing. While Python coding is beyond the scope of this book, many beginner tutorials can be found on the internet.

Another example that may require unstructured data extraction tools is a website with a detailed table of information. How would you extract that table from the website? It seems that it would be easy to use our curser to copy the data and then paste it into a spreadsheet. However, it may end up looking messy in the spreadsheet. The Chrome web browser has an extension tool called "table capture" that allows you to copy html data from a table and paste it to a spreadsheet. In addition to using different tools and techniques for unstructured data extraction, you may have to actually prepare the textual data prior to extracting it. For example, you may need to build a dictionary for words that are of interest to extract from text data. For purposes of this textbook, unstructured data extraction is for awareness purposes only as many computer science and data analytics courses teach Python programming and specific text analytics methods, respectively.

3.3 Data Preparation and Transformation—Stage Three

Learning Objectives

At the end of this section, students should be able to:

1. Describe the two ways data is reshaped.
2. Describe the three ways to join data.

Up to 80 percent of the time required to analyze a business is spent on data preparation. Considered the least-liked task, data preparations is the most important because we need to make sure that the data are in the proper format to analyze in our data analysis software. Recall the characteristics of good data from Chapter 1? It is important to have good quality data to do your analysis, and more times than not, the data need to be "cleaned." Simple examples may be that your numbers are in a text format, but it would be better to analyze if they were formatted as numbers. Cleaning the data to transform text to number format for certain fields of data would be helpful. In addition, we may notice that some of our customers have similar yet different names. Perhaps the company name is in lower case in some places and in all upper case in others. Cleaning the data would also require identifying duplicates and making any other necessary corrections.

Reshaping Data

Data formats can be described as either wide or long. Wide format is what we are more often used to when we see a spreadsheet with a row representing each observation and variables are across the spreadsheet in each column. So, with data in a wide format, we can see the data variables spread out horizontally. Conversely, long format has the variables in one column and the values in another column. With data in a long format, we can see the data variables vertically.

Data may need to be reshaped because the software to do the data analysis requires one format over the other. Figure 3.6 shows the same data in both wide and long formats. As shown in the Figure 3-7, the wide format has four columns; the first column depicts a list of asset categories. Columns two through four are labeled by respective year-end dates for three years. When these same data are reshaped into the long format, there are three columns. Notice how Date is one column and all three years are in this one column.

FIGURE 3.6 Data Formats

Wide Format

	12/31/2017	12/31/2018	12/31/2019
Cash	5,000	8,000	11,000
Inventory	10,000	9,000	8,000
Accounts Receivable	13,000	14,000	16,000

Long Format

Asset Type	Date	Amount
Cash	12/31/2017	5,000
Cash	12/31/2018	8,000
Cash	12/31/2019	11,000
Inventory	12/31/2017	10,000
Inventory	12/31/2018	9,000
Inventory	12/31/2019	8,000
Accounts Receivable	12/31/2017	13,000
Accounts Receivable	12/31/2018	14,000
Accounts Receivable	12/31/2019	16,000

Joining Data

Preparing data for analysis may require the user to combine data from two separate sources. Data joining may come from the same source, such as a relational database or from different sources such as a database and a spreadsheet or a different database. Similar in concept to a relational database where the data tables are already joined together through a common variable between the two tables (e.g., Customer number), you may need to physically join two disparate sets of data to analyze. For example, your customer information resides in your AIS, but your satisfaction survey results are kept in a separate spreadsheet. Joining the data between these two sources would allow you to analyze which customers are satisfied and those who are not satisfied. However, you can still ask more questions of this joined data, such as *"What did the customers that were not satisfied buy?"* The ability to identify trends with a product and satisfaction levels may identify a root problem with a product, allowing for management to make better decisions before a bigger problem occurs.

FIGURE 3.7 Inner Join Condition

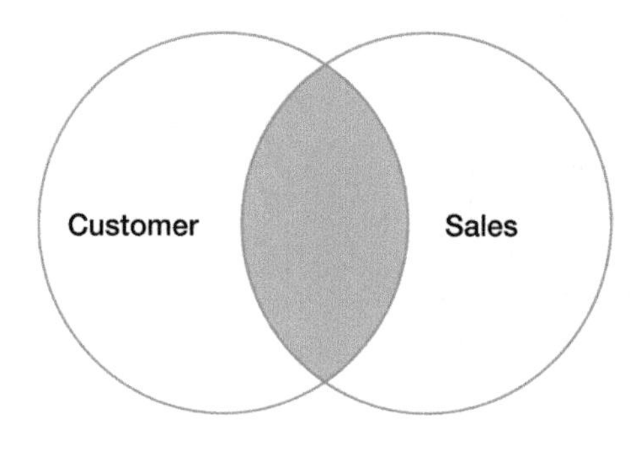

Four types of join conditions can occur between two tables. These are best illustrated thinking about the data between two tables and displayed using Venn diagrams. For the purpose of illustration, the data found in Figure 3.8 is used. In Figure 3.8, two tables have one field in common, Cust_ID (circled in red). It is important to note that the field you want to join for the two tables is consistent, meaning that you cannot join a text field to a number field. To illustrate this, if Cust_ID was all text in one table and alphanumeric in the second table, you would need to reformat one of the fields in a table to make it consistent with the field you intend to join in the other table. Examine the data in these two files. Do you notice anything? In the Customer_File, there are four customers, and in the Sales_Transaction file, there are four transactions. Do you see that one customer does not have any transactions? It is Customer ID C15120. To illustrate the different joins, you will see that the output depends on the join condition.

FIGURE 3.8 Customer and Sales Transaction Tables to Join

Customer_File (Master)

Cust_ID	Names	Address
C15105	J. Adams	15 Main St.
C15108	H. Mart	123 Washington St.
C15112	A. Smith	77 Wentworth Ave.
C15112	M. Malloy	35 St. George Ave.

Sales_Transaction_File

Dates	Cust_ID	Product_ID	QTY	Amount
1/12/19	C15108	P1052599	1	2000.00
1/15/19	C15105	P1052837	1	1000.00
1/16/19	C15112	P1060001	1	2500.00
1/18/19	C15108	P1060001	1	2500.00

In the case of an inner join condition (Cust_ID), the output is the intersection of records from the customer and the sales transaction file where Cust_ID matches. The output would show all four transactions for the three customers C15105, C15108, and C15112. Because customer C15120 has no sales transactions, this customer is not included in the inner join output.

Figure 3.9 displays a Venn diagram of the Left Join condition. Here the output would show all records from the customer table, regardless of if a sales transaction is associated with that customer. A left join is relevant if you are interested in identifying which customers have no sales transactions. Somewhat similar in concept, the Right Join condition would have output of all sales transactions regardless if there is a customer id match. A right join is relevant if you are interested in finding out if a sales transaction does not have a proper customer id and you are trying to identify any errors in your table. Figure 3.10 displays a Venn diagram of a right join. The fourth join condition is the Full Join, which lists all records from both tables, so both circles in the Venn diagram would be fully shaded and list all records, no matter if they match between tables.

FIGURE 3.9 Left Join Condition

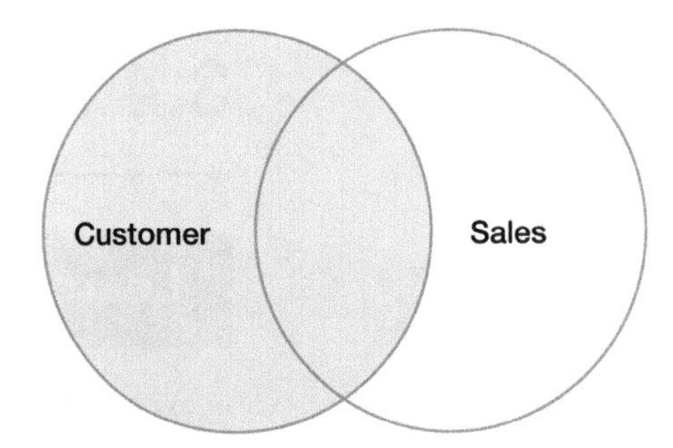

FIGURE 3.10 Right Join Condition

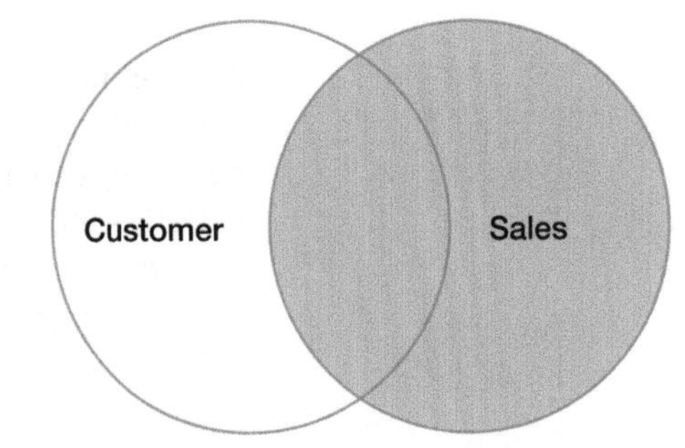

Different Types of Joins

This is a video that explains the four different types of joins with examples.

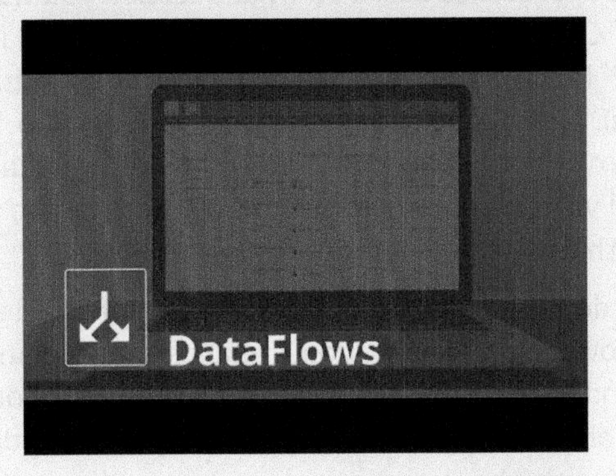

View in the online reader

3.4 Data Analysis—Stage Four

Learning Objectives

At the end of this section, students should be able to:

1. Describe the three types of data analysis.
2. Understand the differences between the three types of data analysis.

After extracting and prepping the data you need, you finally get to analyze the data! If 80 percent of the effort is extracting and prepping the data, 20 percent is spent on analysis. One of the greatest advantages that accountants have, from a data analysis perspective, is that we are trained to be objective and independent. This means that accountants are expected to be objective and free from bias when analyzing the data. There are generally three types of data analytics: descriptive, predictive, and prescriptive.

Descriptive Analysis

descriptive analysis

Simplest analysis that looks to understand questions from the data of *what* happened or *why* it happened.

Descriptive analysis is the most common form of analytics that most businesses conduct today. This type of analysis can be approached based on what question you want to answer, such as *"Why are profits down this year?"* Or more specifically, *"Why are profits down in the northeast region and up in the southeast region?"* Many organizations run their business using measures called key performance indicators (KPIs). Descriptive analysis uses these data to build a data visualization dashboard around several of these KPIs. A dashboard uses the updated organization data and keeps it in a predetermined visualization that continues to be useful to the organization. This way, you do not have to rebuild the visualization each day, week, or month.

A second approach to descriptive analysis is exploration of the data for any interesting patterns. You may not even know what your question is and just want to understand the relationships with your data. You may end up discovering interesting trends that you did not know previously. Skills involved with both of these types of analysis evolve around data visualization software where you would interact with the data to analyze. Interactive data visualization techniques involve aggregating the data, filtering the data on certain variables, creating calculations from the data, etc. Descriptive analytics uses the organization's historical data and asks, *"What has happened?"*

Predictive Analysis

predictive analysis

Uses your data to make predictions or to ask, *"What will happen?"*

Predictive analysis uses your data to make predictions or to ask, *"What will happen?"* Predictions with your data are based on statistical models. One of the most basic statistical models that you may have already encountered in your business coursework is the linear regression model. The best way to describe a linear regression model is that you have a relationship between an independent variable (e.g., average daily temperature) and a dependent variable (e.g., sales). Your model may end up showing that average daily temperature increases sales. Although this is a highly simplified example, it is important to note that these two variables may be correlated, meaning that when average daily temperature is high, so are sales, and when average daily temperature is low, so are sales. Can we conclude that average daily temperature causes sales? Causation would require you to conduct a statistical linear regression test with the hypotheses that average daily temperature causes sales. Although statistics are beyond the scope of this textbook, it is important that an accountant with subject matter knowledge understand basic statistic concepts when doing predictive data analysis.

Other more complex predictive analysis includes developing algorithms and the use of machine learning. The use of massive amounts of data is generally required to develop specific algorithms that are directed toward solving a specific problem. It is important to note that the main difference between descriptive and predictive analytics is that predictive analytics uses statistical techniques to "predict" a future outcome. Both methods use historical data of the organization. Examples of predictive analytics for business organizations is to predict customer churn (cancellations), predict organizational bankruptcy or customer lending risks, etc.

Prescriptive Analysis

Prescriptive analysis takes predictive analytics to a new level by the ability to recommend (prescribe) an action based upon an optimized outcome. The question answered here is, *"What should we do?"* This type of analytics uses the modeling found in predictive analytics and incorporates it with business rules and real-time data to prescribe recommendations of action.

prescriptive analysis

Analysis that seeks to use the data to prescribe an action based upon an optimized outcome or asks, *"What should we do?"*

While many companies have not yet reached this level of maturity with their analytics, the level of sophistication needed to implement the best-prescribed option requires vast amounts of data, statistical tools and data science techniques to provide optimization options and decision support. This means successful organizations using prescriptive analytics can harness potential effective opportunities on how business will be done in the future. Examples include the company FleetPride, who uses prescriptive analytics to manage the supply chain that determines optimal actions for daily customer demand, staffing, and inventory.[4]

Analytics, Data Science, and Optimization at FleetPride

This is a video that explains how the company FleetPride used analytics to solve problems.

View in the online reader

3.5 Data Communication, Sharing Insights—Stage Five

Learning Objectives

At the end of this section, students should be able to:

1. Understand the importance of an organization's data governance.
2. Understand the role of data governance.

data culture

Organization where many employees, not just a few specialists, use data analytics to make their decisions.

data governance

Effective management and use of the organization's data.

Once the data have been extracted, prepped, and analyzed, it is important to summarize and communicate insights. First, what do we mean by insights? Insights are basically your understanding. When you are communicating your insights, you will want to make sure you provide enough information about your data analysis. You can think of this as telling a story with the data. You will want to make sure you identify *what* data were used and *what* problem you are addressing, *why* that problem is important, understand *who* your audience is, and do not assume they understand jargon. Finally, provide conclusions and recommendations of your analysis. Organizations that take data insights into serious actionable insights must understand more about having a **data culture** and the role of **data governance** in their organization.

What Is a Data Culture?

An organization with a data culture is an organization where many employees, not just a few specialists, use data analytics to make their decisions. It is not relegated to a few "experts" in the organization and used only in certain areas, depending upon who is the manager. Instead of management "pushing" data-driven decision-making down to the employees, it should be "pulled" by employees. While this seems fairly commonsense, it is often hard for organizations to make large behavioral shifts in their organizations.

Although it sounds strange, most managers in the past may have made decisions based on their experiences and have not used much data. One of the best examples of data-based decisions is Billy Beane, General Manager of the Oakland A's, who used data, not the intuition of baseball scouts, to make recruiting decisions. This was documented in the book *Moneyball* by Michael Lewis, which later became a movie.

It can be challenging for organizations to make big changes in their organizational culture. While most organizations acknowledge the need for data culture, most are still grappling with how to get there. For the most part, leadership from the top is required in addition to management understanding that an organization's information has value. As accountants, we understand value when we think of the balance sheet; however, the balance sheet does not have an asset line item for the value of an organization's information! In addition to these concepts, an organization cannot get too far unless it has a good handle on the role of data governance in the organization.

What Is the Role of Data Governance?

Data governance is about having effective management and use of the organization's data. Let's go back to Chapter 1 where we first learned about the concept of what makes information useful. It must be relevant, reliable, timely, complete, and understandable. Having good data governance in place allows for that to happen in organizations on a large scale. Although it sounds simple in concept, most organizations actually struggle with where their information comes from and where it is stored because it may have many different repositories.

In addition, once there is a good handle on where the information is located, it needs to be validated. The organization will want to agree on definitions of data. For example, is a sale defined the same for accountants as it is for salespeople? This is known as the single source of truth. The organization needs to have good data security practices in place. We will learn more about data security in Chapter 10 of this book. The basic question here is, *"Who can access the data?"* and *"Who can receive copies of the data to do analysis with it?"* The type of data governance model depends on the expectations of accountability of the data. The data governance model for an organization will be on an accountability continuum somewhere between centralized and decentralized, meaning that a centralized model will maintain accountability of the data within a centralized few people (e.g., IT department) and decentralized would mean data accountability may be spread out over many people (e.g., department heads).

Key Takeaways

In this chapter, we learned how data have become a very important part of an accounting system and how they can be stored. We looked at the progression from file cabinets to "big" data and saw that there is no one best way to store data in an accounting system. We discussed conventional flat files, including their advantages and disadvantages, and compared them to a relational database. Relational databases are capable of integrating data from across the enterprise and allowing users to access it in almost unlimited ways. We learned how to extract data from a relational database using the SQL language. We also learned about how data can be reshaped and used to get them in the format required to do data analysis. In addition, we learned about the three types of data analytics and the importance of organizational culture and data governance.

Reference

- Raschke, Robyn, and Kimberly Charron. "Review of Data Analytic Teaching Cases, Have We Covered Enough?" *Journal of Emerging Technologies in Accounting*, March (2021).

3.6 End-of-Chapter Exercises

Exercises

1. What are the five stages of the data analytic cycle?
2. What are the three types of files in a database? What are the differences between them?
3. What are files made up of?
4. What are records made up of?
5. What is the difference between a conventional flat file and a relational database?
6. What are the four Vs of big data, and what do each of them mean?
7. What is the difference between a data warehouse, data mart, and a data lake?
8. What is the best way for an organization to store transactional data as well as social media data?
9. How is structured information normally retrieved?
10. Describe what the following SQL commands mean.
    a. SELECT
    b. FROM
    c. WHERE
    d. JOIN
11. Using Figure 3.5, what code would you need to find the following information?
    a. list of customer sales less than $2,500
    b. list of customer sales greater than or equal to $2,000
    c. list of customer sales who purchased product #1052837
    d. list of customer sales for January 15, 2019
12. What are the two ways that data might need to be prepared before analysis?
13. How would the data from the table below look if reshaped into the long format? How many columns would you have? Can you do this is Excel using the transpose function?

Spring 2020	Fall 2020	Spring 2021	Fall 2021
1000	100	800	1500

14. What are the four different types of joins between two tables?
15. What type of join would I use if I want only data selected that matches both data in the two tables?
16. Which of the following is a collection of records?
    a. file
    b. field
    c. database
    d. bits
17. Which of the following is a conceptually correct hierarchical ordering of items?
    a. file, record, bit, character
    b. field, record, bit, character
    c. database, file, field, record
    d. record, field, character, bit

18. Which of the following represents semipermanent data, such as ledger accounts, customers, or inventory items, together with their balances in a master file?
    a. field
    b. file
    c. gigabyte
    d. chart of accounts
    e. None of the above
19. Which of the following is not one of the advantages of databases over flat-file systems?
    a. Data are pooled by the whole system instead of owned by individual applications.
    b. Data conflict is reduced.
    c. More sophisticated hardware and software are required.
    d. Data redundancy is eliminated.
20. Which of the following arguments is generally not made for creating data warehouses?
    a. Some operational data may be stored on tape.
    b. They are ideal for storing structured and unstructured data.
    c. The processing burden is placed on operational transaction processing by data analytics.
    d. Possible file locking of needed operational records is caused by data mining.
21. Which of the following is a method for storing data over multiple file servers?
    a. a relational database
    b. a data warehouse
    c. an enterprise resource planning system
    d. a distributed file system
22. Each of the following would likely be a characteristic of big data, except
    a. there will be an unusually large amount of it.
    b. you won't know where it's coming from.
    c. it will occur at a very high rate of speed.
    d. the data will come in many different forms.
23. Which of the following is the least likely form that big data is likely to come in?
    a. email messages
    b. Twitter feeds
    c. sales transactions
    d. surveillance camera footage
    e. web pages
24. Big data are most likely going to be stored in which of the following data management solutions?
    a. relational databases
    b. data marts
    c. data warehouses
    d. data lakes
25. Which of the following statements about data analytical thinking is false?
    a. It is important to recognize that your organization may have access to many forms of data that can be used to improve decision-making.
    b. Part of it is identifying the questions that need to answered and whether you think that there could be data to answer.
    c. You need to understand that there are different ways of analyzing data and figure out which one would be appropriate in the circumstances.
    d. Every business should recognize the opportunities and necessity of using big data.

26. Descriptive analytics are generally the most basic type of data analytics. Which of the following would NOT be a good example of one?
    a. determining the standard deviation of a set of data with a statistics package
    b. summarizing a set of historical data and determining the number of records in it as well as the minimum and maximum value
    c. creating a model that would be capable of describing a customer's credit risk
    d. providing a histogram or density plot of a series of production costs
27. Which of the following statements would be an example of a predictive data analytic?
    a. Create an analysis that can rank three action alternatives and recommend which outcome will provide the best results.
    b. Create a model that can provide the probability of a taxpayer's tax return being in error.
    c. Conduct an analysis to see what factors are related to customer churn.
    d. Provide a visualization chart that shows the prime interest rate for each of the 12 months in a year.
28. Prescriptive analytics answer which of the following questions?
    a. What should be done?
    b. What has happened?
    c. What is going to happen?
    d. Can something help us explain what or why something has happened?
29. Take another look at Joe's Ristoranté in Chapter 1 and identify what information would need to be stored in a relational database. Answer the following:
    a. What information would you like to store? Why?
    b. What information should be stored in a master file?
    c. What information should be stored in a transaction file?
30. How should information that is not internally generated by transactions (e.g., social media posts) from Joe's Ristoranté be stored, if at all?
31. What descriptive analytics would be useful for Joe's Ristoranté (make sure these questions match to the information needed in Exercise 29).
32. What predictive questions would you ask for Joe's Ristoranté?
33. What prescriptive questions would you ask for Joe's Ristoranté?
34. Go to the tableau public page for tableau software.
    a. Click on "GALLERY" at the top of the page and explore the different visualizations and search for visualizations that are business or accounting related.
    b. Describe why the visualization you chose is meaningful in presenting information that is easy to understand (please copy paste the link of the visualization).
    c. In your description, what questions does the visualization help answer?

Endnotes

1. https://www.ibmbigdatahub.com/infographic/four-vs-big-data
2. https://www.abiresearch.com/press/more-than-30-billion-devices-will-wirelessly-conne/
3. Accessed via J. Dixon, Pentaho, Hadoop, and Data Lakes, blog, 2010; http://jamesdixon. wordpress.com/2010/10/14/pentahohadoop-and-data-lakes.
4. https://www.ibm.com/blogs/journey-to-ai/

CHAPTER 4

AIS Beyond the Financial Statements

This chapter covers emerging technologies and emerging topics and how they will affect accounting, specifically as they relate to AIS, and why it is important for students to have an awareness of these emerging areas. Emerging technologies include smart contracts, robotic process automation (RPA), artificial intelligence (AI), and machine learning (ML). Emerging topics that will influence the AIS are integrated reporting, which includes financial reporting with nonfinancial reporting as it relates to an organization's environment, social, and governance (ESG) performance. In addition, innovation and regulation influence an AIS. Regulation and compliance affect an AIS externally, whereas business model innovations affect it internally. As an accountant, you must remain aware of how these technologies and topics will affect information needed for organizational accountability. The overall goal of this chapter is to provide awareness of these technologies and topics because these will continue to evolve in the future.

4.1 Smart Contracts

Learning Objectives

At the end of this section, students should be able to:

1. Understand how a basic smart contract works.
2. Understand how smart contracts can be used in accounting.

We all understand what a contract is: There are two parties, they agree on terms, and a transaction occurs. But what makes a contract smart, and why is it important to accounting?

What Are Smart Contracts?

Smart contracts use software programming to assist with the standard process of contracts and can include verification, enforcement, and performance of the terms of the contract. First envisioned in 1994,[1] computer scientist Nick Szabo stated that the best way to formalize a business transaction is with a contract and programming, which makes it more efficient to satisfy the contractual requirements, minimize exceptions, and eliminate intermediaries. While a smart contract may be useful on its own, a simple example is a vending machine where you put in the money and push a number to get a bag of chips. There is no intermediary; the two parties are you and the vending machine. The vending machine verifies that you put in the money and the selection of chips by the number you pressed. Thus, the contract is performed once you put the money in the machine (specified precondition), and you get the chips.

smart contracts

Contracts that use software programming to assist with the standard process of contracts and can include verification, enforcement, and performance of the terms of the contract.

decentralized applications (DApps)

Software programs used in smart contracts.

However, smart contracts really are just computer code that use business logic (e.g., if-then statements). The potential of smart contracts is built on the blockchain technology that we learned about in Chapter 2. What makes smart contracts more realistic and powerful now is that by being on the blockchain, an intermediary is not needed. The blockchain allows all parties (e.g., buyer and seller in a contract) to see the transaction, and the blockchain makes the transaction immutable, which means it is hard to change it once it is on the blockchain. General examples of smart contracts on the blockchain include property leasing transactions (e.g., real estate and cars), supply chain, financial transactions, and royalty payments. One of the best-known platforms for developing smart contracts is Ethereum. Because we are just talking about pieces of computer code that runs on a blockchain, you may see the term **DApps**, used which stands for decentralized applications.

Smart Contracts—Simply Explained

This is a video about smart contracts.

View in the online reader

The benefits of using smart contracts are efficiency as well as fraud reduction. The drawbacks are that they use programming code and can be susceptible to bugs, leading to security issues. However, smart contract auditing organizations such as Quantstamp.com help organizations reduce the threat of security issues associated with their smart contract applications.

How Will This Technology Affect Accounting?

Many accounting thought leaders believe that some future uses of smart contracts and blockchain will be in the form of "smart audit" procedures. Meaning that the use of "if, then" business logic from a programming perspective can automate smart audit procedures of client's data in a blockchain (Rosario and Thomas 2019; Kokina, Mancha, and Pachamanova 2017).

From an internal organizational perspective, smart contracts can be used to insert programming to invoke automatic controls. Further use of smart contract technology can be used to help with fraud prevention by invoking business logic rules along business processes. For example, smart contract technology can be used to ensure that all conditions are met before booking sales revenue (Dai, Wang, and Vasarhelyi 2017). This is particularly important for us to consider, as we will learn shortly, because the regulatory environment requires us to think more dynamically to adjust to changing regulations. While smart contracts require a well thought-out blockchain, the future promises that how we conduct business transactions with our trading partners may change.

Blockchain Brief—Audit and Assurance

This is a video on accounting opportunities as they relate to smart contracts on the blockchain.

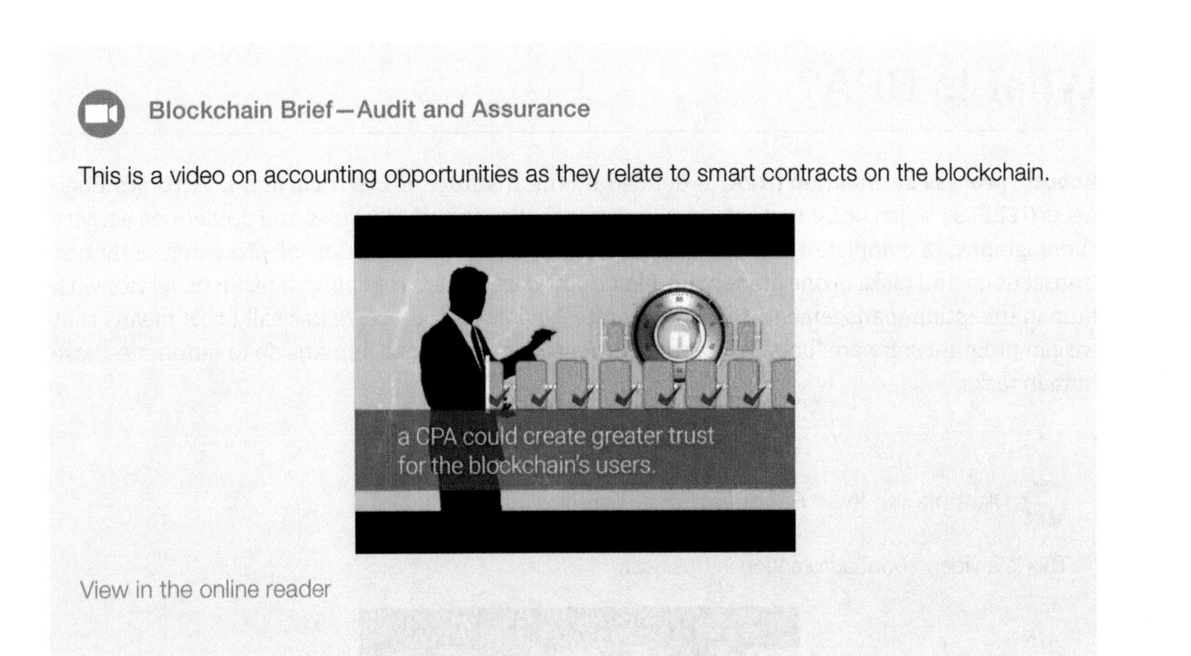

View in the online reader

Want to know more about smart contracts and building skillsets on creating code for smart contracts? Go to Ethereum for developer resources and tutorials to get you started. While these skills are beyond the scope of this book, learning is lifelong. Students who are passionate about any of the topics in this chapter have the ability to build those skillsets that will make them in high demand in the workplace.

4.2 Robotic Process Automation

Learning Objectives

At the end of this section, students should be able to:

1. Understand the basic concepts of robotic process automation.
2. Understand how robotic process automation is used in accounting.

You may have heard that the "robots are coming!" How will this affect you? While robots will not take over your job, they may enhance how you do your job. This means that your role in an organization may change and quite possibly for the better! The repetitive tasks that accountants often complain about will be automated using RPA through the creation of "bots," allowing accountants more time to use their critical thinking skills.

What Is RPA?

robotic process automation (RPA)

Software that uses business rules and a predefined activity to autonomously complete tasks in unrelated software systems.

Robotic process automation (RPA) is defined by the Institute of Electrical and Electronics Engineers (IEEE) as "a preconfigured software instance that uses business rules and predefined activity choreography to complete the autonomous execution of a combination of processes, activities, transactions, and tasks in one or more unrelated software systems to deliver a result or service with human exception management" (IEEE Corporate Advisory Group 2017). Basically, this means that we can program software "bots" to accomplish repetitive work that humans do to automate those human tasks.

Automation in 60 Seconds: What You Need to Know

This is a video about automation in business.

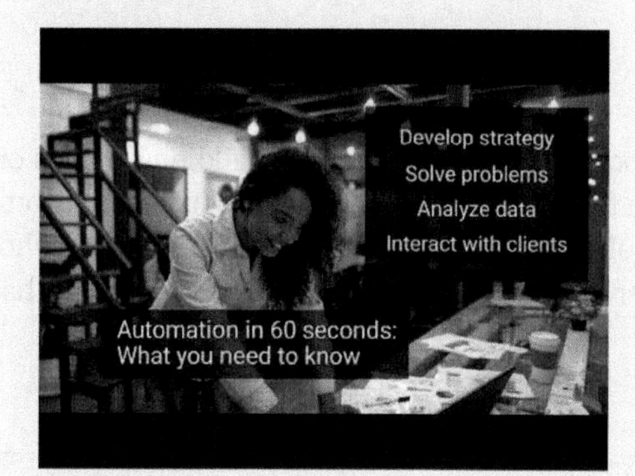

View in the online reader

If we just think about tasks that involve our schoolwork, we can see that there is a lot of repetition. For example, we may check the school's learning platform for any new announcements or assignments. We would then update that information on our electronic calendars. We check our email throughout the day.

Can you think about how certain areas of business might be repetitive? How about coordinating meetings? Documenting travel expenses? Hiring new employees? What about the repetitive tasks that occur in accounting transactions that we do with our trading partners? Processing invoices from our vendors? Creating invoices to email to our customers?

The benefits of using RPA to automate repetitive human tasks are efficiency and cost reduction. This frees up the human component to focus on the areas that are more complex and require critical thinking to solve problems. Some of the drawbacks to think about relate to human behavior. How would our clients and employees feel if they were interacting with a "bot" and not a human? Other areas of concern relate to the data access and quality of the data necessary for the "bot" to perform adequately. How would the organization justify that a program "bot" gain access to confidential data to complete a task?

How Will This Technology Affect Accounting?

RPA use in accounting will continue to grow. In fact, Boston Consulting Group predicts that by 2025 more than a quarter of all jobs will be replaced by bots, with a high likelihood that the jobs being automated would be tax preparers, accountants, loan officers, and credit analysts.[2] In addition, Grant Thornton's recent survey of Chief Financial Officers (CFO) show that approximately 74% of the CFO's are or plan to implement automation in the finance/accounting functions within the next five years.[3] This means the role of the accountant will surely change. Think about the change to your role being elevated to solving problems versus producing financial information. Your role will be as a user of the information, and you will be able to create bots for your organization to handle all of the mundane tasks. This means you may be involved more in the exceptions to the rules, those tasks that will still require critical thinking to resolve. For public accounting, the demand for RPA will grow. A recent study that interviewed Big 4 public accounting leaders notes that not only has RPA been used to help with the internal operations of the firm, but it also is now being deployed to help their clients automate their business processes and automate tax processes (Cooper, Holderness, Sorensen, and Wood 2019).

While there is still potential to use RPA in assurance services, the development of these automation tasks is not as far along as they are with business process and tax automation. Assurance (audits) require following certain audit procedures based on rules and regulations from the Public Company Accounting Oversight Board (PCAOB) auditing standards. However, this does not mean that audit procedures cannot be automated; it just means that the development of these automated "bots" may take longer due to the regulatory requirements.

Processes that are ripe for automation with the most potential for savings include but are not limited to human resources tasks, order-to-cash and source-to-pay transactions, and account reconciliations. Accounting firms will be looking to hire students with RPA-specific skills, the ability to be technology minded as well as having accounting knowledge. Students will need to have critical thinking skills as well as the ability to communicate both in writing and orally. While the scope of this book can provide you with developing critical thinking skills and communication skills, the intent of this section is to provide awareness of RPA and to provide you with enough information on future possibilities.

How to Use RPA for Invoice Extraction and Processing

This is a video that demonstrates how RPA is used to automate invoice processing using the software UiPath.

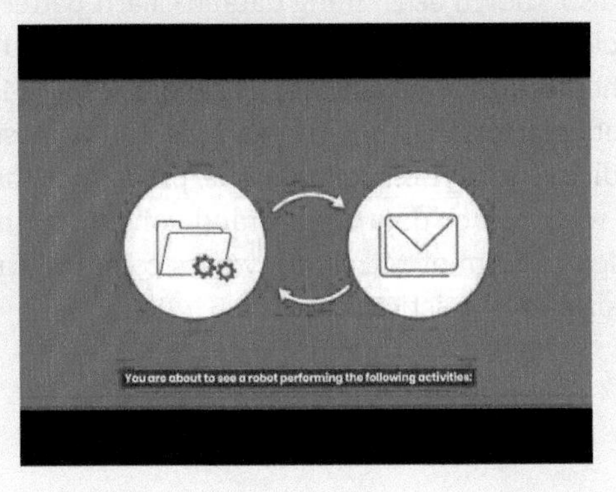

View in the online reader

If you find that you are passionate about this topic and would like to explore more on RPA and programming "bots," UiPath has free software available as well as free learning tools that allow you to program your first "bot" (see https://academy.uipath.com/learn).

4.3 Artificial Intelligence and Machine Learning

Learning Objectives

At the end of this section, students should be able to:

1. Understand artificial intelligence and how it can be used in accounting.
2. Understand machine learning and how it can be used in accounting.

artificial intelligence (AI)

Program code that is intended to mimic human intelligence to accomplish a task.

machine learning (ML)

A subset of AI that relies on large amounts of data to learn patterns to use in algorithms for decision-making.

Artificial intelligence (AI) and the subset of AI, **machine learning (ML)**, have been around for many years. What makes this combination more relevant today is that data storage costs are low and have decreased over time, while the computing capability has increased over time. Meaning, this is a great time to have this combination of inexpensive power to use in leveraging the accomplishment of certain business goals. This is especially true within the context of data analytics.

What Are AI and ML?

Quite simply, AI is program code that is intended to mimic human intelligence to accomplish a task. For example, your apple iPhone has AI named Siri, which allows you to ask questions for Siri to answer. In addition, an increasing number devices used in the home use AI, such as Amazon's Alexa and Google's Home smart speakers. You may have encountered these basic examples in your daily routines. However, in business AI is used in many areas, such as marketing, supply chain, and accounting.

ML is considered a subset of AI, meaning that all ML is AI but not all AI is ML. ML relies on large amounts of data (also known as training data) to learn patterns to use in algorithms for decision-making. An example of ML that we see in our daily lives is the spam filter on our email accounts, which detects whether an email is spam. Facebook using ML to suggest friend tags in photos that you upload to its platform is another example. In business, ML is used in areas such as fraud detection and predictive analytics. For example, predictive analytics uses data generated to understand when parts wear out or data from brand consumption to develop new products. Natural language processing is a form of ML that involves communication between humans and machines where text analysis and linguistics is used.

How Does Machine Learning Work? Simply Explained

This video provides a simple example of machine learning.

View in the online reader

How Will This Technology Affect Accounting?

From an accounting perspective, AI and ML will enhance decision tasks relevant to accounting and will be used in areas such as anomaly detection, forecasting, and compliance. Currently, large accounting firms such as Deloitte have deployed AI to review complex documents for effective audits.[4] In addition, software is available to use AI in audits to identify risk. This allows auditors to focus their attention on examining transactions that are highlighted as higher risk. This type of software is used both for internal as well as external audits.

In addition, ML is used for predictive analytics, as mentioned in Chapter 3. Predictive analytics in accounting means that analytics will help organizations predict "what will happen." While most of our experience with accounting transactions is based on what *has* happened, the exciting part of understanding transactions is to harness this information to develop models of prediction. The benefit to organizations will be in forecasting sales, logistics, hiring, and financing needs more accurately. In addition, predictive analytics will be used for better benchmarking of costs and budgets to more efficient processes.

It is important for accountants to be aware of the value AI has to organizations as well as how to leverage AI to accomplish tasks for organizations to become more effective and efficient. While this technology has great potential, there is also great responsibility. Students should be aware of the ethical responsibility of using AI in organizations because these systems will be more in use in the future. For example, will the organization's customers, vendors, and employees be okay with interacting with an AI-enhanced program? The element of trust is important when using algorithms, and the opportunity for accountants to audit these algorithms will become a part of the future.

 Artificial Intelligence and Human-Computer Collaboration

This is a video that discusses how humans and computers will collaborate and the value of AI.

View in the online reader

While the scope of this book is to help you develop critical thinking and communication skills, the intent of this section is to provide awareness of AI and ML and to provide you with enough information on future possibilities. If you find that you are passionate about this topic and would like to explore more on AI and ML, https://www.mindbridge.ai/ is a specific solution for AI in auditing, with webinars and other resources available.

4.4 Corporate Social Responsibility

Learning Objectives

At the end of this section, students should be able to:

1. Understand the concept of stakeholder theory as it relates to corporate social responsibility.
2. Understand the eight content elements of Integrated reporting.

sustainability

An organization's ability to meet its own needs without compromising future generations from meeting there's.

Corporate social responsibility (CSR) is also known from an investment perspective as Environmental, Social, and Corporate Governance (ESG). The argument that organizations are in business to pursue the singular objective of profit maximization is giving way to a new paradigm of thinking. According to the businessroundtable.org, which is made up of CEOs in the United States, the purpose of a corporation is to serve all stakeholders, which means not only bringing value to investors and customers, but also treating employees and suppliers fairly and to support communities and protect the environment with sustainable practices.[5] Put simply, we define **sustainability** as an organization's ability to meet its own needs without compromising future generations from meeting theirs. So, what does this have to do with AIS? It could be argued that an effective accounting system should provide not only the information an organization needs to operate, but also the information it needs to ensure that such operations are sustainable. AIS is needed to ensure that good information is collected and organized to report on past performance (financial information) as well as what is beneficial for future performance (sustainability information) for a fair representation of how value is created.

SASB—Markets Make the World Go Round

This is a video on how the need for good information has evolved from financial information to include sustainability information.

View in the online reader

Stakeholder Theory

stakeholder

Any individual or group who can affect or is affected by the actions, decisions, policies, practices, or goals of an organization.

Because sustainability is focused on all stakeholders of an organization, it is relevant for us to understand a management theory known as stakeholder theory. A **stakeholder**, according to Freeman (2010) in *Strategic Management*, is "any individual or group who can affect or is affected by the actions, decisions, policies, practices, or goals of an organization." Failing to identify stakeholders such as investors, the planet, or future generations can cause ethical problems. To avoid ethical problems, we must first be able to identify potential ethical contexts. This is where our awareness (our willingness and ability to identify) comes into play. In this regard, knowing who our stakeholders are (or could be in the future) and what ethical principles might come into play and how they may come into conflict is critical.

As mentioned in Chapter 1, organizations have internal and external stakeholders. Internal stakeholders include those who are involved directly with the business, such as the owners, employees, customers, and suppliers. External stakeholders on the other hand may include governments, competitors, consumer advocates, environmentalists, special interest groups, and the media. The question for most business owners is, "How can a business create value when there are so many different stakeholders?" While it's not a one-size-fits-all equation, organizations must first articulate their shared values and how they will deliver on that shared value with their stakeholders (Freeman, Wicks, and Parmar 2004).

Organizations have several resources to use when considering how best to disclose their sustainability practices. While investors want more disclosure on sustainability, there is not one primary resource for how to adequately disclose this information. In addition, the issue of how reliable this information is for investors is also in question. However, resources and guidance that include sustainability frameworks are currently available to organizations, and as this information continues to evolve, the following are worthy of discussing for this topic. These nonprofit organizations often work together with the main theme of helping organizations understand how best to disclose their sustainability practices to stakeholders and include but are not limited to Sustainability Accounting Standards Board (sasb.org), the Global Reporting Initiative (globalreporting.org), the task force on climate-related financial disclosures (fsb-tcfd.org), and the International Integrated Reporting Council (IIRC). To date, in the United States, disclosure by publicly held companies relating to sustainability and climate change is voluntary (unless it meets a threshold of materiality), and it is usually done in separately issued CSR or ESG reports; however, it does appear that the U.S. Securities and Exchange Commission (SEC) is wrestling with disclosure issues in this area, and we may see future public statements and guidance.[6]

Integrated Reporting

integrated reporting

A framework used to communicate with stakeholders on how the organizational strategy and performance relate to value over time.

Integrated reporting is a framework sponsored by the IIRC for organizations to communicate with stakeholders on how the organization strategy and performance relate to value over time (e.g., short term and long term). The framework focuses on a principles-based approach that integrates financial and nonfinancial information into a meaningful report for stakeholders. The overall focus is to interconnect information that is financial and nonfinancial for the long-term benefit of the organization and its stakeholders. It is based on eight areas of content:

1. Organization and external environment
2. Organizational governance structure
3. Organization business model
4. Risks and opportunities
5. Organizational strategy and resource allocation
6. Achievement of objectives
7. Implications and future performance
8. How the organization evaluates what is material to report and how it's measured

To elaborate on these eight areas of content, the organization and external environment is concerned with what the organization does (e.g., what type of business is it in?) and may include metrics relating to key markets that the business operates in, their position in the supply chain, etc. External environment would include a discussion of significant external factors that may impact the organization from achieving value in the short to long term.

The second content area of governance focuses on the organization elaborating on the support structure for accomplishing value in the short and long term. This content may include information on leadership structure, the organization's ethics and values and how key decisions are made, compliance with legal requirements, and how incentives may be linked to value creation.

The third content element of the business model relates to the organization describing key inputs, business transactions, outputs, and outcomes that have a bearing on short- and long-term value. Outputs are what the organization does (e.g., products), and outcomes are what the organization wants to measure (e.g., employee satisfaction).

The fourth content element involves the organization elaborating on specific risks and opportunities that may affect short- and long-term value creation and how the organization is dealing with these potential risks and opportunities. For example, an organization may need highly skilled workers, and if there is a shortage of these workers or if the cost to hire is increasing, how is the organization going to deal with this potential risk? Is the organization going to open up an office in another part of the country where skilled labor is available and for a reasonable cost? For example, Amazon announced a second headquarters because it was finding it difficult to hire skilled workers on the West Coast. So the company set up a second headquarters on the East Coast.

The fifth element relating to organizational strategy allows the organization to describe its short- and long-term strategic objectives to stakeholders as well as describes how it will get there.

The sixth content element of achievement (performance) is a means for the organization to provide measures to show the progress toward the strategic objectives and outcomes.

The seventh content element, implications, relates to the organization providing a discussion of uncertainties and challenges that may be encountered in achieving short- and long-term objectives.

Finally, the eighth content element provides a discussion on what the organization considers important to disclose as well as what frameworks are used and how measures will be quantified. It is important to note that organizations that wish to have an integrated annual report still exhibit management judgment in their discussions incorporated in the eight content elements, meaning there may be differences between two companies in the same industry.

Currently, the United States does not have a high number of publicly held companies adopting the integrated report format. As of now, the SEC does not mandate this report format. South Africa is the only country that mandates integrated reporting. What does this mean for an accountant anywhere else in the world? It means that you will need to understand how well your AIS best supports an organization's strategic objectives. If the organization has a strategic objective of greenhouse gas reductions, how would that information be measured, and does that information need to be assured by an external auditor? What we do know is that more and more investors want CSR information. The question remains just how much will be reported. What is true is that accountants will be involved because accountants are objective and understand the value of data.

Unilever: How Integrated Reporting Is Making a Difference

This video is about a company that uses integrated reporting.

View in the online reader

Want to know more about this topic? The IIRC maintains updated information as well as examples of integrated reports. Southwest Airlines and Clorox are good examples of companies that have adopted integrated reports in the United States. (There are others, too.) The following link provides current examples from the IIRC of reports issued all over the world: http://examples.integratedreporting.org/home. Try looking up a few brands that you are familiar with; you may be surprised how well these companies disclose nonfinancial information that is just as important as the financial information in achieving strategic objectives.

4.5 Innovation and Regulation on AIS

Learning Objectives

At the end of this section, students should be able to:

1. Explain business model innovations.
2. Understand how business model innovations and regulations influence an AIS.

Organizations constantly are innovating their products and processes to remain competitive in the marketplace. In addition, government and industry regulations continue to evolve. This next section intends to provide an accounting student with the awareness that as the environment evolves, both internally from the organization and externally from regulation, the AIS needs to continue to support the organization.

What Are Business Model Innovations?

business model innovation

When organizations innovate by creating new products, changing existing products, as well as creating or changing business processes.

Because organizations may have to respond to competitive pressures in their external environment or be driven internally to increase their market share, organizations will continue to innovate and change their business model to create value. **Business model innovation** is when an organization innovates by creating new products, changes existing products, or creates or changes business processes. This means that organizations can exploit existing products and processes to create new markets or opportunities in existing markets.

Good examples of organizations that were successful in business model innovation are Apple and Amazon. When Apple first began, it made personal computers. Then in 2007, Apple changed its name from Apple Computer Inc. to Apple Inc. because it introduced the iPhone. Before its entry into the cellphone market, Apple created a new market: smartphones and smart mobile devices. Amazon also is a good example of innovation because initially Amazon just sold books. Then to solve its own problems with cloud computing and shopping online, Amazon launched Amazon Web Services (AWS), which was a novel way to create an entirely new market by offering infrastructure for other web retailers and making the infrastructure cheap and accessible. This product line continues to provide a majority of the profits for Amazon.

According to the research of Amit and Zott (2012), managers should ask six questions when considering business model innovations:

1. What customer needs does the new model address?
2. What novel activities help satisfy these needs?
3. How could activities be linked in novel ways?
4. Who performs these activities? The company? A trading partner?
5. How is value created?
6. What revenue model works?

These six questions require a holistic approach for managers to think about creating value overall.

How Do Business Model Innovations Affect AIS?

While executive management is approaching value creation from a holistic perspective, once the decision is made to innovate and create a new product or market, the reality of implementation occurs.

Alex Osterwalder: What Is Business Model Innovation?

This video explains business model innovation.

View in the online reader

From an AIS perspective, the accountant needs to consider, "Does my current system support the new revenue model and the activities from the business model innovation?" For example, suppose an organization is in the leasing industry and leases equipment to construction companies. The revenue model is leasing on a weekly or monthly basis, but the company decides to create a new market where equipment leasing is billed on an hourly basis. Will the AIS be able to handle hourly billing? We will learn more in Chapter 6 about strategic planning and systems development.

How Do Regulations Affect AIS?

While business model innovations are internally driven and affect an AIS, government and industry regulations are external forces. These external forces may give organizations enough time to prepare, or they may end up surprising the company, which realizes it needs more time for compliance. While this book will not provide an exhaustive list, the accountant should be aware of financial regulations and required disclosures. All publicly held organizations in the United States must comply with SEC disclosure requirements and provide financial statements that are prepared under Generally Accepted Accounting Principles (GAAP). Some people may not realize that preparing financial statements changes over time. For example, one recent change requirement is in the area of revenue recognition.

It is important to note that if GAAP changes with a deadline, the organization should begin planning immediately to determine if their AIS can support the new requirement or if a system implementation is needed to support the new requirement. Why is this important? Because system implementation takes time and requires appropriate planning and testing as well as managing costs. To take the revenue recognition example a step further, and to see how well accounting students can think critically and relate topics from their financial accounting courses to their accounting information systems course, let's look at ASC 606 as an example.

ASC 606 is the Financial Accounting Standards Board (FASB) accounting standards codification (ASC) on recognizing revenues from contracts. Originally issued in May 2014, it required publicly held companies to comply by the first quarter of 2018. But wait, don't most publicly held companies provide a comparison from the prior year? Well, that means my AIS has to be ready to go by the end of 2016 so I can be in compliance to report 2018 and 2017. The point is that you have two years to be compliant instead of thinking about four years from the issuance of the standard. This means you need to start sooner as opposed to later to determine if your AIS can handle the required change.

Key Takeaways

In this chapter, topics were discussed to make accounting students aware of emerging technologies such as smart contracts, robotic process automation, artificial intelligence, and machine learning. With emerging technologies come opportunities for accounting that affect the AIS. In addition, topical areas such as CSR and how changes that come internally (business model innovations) or externally (regulations) and the effect on an AIS were also presented. As the business landscape will always evolve, it is important for accounting students to understand how the AIS will also need to evolve to meet the needs of the organization.

References

- Amit, Raphael, and Christoph Zott. "Creating value through business model innovation." *MIT Sloan Management Review* (March 20, 2012).
- Cooper, Lauren A., D. Kip Holderness Jr., Trevor L. Sorensen, and David A. Wood. "Robotic process automation in public accounting." *Accounting Horizons* 33, no. 4 (2019): 15–35.
- Dai, Jun, Yunsen Wang, and Miklos A. Vasarhelyi. "Blockchain: an emerging solution for fraud prevention." *The CPA Journal* 87, no. 6 (2017): 12–14.
- Freeman, R. Edward. *Strategic Management: A Stakeholder Approach.* Cambridge, England: Cambridge University Press, 2010.
- Freeman, R. Edward, Andrew C. Wicks, and Bidhan Parmar. "Stakeholder theory and the corporate objective revisited." *Organization Science* 15, no. 3 (2004): 364–369.
- IEEE Corporate Advisory Group. *IEEE Guide for Terms and Concepts in Intelligent Process Automation.* Piscataway, NJ: The Standards Board, 2017.
- Kokina, Julia, Ruben Mancha, and Dessislava Pachamanova. "Blockchain: Emergent industry adoption and implications for accounting." *Journal of Emerging Technologies in Accounting* 14, no. 2 (2017): 91–100.
- Rozario, Andrea M., and Chanta Thomas. "Reengineering the audit with blockchain and smart contracts." *Journal of Emerging Technologies in Accounting* 16, no. 1 (2019): 21–35.

4.6 End-of-Chapter Exercises

Exercises

1. Explain how crowd-funding websites such as Kickstarter use smart contracts.
2. What are the benefits of smart contracts in accounting?
3. Can smart contracts be trusted? Why or why not?
4. What types of services can CPA firms provide to their clients who use smart contracts?
5. What are the benefits of RPA?
6. Based on your own experience in accounting classes, what areas of accounting appear to be repetitive and a good candidate for RPA?
7. Do you think companies will adopt AI technologies in accounting quickly? Why or why not?
8. What type of accounting applications can use ML?
9. What kind of task is ML better at than humans?
10. Are humans still needed for ML?
11. Are ethics important for AI and ML? Why or why not?
12. What accounting examples can you think of that are good to use AI? To use ML?
13. Why should accountants be involved in integrated reporting?
14. What types of frameworks can be used in integrated reporting?
15. The difference between smart contracts and contracts is that
    a. smart contracts are digital.
    b. smart contracts are on a blockchain.
    c. smart contracts use programming.
    d. All of the above
16. RPA benefits include which of the following?
    a. speeds up processes
    b. reduces errors
    c. inexpensive to implement
    d. All of the above
17. __________ is considered a subset of __________.
    a. ML, AI
    b. AI, ML
    c. RPA, ML
    d. AI, RPA
18. Which one is not an organizational outcome?
    a. employee satisfaction
    b. employee diversification
    c. customer satisfaction
    d. product development
19. What frameworks help organizations with sustainability disclosure?
    a. SASB
    b. IIRC
    c. fsb-tcfd
    d. All of the above

20. According to research by Amit and Zott (2012), managers should ask which question when considering business model innovations?
    a. How much can we invest in new products?
    b. How could activities be linked in novel ways?
    c. How do activities create products?
    d. How do we value products?
21. An organization can create business model innovations by
    a. creating a new product.
    b. updating an existing product.
    c. changing a business process.
    d. All of the above
22. Pull the integrated annual report for Southwest Airlines and compare it to another publicly held airline (United or American).
    a. Can you tell the difference between the two reports in format?
    b. Evaluate Southwest based on the eight content areas of the integrated report as per the IIRC.
23. Create a KWL chart for one of the five major areas of this chapter. A KWL chart stands for "What I know," "What I want to know," and "What I learned." Please provide the sources that you went to as you complete your chart. For more information about KWL charts and how to complete one using Lucid Charts, go here:

    https://www.lucidchart.com/blog/what-is-a-kwl-chart
24. **Reflective Learning**
    a. Based on reading and reflecting on this chapter, what have you learned? Do you feel passionate about a certain emerging technology or topic that you'd like to learn more about?
    b. What was the most difficult concept in the chapter? Why was it difficult?
    c. Does the material in this chapter relate to anything you have covered in another course or seen in any of your prior experiences?

Endnotes

1. www.fon.hum.uva.nl/rob/Courses/InformationInSpeech/CDROM/Literature/LOTwinterschool2006/szabo.best.vwh.net/smart.contracts.html
2. https://www.bbc.com/news/technology-33327659
3. https://www.grantthornton.com/Insights/CFO-insights.aspx
4. https://kirasystems.com/partners/deloitte-alliance/
5. https://opportunity.businessroundtable.org/wp-content/uploads/2019/08/BRT-Statement-on-the-Purpose-of-a-Corporation-with-Signatures.pdf
6. https://www.sec.gov/news/public-statement/lee-mda-2020-01-30#_ftnref2

PART 2

The Designer Perspective

CHAPTER 5

Documenting the Accounting Information Systems

5.1 Systems Documentation

Learning Objectives

At the end of this section, students should be able to:

1. Discuss how accounting systems documentation can be used to design and implement a working accounting system.
2. Identify and explain the accounting system implications of the Sarbanes-Oxley Act as it relates to systems documentation.
3. Understand how a lack of documentation may be considered a significant deficiency or material weakness.
4. Describe the types of accounting systems documentation that can be created.

Systems documentation allows an organization to review and evaluate accounting information system design. Nevertheless, some organizations have little or no documentation. For those that do, documentation makes a system more formalized. In general, documentation is useful in helping management understand and maintain controls with the current state of the system. In addition, external auditors review system documentation as part of their audit procedures. It is important for organizations to keep their systems documentation current. The process of generating documentation, however, can be costly and time-consuming if not maintained on a current basis.

Why Do We Need to Document AIS?

Documentation can be used to communicate how a process works, job responsibilities, and provide a reference for training purposes. When properly designed and communicated, documentation can reduce the number of costly misunderstandings and mistakes. Once a system is documented, continuous review and improvements can be made. Public companies are required to document their accounting systems and controls (Sarbanes-Oxley Act of 2002). While private companies are not required by law to document their accounting systems, if a private company is audited, auditing standards require the auditor to consider the client's internal control system. In this context, a lack of documentation or poor documentation may be interpreted as a significant deficiency or material weakness. Flowcharts are a tool to help effectively document and communicate information systems.

What Types of Flowcharts Are There?

Organizations use several different types of flowcharts, and they each have trade-offs. Specifically, certain types of flowcharts are used to document different views of the organization. The main types of systems documentation used are dataflow diagrams, flowcharts (document, systems, and program), entity-relationship diagrams, resource-event-agent diagrams, business process model notation, and unified modeling language diagrams.

For purposes of this chapter, we will spend time discussing dataflow diagrams and flowcharts. In Chapter 7, we will spend time focusing on entity-relationship and resource-event-agent diagrams. Business process model notation is a graphical representation of a business process and beyond the scope of this textbook. In addition, unified modeling language diagrams are used in system design by software engineers and are beyond the scope of this textbook.

Who Uses Flowcharts?

Both internal and external users employ organization flowcharts. From the internal user perspective, and due to compliance requirements found in the Sarbanes-Oxley Act, management must assess and document their internal control over financial reporting (section 404). Because of this compliance requirement, accountants, auditors, and system users all utilize flowcharts.

1. Accountants use flowcharts to design and monitor (i.e., internal controls) the accounting system.
2. Auditors use flowcharts to understand how a client's system works and to evaluate the effectiveness of the internal control structure.
3. System users employ flowcharts to understand a process and learn how a system works.

Flowchart users use various types of documentation to create their flowcharts, including narrative description, internal control questionnaires (ICQs), copies of job descriptions, and accounting manuals. Different tools can be used to help comprehend, design, and evaluate an accounting system. The general rule for choosing documentation is to choose the technique that gives you the most explanatory value for the least cost.

For example, a simple write up of a system using a narrative memorandum can be a very cost-effective way to document one's understanding of the flow of transactions. Many companies use them because they are the least expensive and easiest to prepare.

ICQs can also be used to document an accounting system. Instead of simply describing the processes in narrative form, an ICQ describes the internal control procedures that would be expected throughout the process of an effective system. ICQs can be very helpful in identifying and documenting whether the controls that need to be there are there and have been implemented. This approach can also be useful in evaluating the system. For example, Figure 5.1 provides an illustration of an ICQ that facilitates the evaluation of a billing and accounts receivable function:

FIGURE 5.1 ICQ for Billing and Receivables

Control Objective: Keep track of who owes you money, how much, and when.

Risks: Customers might be billed, billed the wrong amount, or billed for something not shipped or ordered.

Activity Controls:

1. Do they use a pre-numbered sales invoice for billing?	Yes	No
2. Do they have standard terms of sales?	Yes	No
3. Do they match quantities billed to the shipping report?	Yes	No
4. Do they match the items billed to the approved sales order?	Yes	No
5. Is an up-to-date master price list used?	Yes	No
6. Do they verify the extensions and totals of the invoice?	Yes	No
7. Do they prepare an aged trial balance of receivables on a regular basis?	Yes	No

After collecting narrative information about a system, an approach known as the dataflow diagram is used to understand the logical flow of information without being constrained by physical systems. When you want to understand the processing activities and the files affected instead of merely examining the flow of information, a flowchart is used.

5.2 What Are Dataflow Diagrams?

Learning Objectives

At the end of this section, students should be able to:

1. Explain what dataflow diagrams are used for and who uses them.
2. Understand the symbols used to create dataflow diagrams.

dataflow diagrams (DFDs)

A visual depiction that focuses on the flow of information through the system.

logical DFD

A dataflow diagram that visually depicts the logical flow of information in a process, such as "what" the business activities are.

physical DFD

A dataflow diagram that visually depicts "how" the process works, such as the software programs, hardware, and databases.

Dataflow diagrams (DFDs) focus on the flow of information through the system. There are two types of DFD, logical and physical. A **logical DFD** is the logical flow of information in a process, such as "what" the business activities are, while the **physical DFD** is concerned with "how" the process works, such as the software programs, hardware, and databases. For purposes of this book, we will focus on the logical DFD.

Recall the horizontal block diagram of input-process-output from Chapter 2 (see Figure 2.3); the DFD similarly diagrams the source and destination of the data (input/output), the processes that transform the data (process), the data storage, and the data flow. Using a DFD is a good starting point for systems analysts to communicate systems design to nontechnical users. The logical DFD diagrams the logical flow of the information. Thus, it is not hindered by software, hardware, or database structures.

How Do You Create a DFD?

Creating the DFD requires the use of four basic symbols, described next. The objective of the DFD is to describe what happens to the data, meaning stored data may have both inflows and outflows. The systems analyst may create a DFD just to gain an understanding of how data from a process flows through the system. Note that DFDs can range from a summary (high-level) format to a more detailed level.

When beginning the DFD, the first decision is to determine the level that you want to diagram for the data flows. For example, considering the audience will facilitate the understanding of the diagram. If you are talking to other managers about the major functions of the logical flow of a business process, a high-level diagram may suffice. However, you may want to expand the high-level diagram to more detailed logical flows. The best way to create a DFD is to begin at the high level, then expand it to the functional level. If the DFD begins to become more complex (e.g., more than nine processes), you will want to take each function and create subdiagrams to expand in detail each function separately. This allows a manager who may want to understand what happens within a certain process to look at the subdiagram to understand more of the details of the logical flow of data for that specific area.

Next decide the components for your diagram. What are the sources and destination of the data flows? If we consider the example of ordering inventory, where do we find out what inventory we need to order? Does the data come from the warehouse when stock gets low? At a summary level, we can state that the data source begins in the warehouse when we realize that certain products are low and we need to reorder more. Then the reorder of the inventory (process that transforms the data) should go to the destination, which is generally the purchasing department in a manufacturing company.

What Basic Symbols Are Used?

Only four basic symbols are used to create a dataflow diagram (see Figure 5.2). A square represents the source or destination of data, and a circle represents the process of transforming the data. The Data Store symbol looks like an incomplete rectangle, and finally, the Data Flow symbol is a directional arrow that shows the logical flow of the data. The difference between a data store and a data flow is that the data store represents data at rest, whereas the data flow represents data moving or in motion. A data store may represent data that are in a database file or a part of a file.

FIGURE 5.2 Data Flow Diagram Symbols

INPUT/OUTPUT		
Source or Destination of Data	This symbol is used to define the source or destination of a data flow, meaning where the data are needed (destination) and where it initiated (source).	□
Process	This symbol is used to show that data are transformed.	○
Data Store	This symbol is used to show that data are at rest, including but not be limited to a data file or pieces of a data file, such as a record or attribute from the data file.	(open rectangle)
Data Flow	This symbol is used to show that data are in motion.	⟶

Symbol Logic: Data Flow Diagrams

This is a video on the symbols used to create data flow diagrams.

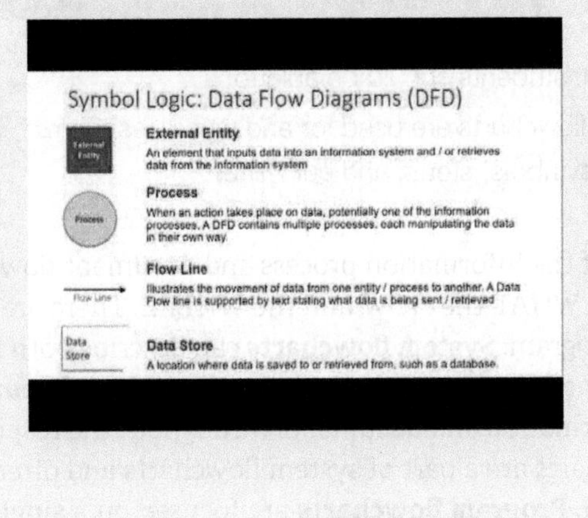

View in the online reader

Guidelines for Creating DFDs

Guidelines for creating DFDs begin with going from a logical left to right as you begin your diagram. Make sure that you have the right level of detail for your audience and do not make one diagram too complex; it is better to have subdiagrams. Examine the data elements needed for the data stores. What data elements flow in and out of the data stores? Are there any redundancies in the data stores? Having the DFD allows you to actually trace the flow of data through the physical system.

Let's look at how we might represent the data flows of a company at a summary level where the customer places an order and then the order processing system notifies the warehouse to pick and pack the goods and ship to the customer. Finally, the order processing system invoices the customer once the information on shipping is updated in the order processing system. Figure 5.3 shows the summary DFD based on this narrative.

FIGURE 5.3 Order Invoice: Summary DFD

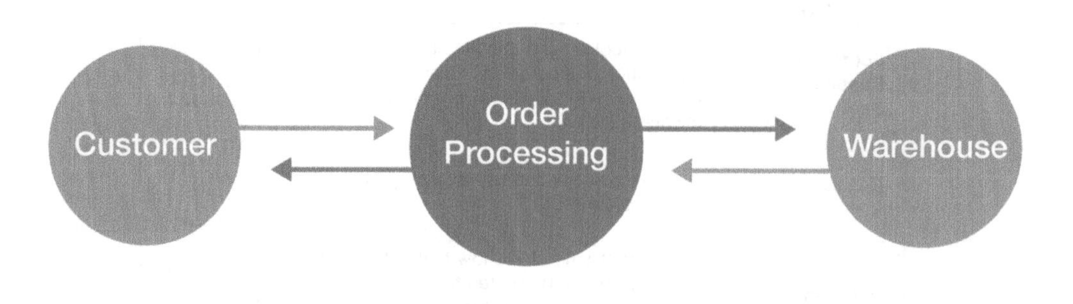

5.3 What Are Flowcharts?

Learning Objectives

At the end of this section, students should be able to:

1. Explain what system flowcharts are used for and who uses them.
2. Identify flowcharting symbols, steps, and guidelines.

flowchart

A visual diagram depicting the procedures and document flows of an accounting system.

system flowcharts

A type of flowchart that visually depicts manual and computerized accounting systems documenting inputs, processes, and outputs.

document flowcharts

A part of a system flowchart used to describe the flow of information and documents throughout the responsibility areas of an organization.

program flowcharts

A type of flowchart that is focused on a single program within the system.

A **flowchart** is a diagram of the information process and document flows of an accounting system representing the WHO, the WHAT, the HOW, and the WHERE. There are three types of flowcharts: systems, document, and program. **System flowcharts** can describe both manual and computerized accounting systems, documenting inputs, processes, and outputs. **Document flowcharts** are used to describe the flow of information and documents throughout the responsibility areas of an organization. Document flowcharts are a part of system flowcharts and often used to describe internal controls of an organization. **Program flowcharts** are focused on a single program within the system. This video describes why flowcharts are useful.

How to Use Flowcharts

This video describes why flowcharts are useful and how to use them.

View in the online reader

What Basic Symbols Are Used?

You need to know and be able to use fifteen symbols to create a flowchart. Figure 5.4 shows the input/output symbols.

FIGURE 5.4 Input/Output Flowcharting Symbols

INPUT/OUTPUT		
Document	Represents any document, form, or report used in the system such as a purchase order, invoice, check, financial statement, etc. (can also be used as an output).	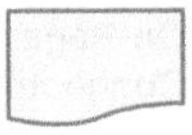
Data Input	This symbol is used when someone is entering data into a computer using either a keyboard, a touch screen, or voice recognition.	
Display	This symbol is used to represent a computer screen.	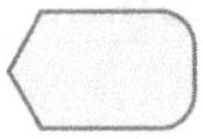

Processes are either manual or computerized and shown in Figure 5.5.

FIGURE 5.5 Process Flowcharting Symbols

PROCESS		
Manual	This symbol is used to represent an activity that is carried out by an employee without the use of a computer.	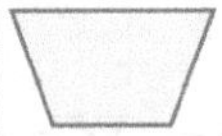
Computerized	Processing of data that is carried out by computers as opposed to being done manually.	

Four symbols are used to represent storage; they are shown in Figure 5.6.

FIGURE 5.6 Storage Flowcharting Symbols

STORAGE		
Manual File	This represents a file cabinet or folder in which documents such as checks, invoices, purchase orders are kept. A letter in the small triangle at the bottom indicates whether the filing was done Alphabetically, Chronologically, or Numerically.	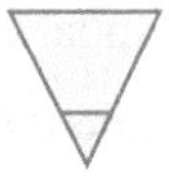
Accounting	A parallelogram is used to represent a journal, register, or ledger. Note: This symbol is used to represent input/output for programming flowcharts. AVOID using it for system flowcharts.	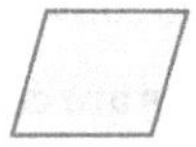
Direct Access	Can be used for magnetic or solid-state disk storage.	
Storage Disk Magnetic Tape	Use when told that the processed information is stored on magnetic tape. This is a sequential-access storage medium.	

Data flow symbols show the flow of information and the beginning and end of the flowchart. In addition, connectors are used when your flowchart becomes complex and you need to break the flowchart into smaller pieces on the same page or if it expands to another page because it does not fit. These symbols along with the symbol for comments and decisions are shown in Figure 5.7.

FIGURE 5.7 Data Flow and Other Flowcharting Symbols

DATA FLOW		
Terminal	Symbolizes the beginning or the end of the flowchart such as something you just received from a customer or sent to the Treasurer or Controller.	
Arrow Lines	These solid lines are used to connect all symbols. Arrowheads are necessary when the flowchart does not follow the normal left to right top-down convention.	⟶
On-Page Connector	Keyed with a number that indicates the point where the flow is being interrupted. Another connector keyed with the same number indicates where the flow picks up.	
Off-Page Connector	We use this connector when the flowchart of a subsystem does not fit on one page. Use an off-page connector at the end of the page and another on the following page.	
OTHER		
Comment	This symbol is used to provide further explanation. For example, if the area of a symbol is insufficient to explain the whole process, this symbol can be used for the full explanation.	
Decision	This symbol is used ONLY for programming flowcharts where alternative steps may be taken based on the result of some decision. We will NOT be using this symbol in systems flowcharts.	

How Do You Create a Flowchart?

Six steps are involved in preparing flowcharts:

1. **Determine the nature of any processes.**

   Are they manual or are they computerized? For example, if the process is manual, use an upside-down trapezoid to depict it. Computerized processes are represented with a rectangle.

2. **All processes should be "sandwiched" between an input and an output.**

   Both manual and computerized processes have inputs and outputs.

3. **Flowchart should flow logically.**

   Generally, the flow should be from left to right, top to bottom. When you are unable to follow this convention, you should use arrowheads on your flow lines.

4. **All symbols are connected with flow lines.**

   The flow lines should always physically connect to the symbols.

5. **Use the appropriate symbols.**

   Select them from an appropriate source such as shown in Figure 5.4 through Figure 5.7. Be careful if you are using a general flowcharting template that can also be used for program flowcharting. The symbol explanations can be misleading.

6. **Label the symbols with explanations that are meaningful.**

   Since we already know it is a manual process by the trapezoid, labeling it a manual procedure is redundant. A more descriptive explanation like "prepares invoice" is generally more appropriate.

For document flowcharts, follow these additional steps:

1. **Identify the internal and external agents.**

   Since the document flowchart is focused on when a document begins up until it ends (e.g., stored in a file), it is important to determine who is responsible for the document at each stage of the process.

2. **Divide the flowchart into columns to show each internal agent involved in the process.**
3. **Connect external agents as sources or destinations of documents.**

Guidelines for Creating Flowcharts

1. **Flowchart reads left to right, top down.**

   Just how we read a page on a book, the flowchart symbols should be laid out so that flowchart activities flow from left to right, top down. Figure 5.8 demonstrates the preferred method.

FIGURE 5.8 Example of Activity Flow

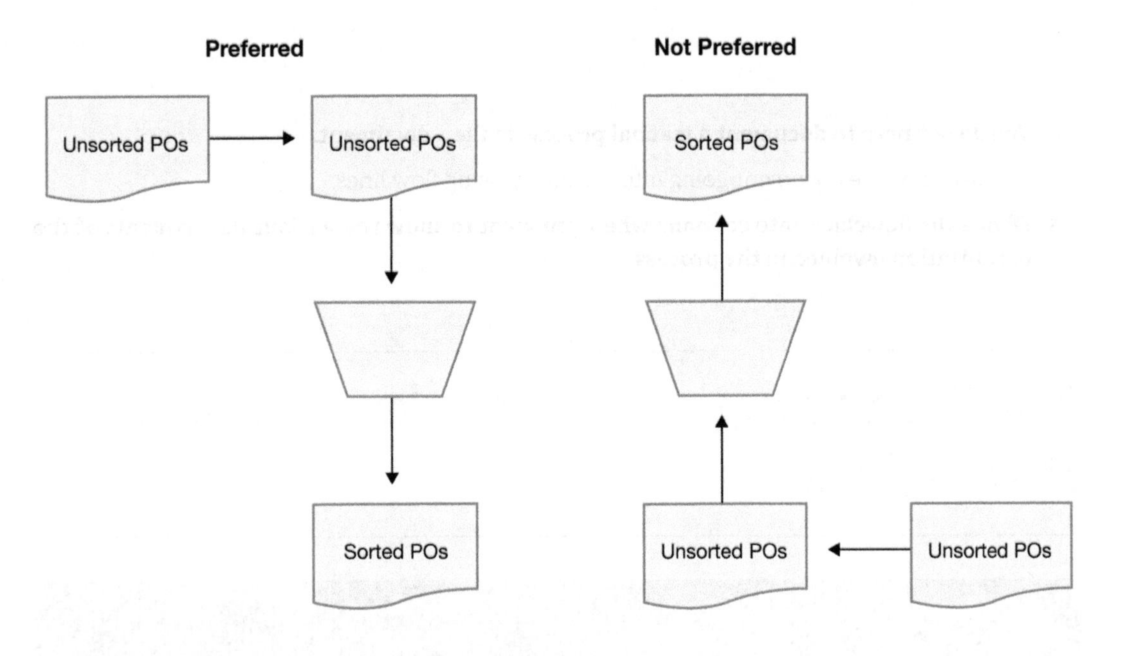

2. **Label all symbols with the process performed.**
3. **Sandwich Rule:**

   A process should be sandwiched between an input AND an output. Thus, a document coming out of a manual procedure before filing it. Remember "docs-in," "docs-out." Figure 5.9 provides the correct and incorrect examples.

FIGURE 5.9 Example of Sandwich Rule

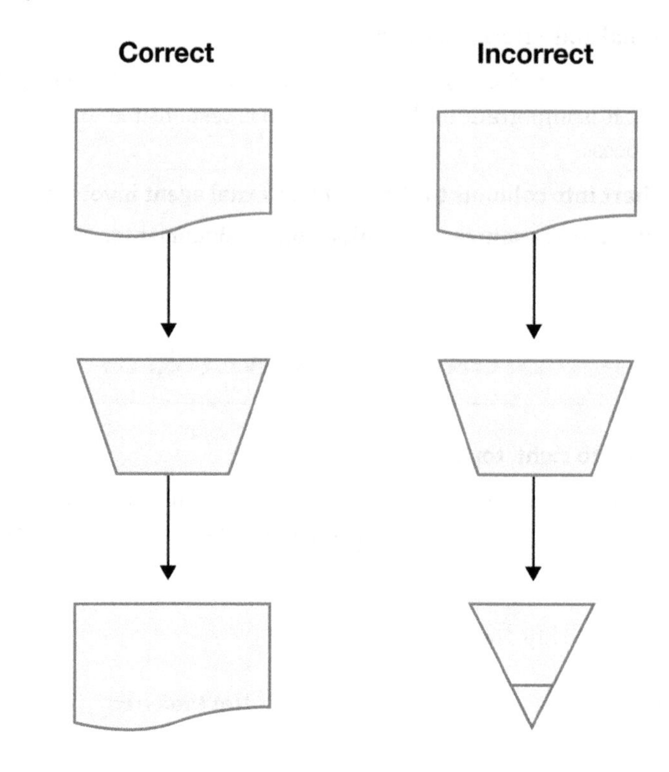

4. **You do not need to document a manual process to file a document.**

   Just show the document going into the file by using flow lines.

5. **Divide the flowchart into columns when you want to show the various departments of the organization involved in the process.**

5.4 Flowcharting a Simple Accounting Procedure

Learning Objective

At the end of this section, students should be able to:

1. Create some basic system flowchart segments similar to the examples in this chapter.

Many different software programs can be used to create a flowchart. For example, Microsoft products have flowchart shapes to build flowcharts in Excel, Word, and PowerPoint. In addition, many online tools are available that make it easy to draw flowcharts. Following is a video using an online program to create a flowchart of the bank teller process.

How to Draw Process Flowchart of a Bank Teller

This is a video using an online flowchart software.

How to Draw Banking Flowchart

View in the online reader

Simple Flowchart for Revenue Cycle

Let's say that a billing clerk manually prepares a sales invoice by referring to a shipping report, price list, and customer record. What would that look like in a system flowchart? How would we begin to construct this chart? When getting started, it is usually prudent to identify the nature of the process involved in the accounting procedure. Ask: Is it manual, or is it computerized? In our example, the procedure is manual, and so we would select the manual procedure symbol (a trapezoid from the list of available symbols shown in Figure 5.5) and place it in the center of our simple flowchart.

Then, we would identify the inputs to this manual process: (1) shipping report, (2) price list, and (3) customer record. Each of these three inputs are manual source documents, and so we should show each of them (using document symbols) entering into the process to the left of the manual procedure (assuming that flowcharts normally flow from left to right, top down). The problem with what we have created so far is that we cannot tell what the three items to the left are and that they are inputs to the manual process. To remedy this, we must label all symbols in our flowcharts using their proper business names (not the flowchart symbol names, since that would be redundant) and add some flow lines.

Please note that arrow heads on the flow lines are optional unless the flow breaks from the normal left to right, top down. Otherwise, they are required. However, you can use them all the time if that is your preference. Finally, we need to add the output from the manual process, which in this case is a sales invoice. The sales invoice (on the right) should be shown on a document symbol. The finished flowchart is in Figure 5.10, showing the manual process in the center, with the three documents to the left of the process, properly labeled, and the flow from documents to the manual process.

FIGURE 5.10 Simple Flowchart Billing

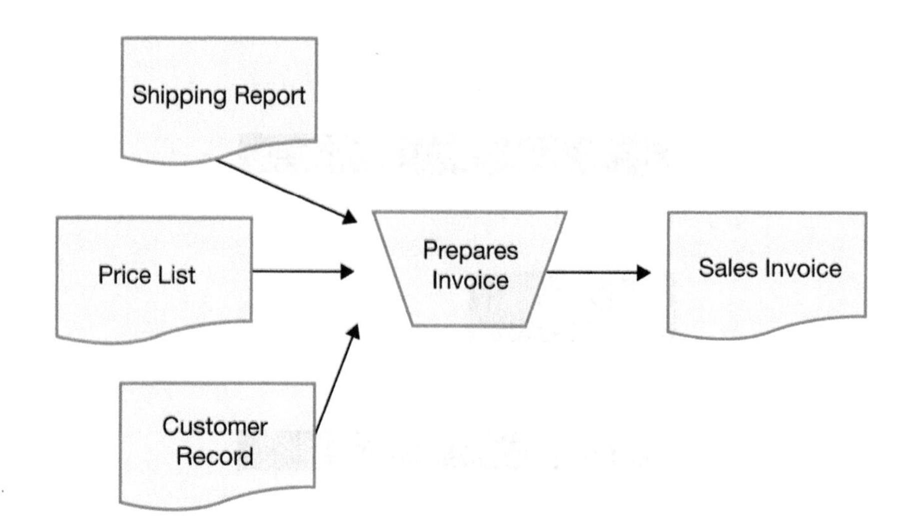

Simple Flowchart for Expenditure Cycle

So now that we have seen an illustration of a manual procedure, what would a basic example of someone entering data into a computer look like in a flowchart? In this example, we illustrate an accounting employee manually matching the source documents to process a vendor invoice with a computer process that posts the accounts payable to the subledger. So, again, we start by asking, "What is the nature of the process?" Because we have a manual process and a computerized process, we must use both symbols found in Figure 5.5. We then apply the sandwich rule to guide us in finding the input and output for both the manual and computerized processes we just identified. For the manual process of compare and approve source documents, our input is from three source documents that are matched and approved in the manual process. These three source documents are the Vendor Invoice, Purchase Order, and Receiving Report. The output is the approved voucher package that includes these three documents. Notice in Figure 5.11, which shows the simple flowchart, that the computerized process of posting to the Accounts Payable subledger uses the voucher package as the input and the output is the Account Payable posting report.

FIGURE 5.11 Simple Flowchart Vendor Invoice

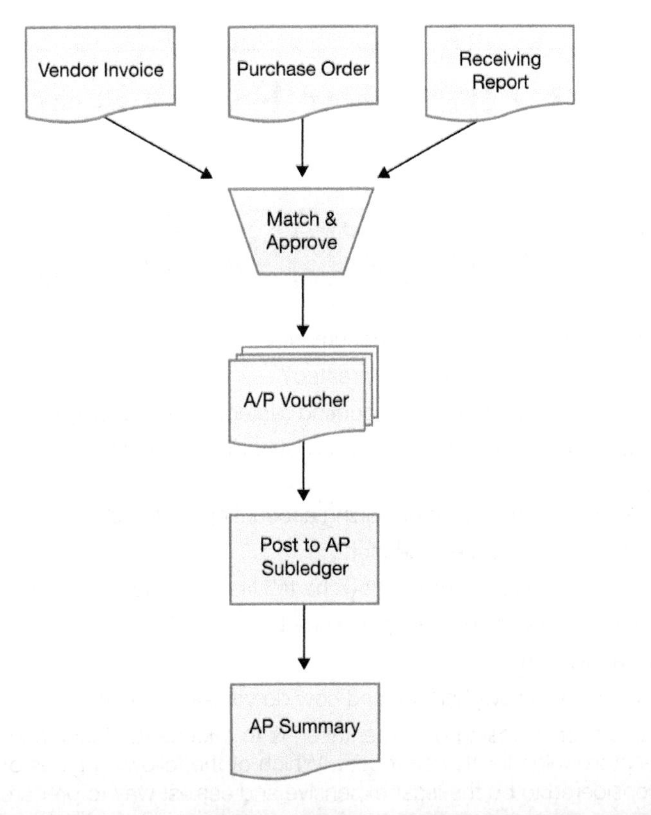

Key Takeaways

In this chapter, we learned about the benefits and costs of proper documentation for an accounting system. We began by examining the different types of documentation that can be used to communicate the interworking of an accounting system and when each should be used to provide the most explanatory value for the least cost. Through studying examples of effective flowcharts, we learned how to use and interpret a variety of symbols to correctly understand the procedures involved in processing a transaction and their corresponding inputs and desired outputs. Finally, we focused on the do's and don'ts of flowcharting in an effort to ensure that our own flowcharts are effective at communicating their intended message.

5.5 End-of-Chapter Exercises

Exercises

1. Why should accounting systems be documented?
2. What types of documentation can be created?
3. Do all companies document their accounting systems? Why or why not?
4. To what extent will auditing standards likely affect the documentation of systems in private companies?
5. How important is flowcharting in designing accounting systems?
6. What are DFDs? What are they used for?
7. What are the three different types of flowcharts? How are the different?
8. What are the guidelines for preparing flowcharts properly?
9. What is the sandwich rule?
10. What is redundancy in flowcharting, and how do you eliminate it?
11. The general rule for choosing documentation is to choose the technique that gives you the most explanatory value for the least cost. Which of the following types of documentation is generally considered to be the least expensive and easiest way to prepare a walkthrough?
    a. system flowchart
    b. ICQ
    c. hierarchical block diagram
    d. narrative memorandum
12. Which of the following statements about documenting an accounting system is true?
    a. The Sarbanes-Oxley Act has made documenting an accounting system required for all companies.
    b. Documentation can make an accounting more informal and repeatable.
    c. Lack of documentation in an accounting system could be considered a material weakness.
    d. When a more visual approach is desired, ICQs are often the preferred documentation technique.
13. A system flowchart is a diagram depicting the
    a. procedures of a system.
    b. document flows of a system.
    c. procedures and document flows of a system.
    d. procedures, decisions, and document flows of a system.
14. Which of the following would not be one of the six guidelines to be used in preparing segments of a system flowchart?
    a. Always sandwich processes between system inputs and outputs.
    b. Arrowheads must be used to designate the direction of flow lines.
    c. Flowcharts should normally flow logically from left to right, top down.
    d. Fill in symbols with explanations that add meaning, not redundancy.
15. What does the flowchart segment below depict?
    a. a manual process that files a document
    b. a manual process that generates a report

c. a computer process that files a document
d. a computer process that generates a report

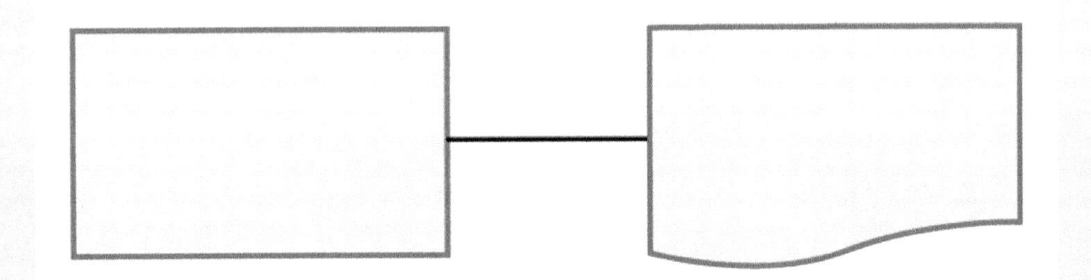

16. Which of the following is the most accurate representation of the chronological steps involved in creating a systems flowchart?
    a. Determine the nature of the process; use the appropriate symbols; fill in the symbols with meaningful explanations; ensure the flowchart flows logically.
    b. Determine the nature of the process; identify the outputs to the process identified; identify the inputs to the process identified; use the correct symbols; fill in the symbols with meaningful explanations.
    c. Determine the nature of the process; identify the input related to the process; identify the output related to the process; use the correct symbols; fill in the symbols with meaningful explanations.
    d. Identify the nature of the process; identify the input related to the process; identify the output related to the process; ensure the flowchart flows logically.
17. Draw a flowchart for each of the following:
    a. Manually prepares invoices in five copies, by reference to a customer's order file and a product pricing file.
    b. Manually sorts purchase orders by assigned numbers and then files.
    c. Processes by computer a batch of sorted sales transactions (on magnetic tape) to update a customer master file (on magnetic tape). Assume that a new master file tape must be generated because of computer magnetic tape technology.
    d. Processes by computer a batch of cash receipts transactions (on magnetic tape) to update a customer master file (on magnetic disk). Assume that the old master file can be directly updated without needing to generate a new file.
    e. Manually compares the purchase order and receiving report with the pertinent supplier's invoice; concurrently marks the invoice approved and files all documents together in chronological order in ready-to-pay file.
    f. Manually posts a batch of check vouchers to the accounts payable subsidiary ledger; resorts the batch by supplier's name and files in supplier's folders.
    g. Combines a sales transaction file and cash receipts transactions file, both sorted by customer account numbers and stored on separate magnetic tapes; sequentially updates the accounts receivable master file, stored on magnetic disk, and concurrently prints an accounts receivable aging report.
    h. Processes by computer in order to extract data from an employee earnings file and an employee history file (both on magnetic disks) onto a report file (on magnetic disk), and then prints two copies of a human resources report from the filed extracted data with one copy going to the controller and the second copy going to the human resources manager.
    i. A customer enters an order for books online. The website's server validates the order and checks to see if the items are in stock by referring to an online inventory master file. When the order process is complete, the website posts the sales data to an online sales order file and emails an order confirmation to the customer.

CHAPTER 6

AIS Strategic Planning and Systems Development

Developing and keeping an accounting system up-to-date is a matter of concern for every enterprise. For most companies, the cycle begins with a study of what they currently have and determining whether it is adequate. Then, they make any necessary changes. In this chapter, we will illustrate the traditional activities involved in accounting systems development. Although the phases of this process may seem relatively straightforward, not all system development projects are successful. In fact, many turn out to be partial or complete failures. Problems often occur because so many uncertainties are connected with such a complicated process. For example, Revlon shareholders filed a class-action lawsuit against the company in 2019 for failure to adequately plan and monitor an enterprise resource planning (ERP) implementation.[1] The failure caused disruptions in the supply chain that increased costs and lowered sales.

In reality, computer system development failures are common. A research report from the Standish Group in 2020[2] studied more than 8,000 projects in the United States, ranging from minor enhancements to major systems re-engineering implementations. Of those surveyed, approximately 84 percent of all projects were either challenged or failed. Hence, only 16 percent were successful. The success rate also depended to a large extent on the size of the project, where of the 16 percent success rate, 9 percent were large companies, 16 percent were medium, and 28 percent were small). While system implementations have great risk, proper planning can mitigate the risk. View a short video here on why IT projects fail.

Have You Ever Wondered Why IT Projects Fail?

This is a video from the Standish Group on IT project failure.

View in the online reader

6.1 Why Is AIS Strategic Planning Needed?

Learning Objectives

At the end of this section, students should be able to:

1. Define strategic planning and understand the need for it.
2. Understand why accounting systems strategic planning is necessary.
3. List and explain the three phases of the system development process.

strategic planning

The basic long-term goals of an enterprise and the adoption of courses of action and the allocation of resources necessary for carrying out these goals.

Chandler in 1962 defined **strategic planning** as the determination of the basic long-term goals of an enterprise and the adoption of courses of action and the allocation of resources necessary for carrying out these goals. This process should yield a flexible and continually updated SWOT analysis (strengths, weaknesses, opportunities, and threats).

Now that information has become an important resource, strategies must be formulated for acquiring and utilizing the information necessary to support future activities. The purpose of systems strategic planning is to create an unfolding master plan for the organization's information needs and the means of meeting those needs. Accounting systems strategic planning allows organizations to be more proactive and to establish initiatives such as

1. tracking technological developments in computer hardware and software and
2. encouraging user involvement in systems projects.

This is different from a reactive response to problems, which many organizations follow.

AIS has several "typical problems":

- Processing bottlenecks and inefficiency
- Unreliable output
- Inability to handle certain types of transactions or access information
- Customer and employee complaints and turnover

The main reason for these "typical problems" in most organizations is a lack of a chief information officer (CIO) responsible for providing leadership in the systems area.

Evolving Role of the CIO

This is a video describing the role of a CIO in an organization.

View in the online reader

Consequently, an organization without a CIO means those responsibilities fall on general management, controllers, or auditors. Those in charge not really understanding the difference between a strategic asset or investment and overhead is also a serious problem. IT expenditures in some organizations are viewed as administrative overhead instead of strategic investments.

Understanding Business Needs and Strategy

Planning the development of new systems should not wait until the old system is at or beyond its useful life because there may not be enough time to adequately plan a new system and get it going before the old one dies or causes the organization to lose profits.

Systems strategic planning should look as far into the future as possible to anticipate changes in advance. This process includes understanding the current business needs and strategy as well as the future needs and strategy. As part of this process, a number of speculative questions should be asked:

Q: Will the evolution and innovation of technologies affect our business?

Q: Should we be taking advantage of new technologies?

Q: Will we be able to comply with upcoming regulations without having to spend an inordinate amount of money?

Ultimately, technology strategic planners need to know where an organization is relative to the Systems Technology Maturity Model (STMM; described in Chapter 2) and then take a look at the costs and benefits of moving to where they should be. The STMM can help an organization see where it could be in terms of technology sophistication. An organization must then decide where it should be on the scale given its environment and resources.

Legacy System and Business Model Innovation Situations

An effective accounting system must be carefully planned, designed, and implemented to meet the needs of a company and its users. This is true whether you have a legacy system that you are going to enhance or, as we found out in Chapter 4, the organization's business model changed because of a change in strategy.

application programming interface (API)

The interface between two software applications that allow them to interact.

For legacy system situations, the organization may find that the AIS is fine for producing financial statements but may need to be modernized so users have better access to the financial information, providing more efficient processes. For example, a legacy system can be modernized by using the data and functions of the legacy system to create a services platform. This may be as simple as creating a new **application programming interface (API)**. The interface may involve a new way to input data into the system, requiring a new form design to make it more user friendly and efficient. For example, if the legacy system required entering data into three different areas of the AIS, it would be much more efficient to create an API that allows one form to input all the data and have that dispersed to the proper database tables.

Additionally, output may be considered as a service for various users. It would be much more efficient to modernize the legacy system and create better reports for the various users, such as sales, marketing, and finance.

Other ways legacy systems are getting modernized is the ability for organizations to redeploy the application to a hosted cloud-based solution. This provides an opportunity for the organization to have more efficient access and potential cost savings for their systems. Of course, much testing is needed to ensure that the migration to the cloud is successful and proper security controls are implemented as well. While beyond the scope of this book, as accountants, it is important to work with the IT and development folks from a business perspective to ensure successful implementation.

Business model innovation situations also leverage existing capabilities of a legacy system but may require additional code to improve the capabilities of the system. For example, if an organization has different compliance requirements for financial reporting, such as componentizing assets for depreciation using International Financial Reporting Standards (IFRS), system developers will need to examine how this change would affect the existing system of currently accounting for depreciation and how moving to componentized depreciation would require any additional rebuilding or rewriting of the application.

For the most part, an organization would consider three steps for systems development, which we will expand upon further in this chapter. System development has traditionally been performed in three phases, as illustrated in Figure 6.1:

FIGURE 6.1 Systems Development

Analysis is the process of gathering data to identify what type of system is needed, what the existing system does, and how it can be improved.

Design is the process of creating a paper (theoretical) model of an improved system.

Implementation is the process of turning the paper (theoretical) model into a working accounting system.

analysis

The process of gathering data to identify what type of system is needed, what the existing system does, and how it can be improved.

design

The process of creating a paper (theoretical) model of an improved system.

implementation

The process of turning the paper (theoretical) model into a working accounting system.

6.2 What Is Involved in Systems Analysis?

Learning Objectives

At the end of this section, students should be able to:

1. Explain the purpose of accounting systems analysis.
2. Know what system analysis is and what it involves.
3. Describe the ROI model and provide examples.

The overall purpose of accounting systems analysis is to see what accounting systems will be required over the long term and then to evaluate the existing systems to see what improvements must be made to meet the plan.

A well-thought-out user-oriented information system can increase productivity, reduce inventories and related costs, improve customer service and management decisions, and coordinate activities throughout the organization.

The system analysis process is illustrated in Figure 6.2:

FIGURE 6.2 System Analysis Process

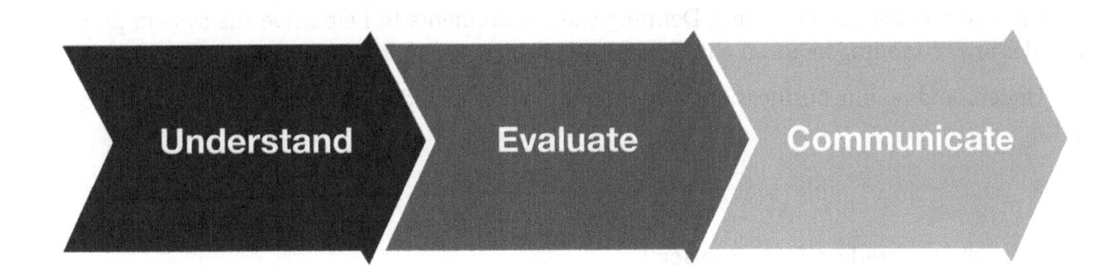

In other words, understand your situation, evaluate the alternatives, and then communicate your recommendations.

Assessing Information Needs

Assessment of information needs includes identifying the informational needs of the organization on three dimensions: operating, decision-making, and reporting. In assessing operating information needs, one should consider evaluating the business process. A business process is how things get done in the organization. As we learned in Chapter 1, processes are tasks that people perform to get things done in an organization. To analyze the process, one may want to do a walk-through of the process from beginning to end. For example, when doing business with customers, we may want to start at the very beginning of the sales process with our walk-through and find out what information the sales department needs prior to booking the sale with the customer. Next, we would seek to understand what the accounting department and the warehouse need when the order is booked and the goods are shipped to the customer. We would then continue our walk-through by looking at the billing process when we invoice the customer and finally what customer service support the customer might need after the sale is made. As you can see, the process does not begin in the accounting department, but from end to end, it affects many departments in an organization, so it is important to have adequate informational hand-offs from one department to the other.

In addition to a walk-through of the process, information assessment also includes interviewing key personnel in the organization. The interview process should be neutral and ask questions starting with broad open-ended questions, such as, "Explain to me how you get this task done," and then more specific questions to make sure you understand.

Assessment of informational needs from a decision-making and reporting perspective means that you should interview management to understand how the information needs map to the organizational strategy. For example, a manager may tell you during an interview, "I could really use two more pieces of information to make better decisions, but that information is not included on any of our reports." Additionally, a dataflow diagram may be used to understand informational needs.

After assessing informational needs, the next step is to evaluate the system strengths and weaknesses. This will then help one with the direction of developing an adequate system to meet the organization's informational needs.

Defining Business and User Requirements

After identifying weaknesses in the system from the informational needs assessment, the next step is to ask, "What needs to be done to solve the problem?" The specific business and user requirements are based on the scope and objectives of how to solve the problem (sometimes you cannot solve all the problems at one time). Defining the requirements to help solve the system problem includes understanding requirements for people, processes, technology, and controls.

Understanding our business and user requirements includes answering the following questions:

What should we have in place?

This can be determined by conducting interviews or studying best practices of model systems.

What do we have?

This should be documented with system narratives, diagrams, and system flowcharts.

Can we do it better?

This involves comparing what you have to what you need and identifying any gaps. Then using creative and critical thinking, consider the alternatives, weigh their pros and cons, and make recommendations.

Do we have the need to change how we are currently doing business with our customers and vendors?

Systems analysis should end up with a system proposal containing formal recommendations for improvement. In general, they normally include one of the following:

- Develop a brand-new system.
- Modify the existing system.
- Do nothing.

As with most system recommendations, the conclusion will be based on costs and benefits. Unfortunately, basic cost-benefit analysis based solely on financial data can result in poor decisions. When an analysis fails to consider quality or other potential intangible costs, misleading results may occur. Consider the following examples:

Ford Motor Company once selected Firestone tires as their low-cost bidder. Unfortunately, the treads peeled off the tires at high speeds on several Ford Explorers, causing rollovers and many serious accidents.[3] Were Firestone tires really the lowest cost?

Joe Student selects Prestigious U because of its outstanding name recognition only to find out later that he could have obtained an equivalent education at a state college. Did Joe really achieve the expected net benefit?

Company A selects software from Vendor B because it has a big name in the industry when Company A could have acquired the same software features from an open-source alternative and met substantially all of its needs for much less money. Was the big-name software really worth it?

Evaluating Feasibility

Alternative solutions are evaluated based on the following four dimensions of feasibility:

- Technical—the technology to do the implementation exists
- Economic—the benefits exceed the costs
- Operational—acceptable by the organization
- Time—can be available by the time you need it

The feasibility study would examine all the alternatives and provides a system analysis report that includes the following parts:

- Background
- Strengths and weaknesses
- Alternative solutions—new system, modify, leave as is
- Recommendations—presentations

As you probably know, billions of dollars have been spent on technology projects over the last decade. To some executives, the benefit of technology expenditures is unclear. Many feel that such expenditures are unnecessary or simply too costly. In some cases, however, management is shortsighted and views technology expenditures as overhead when, in fact, they are strategic investments.

The return on investment (ROI) model has become popular because it forces system analysts to demonstrate the benefits of technology expenditures. For example, if a project cannot produce equivalent revenue increases or cost savings within two to three years, management may be justified in saying no to the proposal. Conversely, a well-documented ROI analysis can help save a project that management may have otherwise rejected because the net benefits were unclear.

Following is an example of a simple ROI analysis used to assess how many months it will take to payback the outlay for a point-of-sale-based, online, real-time inventory system with programmed reorder points. Such systems can be expensive and possibly difficult to justify. The following analysis illustrates whether such a system could be justified given a two-year payback requirement:

Outlay	$ 1,200,000
Year 1 Effect:	
Reduced purchasing costs	200,000
Reduced inventory carrying and reorder costs	100,000
Increased sales	150,000
Year 2 Effect:	
Reduced purchasing costs	$ 220,000
Reduced inventory carrying and reorder costs	150,000
Increased sales	250,000
Year 3 Effect:	$ 240,000
Reduced inventory carrying and reorder costs	180,000
Increased sales	300,000

If management required a 24-month payback for this project, would it be funded?

No, the payback here is approximately 27 months: In the first 12 months, they recover $450,000 ($200,000 + 100,000 + 150,000). In the next 12 months, they recover another $620,000 ($220,000 + 150,000 + 250,000) or $1,070,000 ($450,000 + 620,000) in total. The remaining $130,000 will take another three months to recover if you round up given that the third-year recovery is $60,000 ($720,000 / 12) per month.

Of course, ROI can be more complex by factoring in a discounted rate of return and the impact of inflation. For purposes of this textbook, we focus on simple ROI.

6.3 Effective Systems Development

Learning Objectives

At the end of this section, students should be able to:

1. Describe the overall objective of systems development.
2. Define what is involved in systems design and its output.
3. Explain what is involved in systems implementation.
4. Identify and describe the critical success factors to systems development.

The system development process is important because of a need to cope with change. Such change often results from things like new laws, new technology, internal growth, acquisitions, restructuring, and competition. Failure to adapt should be of concern to managers, who may see their profits decline, and to their auditors because someone may be motivated to engage in fraud to cover up his or her financial problems.

System development includes modifying existing systems and building new systems. Because systems evolve as a business evolves, this process is often referred to as the system development life cycle.

system development
The development of new systems and the modification of existing ones.

System design is a blueprint of how to build the system and includes decisions such as system structure, information flows, required measures, and controls. Materials include the following:

- Narrative descriptions of the process
- System flowcharts
- Input designs
- File designs and record layouts
- Report and screen layouts
- Description of IT infrastructure, such as networks or cloud

Build versus Buy

The options for system implementation have dramatically changed in the last few years. Traditionally, hardware would be installed and managed internally, and the software would either be written internally (often with the help of consultants) known as a "build" method or purchased, aka the "buy" method.

Both the build versus buy methods may include the following steps:

1. Development of software in-house (build) or acquisition of computer software (buy)
2. Acquisition of computer hardware
3. Installation, systems testing, and training
4. Conversion to the new or modified system

Conversion may be immediate for simple low-risk systems or parallel when it's too risky to retire the old one until you are sure the new one is working. Parallel conversion obviously involves more cost and time since you are maintaining two systems, but the trade-off is often very beneficial when conversion risks are high. Another approach to conversion is called incremental, where you bring on your new systems a little bit at a time.

Buy or Build Software? Forbes Technology Council—Russell Smith

This is a video that discusses the logic in deciding to buy or build software applications.

View in the online reader

Development Methods

When the structure of the information to be used or reported is high, we can use a traditional top-down approach. When the information is only partially structured, a prototyping approach can work better. When there is little to no structure, companies have recently discovered that data mining, artificial intelligence, and data analytics can be used to generate information.

Traditionally, when systems were developed using a structured top-down approach, an organization would identify its information needs and system requirements. This was generally the case when designing a system to produce necessary reports with known requirements. The reports would then be designed along with the necessary databases and data inputs. Accounting system output is usually designed first because we must satisfy the operational and information requirements of the organization. Next, we identify the fewest input data elements necessary to support the required outputs. Users will be reluctant to accept a system if its inputs are poorly designed, making data entry difficult to understand or causing mistakes.

What data elements to include on a form must be determined as well as how the data can best be represented, how to arrange the various items, and what explanatory legends and instructions must be added to provide an effective, efficient basis for communication and use. A form can include a report, touch screen, presentation slide, and even a web page as well as a traditional source document.

Keeping the following in mind will improve an organization's forms design:

- **Clarity of presentation**

  This means that the design should be simple and understandable.

- **Logical grouping and flow of data**

  In other words, put things together that belong together and try to stay with the normal left to right top-down flow that people are used to.

- **Effective use of space**

  This means to fill the surface without overflowing the boundaries. For example, try not to put too much on a web page because people do not like to scroll down to see the rest of the page.

- **Conformity with size constraints**

  In other words, plan for size, such as an envelope or paper (portrait or landscape) or computer screen (columns and rows).

- **Ease of use**

  Effort and possible errors should be minimized.

- **Tasteful use of graphic effects**

  Consider elements such as fonts, colors, and graphics (like charts and logos) carefully.

After the top-down design process was complete, systems documentation could be used to facilitate implementation and provide a record of the development process. This type of approach is normally used to generate a company's financial statements.

When a company is designing a system to support decision-making, the information needs may not be clearly known. In such cases, prototype systems are often created using spreadsheets, for example, and tested until a satisfactory model can be achieved. This iterative process is called prototyping.

After experimentation with the prototype is complete, documentation of the system should be created. The documentation should explain how the system works and how to maintain it. In the real world, however, sometimes this does not happen, and when the person using the spreadsheet leaves the company, it can be a problem for the next employee to pick up where the last person left off.

Recently, research has indicated that the majority of corporate information is unstructured. Word documents, emails, spreadsheets, and even image, audio, and video files may have some information value to them, but they are essentially free form and cannot be queried and reported on like a structured database. Some firms are now using data mining, text analytics, and advanced artificial intelligence techniques to infer information in such data and to create reports.

Critical Factors to Successful Development

Success can be understood in terms of six critical success factors (CSFs):

User Acceptance

- Satisfies users' needs
- Makes users' job easier
- Users like it and want to use it
- Compatible with organizational environment

Cost Effectiveness

- Low initial cost
- Low maintenance cost

Flexibility

- Able to adapt to changing requirements and growth
- Not restricted to one hardware or software product line

Reliability

- Little downtime
- High-quality information
- Able to handle exceptions

Management Commitment

- Support for the project
- Commitment communicated to lower levels
- Prompt response to actual or potential people problems

Key Takeaways

In this chapter, we emphasized the importance of keeping an accounting system up-to-date through strategic planning. The purpose of a strategic plan is to identify an organization's information needs and the means for meeting those needs. We looked at the steps involved in accounting systems analysis and thoroughly examined how the process would ideally work. We also outlined the components of a system analysis report. We learned about the accounting systems development process. We saw that it generally takes place in three phases. Its objective is to carefully plan, design, and implement an effective accounting system to meet the needs of a company and its users. The systems development process is important because it allows organizations to adapt to changing system requirements. We learned that planning the development of new systems should not wait until the old system is no longer capable of performing at an appropriate level. We examined the three phases of the system development process: analysis, design, and implementation. We saw how system analysis results in a set of recommendations and how design turns those recommendations into a theoretical model. Implementation then turns the theoretical model into a working system. Lastly, we discussed the critical success factors of system development.

Reference

- Chandler, Jr., Alfred D. *Strategy and Structure: Chapters in the History of the Industrial Empire.* Cambridge, MA: Massachusetts Institute of Technology, 1962.

6.4 End-of-Chapter Exercises

Exercises

1. What is the overall objective of systems development?
2. Why is the systems development process important? Can you provide some examples?
3. Why is strategic planning for accounting systems necessary?
4. How does the systems development process work?
5. What does system analysis involve? Can you give an example of a company going from a desktop accounting package to using cloud computing for its accounting system?
6. What is involved in systems design? Can you give an example?

7. What do you think is the most important factor to successful systems development?
8. Why do systems development projects fail?
9. Are trade-offs necessary in controlling system development projects? Can you give any examples?
10. What is ROI? What is it used for? Can it be calculated? Provide an example using a spreadsheet.
11. Which of the following phases is not included in the systems development process?
    a. implementation
    b. reporting
    c. analysis
    d. design
    e. None of the above
12. Which of the following is considered a critical factor to successful development?
    a. reliability
    b. simplicity
    c. cost effectiveness
    d. flexibility
    e. All of the above
13. Which of the following is not considered an objective for user acceptance when developing a system?
    a. satisfies organizations needs
    b. makes users' jobs easier
    c. makes the economy more stable
    d. satisfies users' needs
    e. None of the above
14. Which of the following is not involved in system analysis?
    a. determining what is needed
    b. identifying what you already have
    c. recommending how to improve things
    d. acquiring basic features
15. Which of the following would not normally be involved in the system implementation phase?
    a. training users
    b. identifying needed features
    c. acquiring hardware
    d. systems testing
16. Which of the following is generally the riskiest approach to system conversion?
    a. immediate
    b. incremental
    c. parallel
    d. incremental/parallel
17. In performing an ROI analysis, an analyst determined that a new system feature would cost $50,000 but would also reduce operating costs by nearly $22,000 per year. Accordingly, the expenditure would have an ROI of how many months?
    a. 25
    b. 27
    c. 28
    d. 29
18. **THE SYSTEM DEVELOPMENT PROCESS: Identifying the Pertinent Phases**

System development refers to the process of analyzing, designing, and implementing new accounting systems or modifying exiting ones.

Required:

Given the description below, please identify whether the development activity described would be performed in the analysis, design, or implementation phase of the system development process.

a. Interviews are conducted to determine what type of system the organization should implement.
b. Computer hardware is acquired.
c. A system proposal is formally documented.
d. A narrative description illustrating the system's structure, information flows, and required level of performance is created.
e. The proposed system undergoes a rigorous testing phase.
f. System flowcharts are created to adequately document the information flows pertaining to the proposed system.
g. Employees are trained to use the new or modified system.

19. **CRITICAL SUCCESS FACTORS: Identifying the Pertinent Ones**

The six critical success factors of system development include user acceptance, cost effectiveness, flexibility, simplicity, reliability, and management commitment.

Required:

Please identify which system development success factor is associated with each example characteristic below.

a. Users like it and want to use it
b. Support for the project
c. Not restricted to one hardware or software product line
d. Easy to service
e. Little downtime
f. Prompt response to actual or potential people problems
g. Low maintenance costs
h. Compatible with organizational development
i. Able to adapt to changing requirements and growth
j. Able to handle exceptions

20. **PROBLEM-SOLVING IN THE REAL WORLD: Thinking and Generating Solutions that Answer Questions and Improve Profits**

After leaving your position in public accounting, you accepted a job in the accounting department of a publicly held company. Despite some problems early on at the new job, you decided to stay on and help your company consider changes to their accounting system. Over the next several months, you encounter the following situations:

a. Although you and your chief financial officer (CFO) were convinced that the company needed a new ERP system, the chief executive officer (CEO) was reluctant to initiate any new IT projects after the company's recent fiasco with a failed acquisition. The CFO wanted to purchase an Oracle database and install Oracle's ERP system and related computer hardware for an upfront cost of $1,200,000 plus approximately $600,000 for consultants to setup up the chart of accounts and database design including tables for customers, vendors, employees, and all other entities of interest. If the Oracle ERP system were implemented, the company would improve its sales and reduce costs by approximately $60,000 a year for the next 5 years, but the system would require approximately $10,000 a year for maintenance, backup, and security consulting services. You think the company would be better off using NetSuite's cloud-based ERP system, which would cost approximately $150,000 to have consultants set up the chart of accounts and database. Thereafter, NetSuite would cost approximately $200,000 a year for usage fees and result in roughly the same $60,000 in improved sales and reduced costs. If the Oracle solution is chosen, the company would also have to spend approximately $150,000 for software licenses and labor to upgrade its operating systems to support the new system. According to the CEO, both of the proposals were unnecessary increases to the company's overhead.

b. Despite the CEO's objection to a new IT project, she decided to approve the CFO's proposal. The CFO was then authorized to contact the sales office at Oracle. In preparation for his conversation with Oracle, the CFO ordered three single processor quad-core servers for the Oracle software: (1) the main production server, (2) a backup server, and (3) a test server. The CFO also contacted the consulting group at the public accounting firm he used to work for and engaged a team there to design and setup the new chart of accounts and database. The hiring process was expedited because he knew the backgrounds of the team members from his experience at the firm. He then called Oracle and ordered three copies of the Oracle Database for the three servers.

The following month, the accounting system consultants arrived and began designing the chart of accounts and database tables based on their projection of what the company needed. During the process, they decided to begin testing their preliminary design on the test server and found that the software required at least dual processors to handle the design that they had created. The project was moving along well until one of the consulting team members took ill, which sidetracked him for more than 2 months, and another consultant was pulled from the system development project several times to return to a previous job that was unraveling. To tweak the design, the consultants proposed a number of customizations, which the CFO approved, including one that would help the database run on a single processor. Several more months went by, and the consultants brought in some other consultants to begin training the staff.

Although the CEO was getting anxious about the time it was taking to design the new system and wanted an immediate implementation, the CFO convinced her that it should be implemented in parallel with the current system. This way the output from the new system could be compared to the old system and any necessary adjustments could be made. During the first 2 months of the implementation, the accounting department was required to work 15 hours a week of overtime, including Saturdays. In addition, several of the employees found the new system to be overly complicated and slow, allegedly due to all of the customizations. There was also unexpected downtime, and everyone's nerves were wearing thin. After a year and a half, the consultants were still trying to work out the bugs and were asking for an additional $50,000 on top of the $100,000 they were already over their fee estimate.

Required:

Complete the following for each of the scenarios above:

i. Analyze and indicate whether you think there is a problem (including your rationale).
ii. If so, explain what you believe is the cause, or if not, why not.
iii. If so, propose a solution (including alternatives, if any).

21. **ROI ANALYSIS: Manz Corporation**

Management at Manz Corporation is in the process of determining whether the company should invest in a more sophisticated inventory tracking system that includes programmed reorder points. Although implementing such a system is not inexpensive, in the long run it should be able to reduce their costs and possibly increase their revenues. The outlay for the inventory tracking system is $1,750,000, and the firm expects to reduce its purchasing costs by $150,000, its inventory carrying and reorder costs by $125,000, and for its sales to increase by $175,000 within the first year of implementing the system as a result of fewer stock-outs. By the end of year 2, the firm estimates its purchasing costs to be reduced by $200,000, its inventory carrying and reorder costs to be reduced by $165,000, and its sales to increase by $250,000. By the end of year 3, purchasing costs are expected to be reduced by $225,000, inventory carrying and reorder costs by $195,000, and sales increased by $310,000.

Required:

a. What is an ROI model and who uses it?

b. What are some of the benefits of using an ROI model?

c. In the scenario described above, if management of Manz Company required a 36-month payback for the project, would it be funded?

22. **Reflective Learning**

a. Based on reading and reflecting on this chapter, what have you learned?

b. What was the most difficult concept in the chapter? Why was it difficult?

c. Does the material in this chapter relate to anything you have covered in another course or seen in any of your prior experiences?

Endnotes

1. Accessed online at https://www.businesswire.com/news/home/20190514006078/en/.
2. Accessed online at https://www.projectsmart.co.uk/white-papers/chaos-report.pdf.
3. Accessed online at https://en.wikipedia.org/wiki/Firestone_and_Ford_tire_controversy.

CHAPTER 7

Database Design

In Chapter 3, we learned about relational databases from a user perspective, meaning that we needed to understand the basics of how information is stored in the data table and how tables are logically connected with relationships. In this chapter, we now consider the designer perspective of databases.

7.1 How Are Databases Normally Designed?

Learning Objectives

At the end of this section, students should be able to:

1. Explain the entity integrity and referential integrity rule for database design.
2. Understand how to normalize a set of database tables.
3. Explain primary keys, foreign keys, and concatenated keys in a database table.

In the real world, most companies attempt to identify, through extensive information needs analysis, the information that is relevant for them to collect and store. The information elements, as we learned in Chapter 3, are called **attributes** (such as part numbers, quantities, etc.). These attributes are then associated with the logical **entities** that they pertain to (the database tables).

attributes
Information elements in a table (e.g., customer name).

entity
Data table in a database.

To assess needs, organizations may use source documents to capture information in their database. For example, a sales order is a source document generated from the sales department that shows what the customer is authorizing to transact business with the company. This source document would tell us who is buying inventory from us, the date the sales order was made, and how much inventory the customer wants to buy and at what price. In addition, other terms may be stipulated in the sales order, such as date the inventory is needed by, any negotiated discounts, etc. Just from this one source document in the sales process, we already would classify the area of interest in entities of customer, sale, and product.

Once all of the informational needs are assessed by the organization, generally through the analysis of business processes, information needed to make decisions (which may be captured from source documents), the design of the database begins. The design process conceptualizes how this information will be captured using entities that capture an area of interest (e.g., customers) and the relationships with other entities (e.g., sales, and products) to capture the transaction. The design of the **conceptual database** is known as a data model.

conceptual database
Business view of the data model.

Data Modeling Concepts

E-R modeling

Entity-Relationship diagram which is a visual representation of how the entities (tables) are related to one-another.

For purposes of this book, a data model is a conceptualization that shows the entity associations (traditionally referred to as entity-relationship or called **E-R modeling**). It is a visual representation of how the entities (tables) are related to one-another. Another way to think about the data model is as a blueprint that you use to build the database. You wouldn't hire a contractor to just start building your house. Could you imagine what that would look like? The contractor would need a blueprint on how to build the house, with the details of where to put in the electric outlets, windows, doors, etc. Thus, in an organization, a conceptual model would be the blueprint used to build a database.

Once you have decided on the relevant data you need in each entity (table), you need to consider how these tables are related to one another. Let's take a look at our example using the sales order. We know we want to capture information about customers (customer table), the activity that is transacted over time with our customers (sales table), and what we sold them (products table). Relationships between tables are designed according to one of three options: one-to-one, one-to-many, or many-to-many. Further in the chapter we will explore this concept to understand how our database design may change because of our business processes and the policies used to transact business with our trading partners (e.g., customers and vendors).

The conceptualized model provides business users a means to communicate their needs with the IT professionals who will actually build the database. While the design perspective is somewhat abstract at first, you are actually thinking about the data you need with the goal of only capturing it once. This provides an efficient manner to the design and requires data integrity, which is achieved by following the fundamental rules of database design. These rules are the *entity-integrity rule* and the *referential integrity rule.*

entity-integrity rule

Reduces duplication of data in a data table where a primary key must be present in the table and have unique values.

The **entity-integrity rule** helps reduce data duplication. The entity-integrity rule has three requirements when creating each entity (table):

1. All tables must have a primary key.
2. All primary keys must have unique values.
3. Primary keys cannot be blank (null).

primary key

Attribute in a table that is the unique identifier.

To continue with our example of the sales order, we know that the business sells products to customers. For the customer table, we capture all the information we need about our customers. We will need a **primary key** that is a unique value for each customer. That means, no two customers can have the same value. Generally, a unique value is a number or a combination of text and numbers. For our example, we would recommend that each customer be given a unique sequence of numbers. Why numbers and not just the business name itself? Because if you conduct business throughout the country, there may be duplication of business names. Business names are based on state filing requirements. To demonstrate this phenomenon, type in "ABC Movers" into your internet search engine and see how many different moving companies throughout the United States have that name but are not related. Using the name of the company as the primary key in this case would violate the second rule of entity integrity.

referential integrity rule

Maintains the integrity of the data between a foreign key and the primary key in the related table.

The **referential integrity rule** is focused on the relationship between two tables to maintain the integrity of the data. Thus, the use of the primary key from one table would be considered a foreign key in the related table. Figure 7.1 visually shows the referential integrity rule.

FIGURE 7.1 Referential Integrity Example

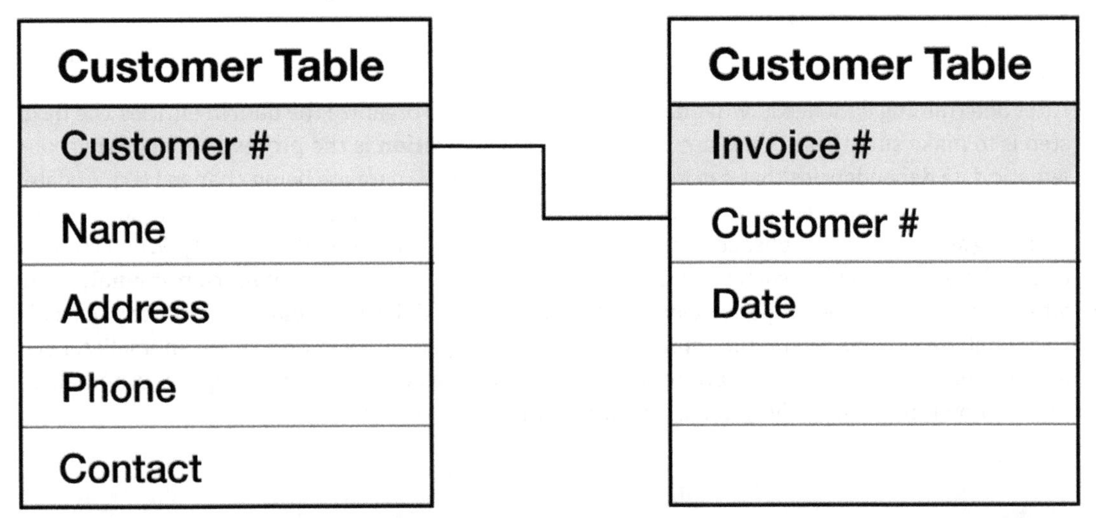

Figure 7.1 shows two entities: Customer Table and Sales Table, which inter-relate with one another. The unique primary key in the Customer Table is the Customer # attribute (shaded blue). Notice that Customer # is also an attribute in the Sales Table. Customer # in the Sales Table is defined as the **foreign key** in the related tables (Sales Table). The Sales Table primary key is the Invoice # (shaded blue). Referential integrity therefore ensures reliability that a Customer # in the Sales Table actually is a Customer # found in the Customer Table. Having the foreign key of Customer # in the Sales Table allows us to physically connect these two tables together, creating a relationship in the database.

foreign key

A field in one table that refers to the primary key in a related table.

Referential Integrity in Microsoft Access

This is a video showing an example of referential integrity in a database.

View in the online reader

Data Anomalies and Normalization

normalization

The process of removing problematic data dependencies that can create problems when the data are being changed.

update anomaly

Occurs when a database is not properly normalized; multiple updates are needed when only one update should suffice.

insertion anomaly

Occurs when a database is not properly normalized and new records cannot be added due to the absence of other data.

deletion anomaly

Occurs when a database is not properly normalized and records with certain attributes shouldn't be deleted.

After determining data needs, what data to store, and how to organize the data in entities, the next step is to make sure these tables are normalized. **Normalization** is the process of removing problematic data dependencies that can create problems when the data are being changed (e.g., update, delete, add). For example, an improper design that requires multiple update operations when updating should be accomplished in one operation is known as an **update anomaly**. When records cannot be properly added, such as for new customers, this is known as an **insertion anomaly**. And when records cannot be properly deleted, this is known as a **deletion anomaly**. A properly normalized database ensures referential integrity and removes update, insert, and delete anomalies. Let's assume that the following data are captured from our Sales Order shown in Figure 7.2 and all of this information is currently stored in one table, which is shown in Figure 7.3.

Basic Concept of Database Normalization—Simple Explanation for Beginners

This is a video that explains the different anomaly problems in a database.

View in the online reader

FIGURE 7.2 Sales Order Example

Sales Order

SO#: 1918
Date: 23-Sep

Customer #: 5965

Customer #: 5965
Address: NY, NY
Contact: A. Malloy

Item #	Description	QTY	Price	Extended Price
5560	Energy Management Device 8"	8	39.98	319.98
2723	Smart Home Controller 240v	9	499.99	4499.91
			Total	4819.75

FIGURE 7.3 Data Table of Sales Order for Figure 7.2

Sales Order	Date	Customer #	Customer Name	Address	Contact Name	Item #	Description	Qty	Price
1918	23-Sep	5965	ABC Electrics	NY, NY	A. Malloy	5560	Energy Management Device 8"	8	39.99
1918	23-Sep	5965	ABC Electrics	NY, NY	A. Malloy	2723	Smart Home Controller 240v	9	499.99

We can already see from the data table in Figure 7.3 that the entity integrity rule is violated by capturing the sales order information in one table. We see that the Sales Order number is repeating summary information, such as Sales Order number, Date, Customer number, Name, Address, and Contact Name. If this customer changed its address, you would have to go in and update this throughout the table, which is problematic and time-consuming. With the data in one table, the repetition requires us to normalize this table into four tables. Figure 7.4 provides how these four tables would relate to each other and not violate the entity integrity rules and be fully normalized, removing anomalies. Note that the attributes shaded in blue are the primary keys for the table. Figure 7.5 shows the data for the sales order record in Figure 7.2 for each of the tables that are normalized using the structure from Figure 7.4.

FIGURE 7.4 Normalized Database Example

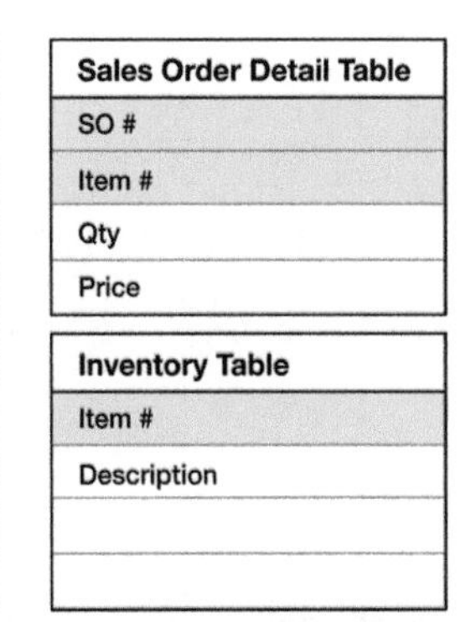

FIGURE 7.5 Normalized Data Records for SO #1918

Sales Order Table

SO #	Date	Customer #
1918	23-Sep	5965

Customer Table

Customer #	Name	Address	Contact #
5965	ABC Electrics	New York, NY	Alice Malloy

Sales Order Detail Table

SO #	Item #	Qty	
1918	5560	8	39.98
1918	2723	9	499.99

Inventory Table

Item #	Description
5560	Energy Management Device 8"
2723	Smart Home Controller 240v

concatenated key
A primary key formed by two foreign keys between two related tables to create the unique primary key.

Look at the data record for the Sales order #1918 found in Figure 7.5; we can see that the *Sales Order Detail Table* has both Sales Order # and Item # shaded blue as the primary key. This is known as a **concatenated key**, which means that these two foreign keys (from Sales Order Table and Inventory Table) are put together to create a unique primary key for the Sales Order Detail Table. Meaning, 19185560 is the unique primary key (this is the first row in the table showing SO # 1918 with Item # 5560).

Do you notice anything else that is different in the tables in Figure 7.5 compared to the Sales order in Figure 7.2? The extended price and the total price of the sales order is not captured in our data tables. Why? If you recall in Chapter 3, a query can calculate the (price * quantity) and provide a calculated total; therefore, it is not necessary to have a field for calculated total in our data tables.

Once the tables are normalized, the actual physical database is constructed. While this may seem logical, it is important to consider the rules of database design. A fully normalized database requires several steps, as seen in Figure 7.4, which is technically known as the third form of normalization (3N). What about the first two forms then? Consider the first form (1N) and the second form (2N) as steps needed to get to the third form (3N), which is commonly known as following rules of good database design.

First normal (1N) form step rules are as follows:

a. Each column must have single values.
b. Each column should have same type of data and not mix data types.
c. One column in the table should be unique to identify the row of data (primary key).

View a video here on first normal form.

First Normal Form (1NF) | Database Normalization | DBMS

This is a video example of the first normal form for database normalization.

View in the online reader

Then second normal form (2N) has the following steps:

a. Fulfill requirements above for 1N.
b. Each nonprimary key field in the table should be **functionally dependent** on the primary key.
c. No nonprimary key fields in the table should be **partially dependent** on other fields in the table.

functionally dependent

Every nonprimary key attribute in a table uniquely determines the value of the primary key.

partially dependent

A nonprimary key attribute in a table is partially dependent on a set of attributes that uniquely identifies records in a table.

We can see that for example, the customer table in Figure 7.5 shows that all the other fields in that table (nonprimary key) are functionally dependent on the primary key of customer # and that no nonprimary fields are partially dependent on other fields in the table. View a video here on the second normal form (2N):

Second Normal Form (2NF) | Database Normalization | DBMS

This is a video example going to the second normal form.

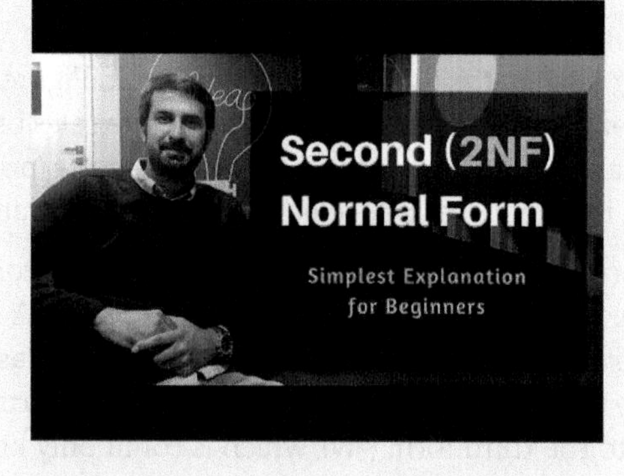

View in the online reader

The final step achieves third normal form (3N):

a. Fulfill the requirements above in (2N).
b. Each nonprimary key field in a table depends only on that primary key.

View the video here for the example to third normal form:

Third Normal Form (3NF) | Database Normalization | DBMS

This is a video example going to the third normal form.

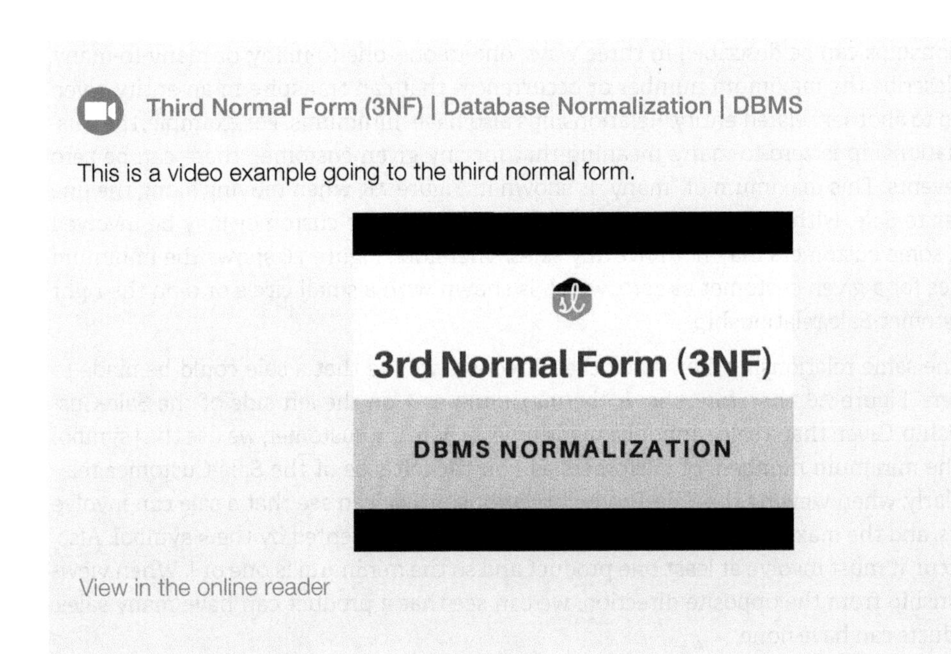

View in the online reader

7.2 Design Approaches

Learning Objective

At the end of this section, students should be able to:

1. Understand how to create a simple Resource-Entity-Agent diagram.

This chapter presents two design approaches: the classic **entity-relationship (E-R) diagram** that you may have seen in management information system courses and the accounting-specific design approach known as **resource-entity-agent (REA) diagrams**, which can be considered an enhanced E-R diagram for understanding accounting information.

entity-relationship (E-R) diagram

A visual representation of how the entities (tables) are related to one-another.

resource-entity-agent (REA) diagram

A visual representation for accounting information systems.

E-R Modeling Approach

FIGURE 7.6 Example E-R Diagram

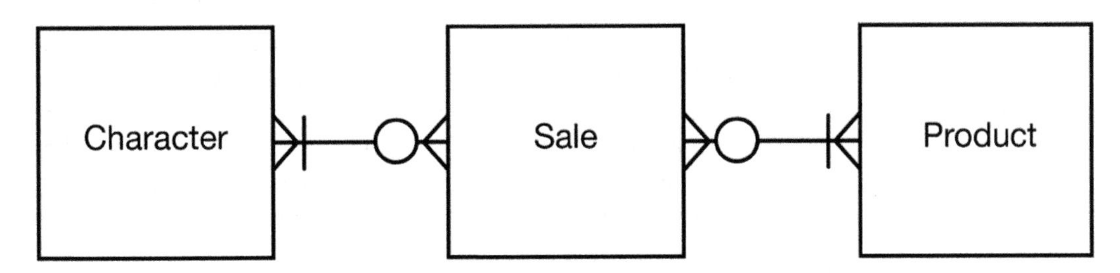

E-R diagrams contain entities of interest and their relationships. Understanding the relationships is important to properly creating the links among database tables. Without these links, users cannot access data from more than one table at a time.

The relationships can be described in three ways: one-to-one, one-to-many, or many-to-many. These terms describe the maximum number of occurrences that can transpire in an entity given its relationship to another related entity. Relationships also have minimums. For example, the Customer-Sale relationship is zero-to-many, meaning that for any given customer, there can be zero or many sale events. This maximum of "many" is shown in Figure 7.6, when moving along the line from Customer to Sale, with the < symbol. In addition, although one customer may be involved in many sales, some customers may not have any sales. Therefore, Figure 7.6 shows the minimum number of sales for a given customer as zero, which is shown with a small circle or o on the right side of the Customer-Sale relationship.

Viewing the same relationship from the other direction, we see that a sale could be made to many customers. Figure 7.6, therefore, shows the maximum as > on the left side of the Sale-Customer relationship. Given that a sale cannot be made unless there is a customer, we use the | symbol to represent the minimum numbers of customers as 1 on the left side of the Sale-Customer relationship. Similarly, when viewing the Sale-Product relationship, we can see that a sale can involve many products, and the maximum in that relationship is many represented by the < symbol. Also, for a sale to occur, it must involve at least one product and so the minimum is one or |. When viewing the relationship from the opposite direction, we can see that a product can have many sales, and some products can have none.

events

Activities that increase or decrease resources directly or planning, control, and management activities that indirectly relate to economic events, but do not change the resources.

resources

Things of economic value to an organization and the objects of exchanges with agents (e.g., cash, inventory).

agents

Internal or external participants who are involved with the transaction.

Historically, entities in a database system were modeled after what accountants did in manual systems based on double-entry bookkeeping instead of modeling what could be more broadly construed as important business events. Instead of just modeling the artifacts of journals and ledgers, a new form of modeling was introduced in 1982 by McCarthy, called REA modeling, which expanded the notion of entities to include two types of **events**. As a theoretical model for accounting information systems, the REA model proposed that both economic and support events be captured and tracked in the system and be connected to other entities defined as **resources** and **agents**. This expanded model is intended to create more useful information for all users in the enterprise.

REA Modeling Approach

REA modeling is a way of expanding the traditional E-R modeling approach by describing entities as resources, events, and agents. Resources are things of economic value to an organization and are the objects of exchanges with agents. Events are activities that increase or decrease resources directly or planning, control, and management activities that indirectly relate to economic events but do not change the resources. Therefore, we can have economic events and support events. Agents are the people inside and outside an organization who are involved in the events.

cardinality

Describes the nature of the relationships between two tables.

When using REA modeling to describe entity-relationships, the entities are organized into columns with events in the middle, agents on the right, and resources on the left. Lines (relationships) are then drawn between the entities with symbols at the ends, which describe the nature of the relationships. This is also known as a **cardinality**, and we will spend more time later in this chapter understanding how to interpret these cardinalities as business process policies.

Using an example of a single business process to simplify the explanation, let's see how we can develop a REA diagram for Joe's Ristoranté's process (the short case in Chapter 1) for acquiring inventory and paying the related bills. Joe is considering upgrading his shoebox accounting system. Joe has more than one vendor and usually places orders for more than one product at a time. These vendors usually fill the orders in one shipment. When the items and a sales invoice are received at the restaurant from the vendor, Joe usually writes a check for the full amount when the bill is due.

To create the diagram, we must adhere to the following guidelines:

1. Each event should be linked to at least one related resource.

2. Each event should be linked to at least one other related event.
3. Each event should be linked to at least two related agents.

Now, let's begin by identifying the relevant events that Joe (management) needs to track and collect information on. In our case, the first event involves ordering items to make the food and drinks, which will be illustrated in Figure 7.7. The second event involves receiving the inventory, which will be illustrated in Figure 7.8, and the third event involves writing a check to pay the bill in Figure 7.9.

Next, we need to describe the relationships between each event and the related resources as well as the events and the related agents (people needed to make these events happen). Beginning with the order products event in Figure 7.7, we must show that an order will have a minimum of one product resource, but the maximum could be more than one (many) products ordered. From the product entity side on the left, a particular product may not be ordered or received and thus the minimum is 0. Alternatively, a particular product may be ordered or received many times and thus the maximum is > (for many). On the right side of the order products event, we must show that an order will have a minimum of one employee (Joe, acting as a purchasing agent) involved in making the order as well as a maximum of one employee (Joe). From the employee-agent perspective on the right, we need to show that Joe (the purchasing agent) may be involved in a minimum of 0 orders to a maximum of many (>). Moreover, the order product event is associated with a minimum and maximum of one (|) vendor to accept the order. From the vendor agent perspective on the right, we need to show that a vendor may be involved in a minimum of 0 orders to a maximum of many (>).

FIGURE 7.7 REA Diagram of the Ordering Process

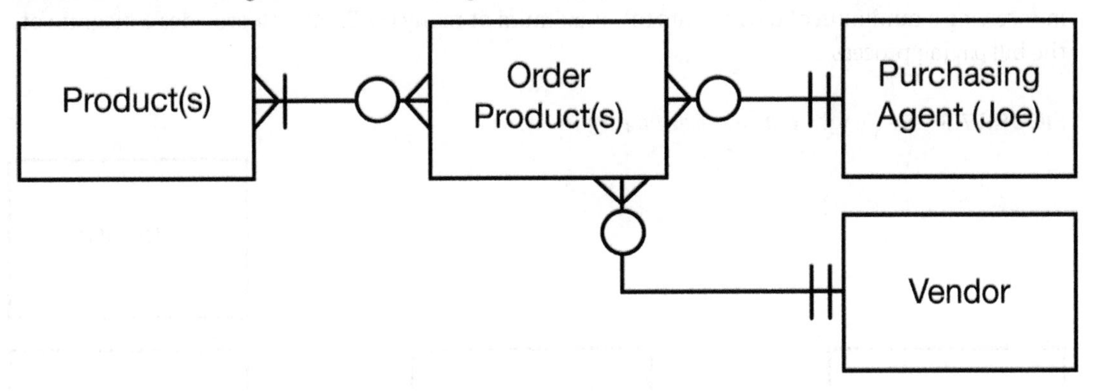

Continuing with the receive products event in Figure 7.8, we must show that a receipt will have a minimum of one product resource, but the maximum could be many (>) products received. From the product entity side on the left, a particular product may not be received, and thus the minimum is 0. Alternatively, a particular product may be received many times, and thus the maximum is > (for many). Please note that it looks like "< " in the figure because you are reading from receive products to products. On the right side of the receive products event, we must show that an order will have a minimum of one employee (receiving clerk) involved in receiving the order as well as a maximum of one employee (receiving). From the employee agent perspective on the right, we need to show that the employee (the receiving clerk) may be involved in a minimum of 0 orders to a maximum of many (>). Moreover, the receive product event is associated with a minimum and maximum of one (|) vendor to accept the order from. From the vendor agent perspective on the right, we need to show that a vendor may be involved in a minimum of 0 received products to a maximum of many (>). Figure 7.8 illustrates the receiving process.

FIGURE 7.8 REA Diagram of the Receiving Process

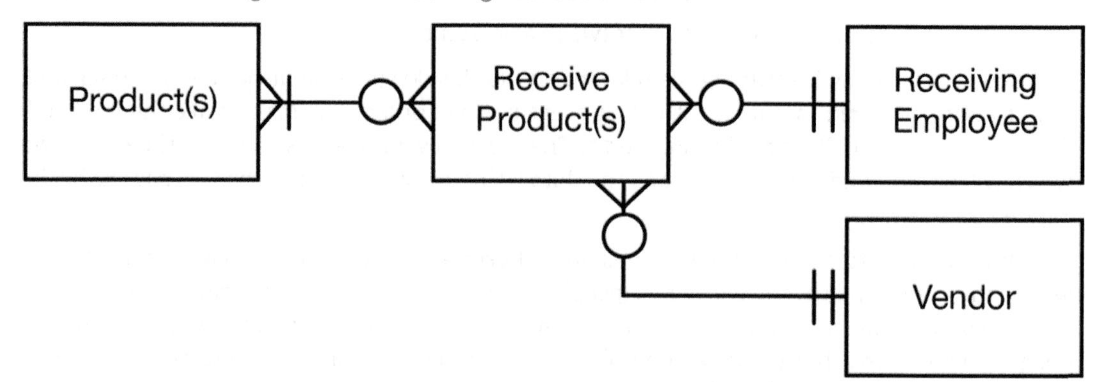

Following with the pay bill event, we must show that a cash payment (check or transfer) can only come out of one account at a time. Therefore, both the minimum and maximum cash resource must be one (|). From the cash resource entity side on the left, cash payments may not be made, and thus the minimum is 0. Alternatively, cash may be disbursed many times, and thus the maximum is < (for many).

On the right side of the bill payment event, we must show that a payment will have a minimum of one employee (Joe) involved in writing a check as well as a maximum of one employee (Joe). From the employee agent perspective on the right, we need to show that the employee (Joe) may be involved in a minimum of 0 cash payments to a maximum of many (>). In addition, the pay bill event is associated with a minimum and maximum of one (|) vendor accepting a payment at a time. From the vendor agent perspective on the right, we need to show that a vendor may be involved in receiving a minimum of 0 payments to a maximum of many (>). Figure 7.9 provides a diagram of the bill paying process.

FIGURE 7.9 REA Diagram of the Bill Paying Process

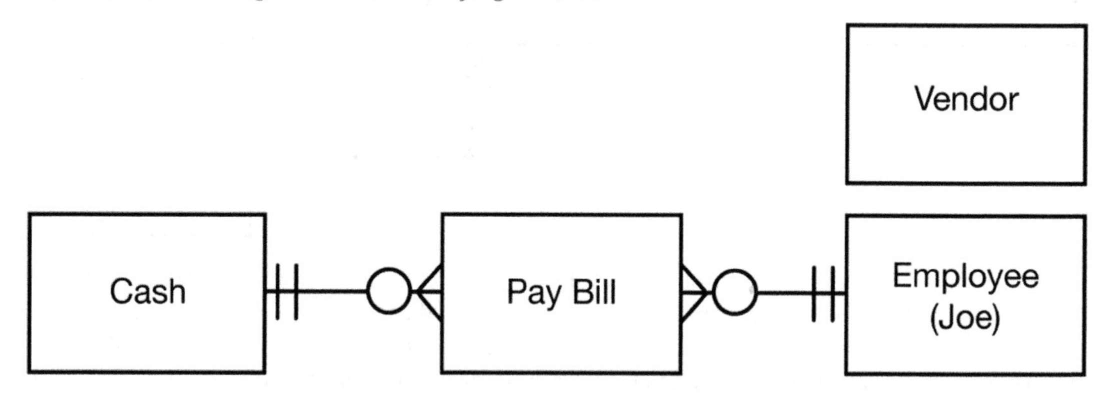

Finally, we need to connect the three event entities in Figure 7.7, Figure 7.8, and Figure 7.9 together into one overall REA diagram. This is done in Figure 7.10. For Joe's Ristoranté, we are assuming that each order will result in a minimum of one (|) receipt and a maximum of one (|) receipt of the products ordered. This assumes that it is not possible for ordered goods to be out of stock. So in Figure 7.10, we see the Order Product(s) event from Figure 7.7 connected to the Receive Product(s) event from Figure 7.8 with a vertical connecting line. From the receive product(s) perspective, we are also assuming that each receipt of goods must be accompanied by a minimum of one (|) valid order and a maximum of one (|) valid order. This is also shown in Figure 7.10 by connecting the Receive Product(s) event to the Order Product(s) event from Figures 7.8 and 7.7, respectively.

In addition, for each receipt of product(s) event, we are assuming that each product delivery will result in a minimum of one (|) payment and a maximum of one (|) payment for the products received. This is shown in Figure 7.10 by connecting the Receive Product(s) event to the Pay Bill event from Figure 7.7, Figure 7.8, and Figure 7.9, respectively. From the bill payment perspective (Pay Bill event), we are also assuming that each cash payment for goods must be accompanied by a minimum of one (|) and a maximum of one (|) valid receipt of goods. This is because the Ristoranté inspects the incoming goods and tells Joe whether they are acceptable or not. This is shown in Figure 7.10 by connecting the Pay Bill event to the Receive Product(s) event from Figures 7.9 and 7.8, respectively. Figure 7.10 shows how the three events from Figures 7.7, 7.8, and 7.9 come together to model Joe's ordering and bill paying process overall.

FIGURE 7.10 REA Diagram of the Ordering and Bill Paying Process

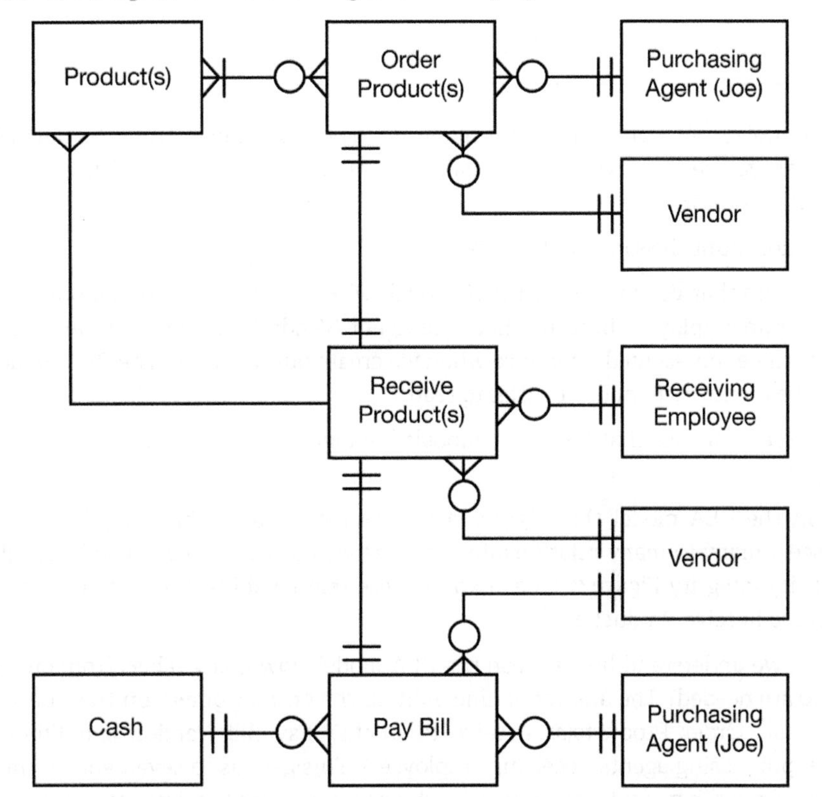

Ultimately, all REA diagrams for all processes are integrated. Each entity (represented by a box in the REA diagrams) is then turned into a database table. Attributes for each table are then added, including the appropriate primary keys.

7.3 Using the REA Model to Create a Database

Learning Objectives

At the end of this section, students should be able to:

1. Understand the importance of a data dictionary.
2. Create an REA database using the data dictionary in Microsoft Access.

The REA model essentially provides a theoretical bridge between legacy flat-file and closed database systems to the modern ERP system by showing how accounting and nonaccounting information can be integrated into a single database system. If we examine the Ordering and Bill Paying process in Figure 7.10 for Joe's Ristoranté, we now have a blueprint to create a database. From this blueprint, we would first determine how many tables (entities) we need to create for our database. Before we start building tables in our database, we need to step back and figure out all the specifics of each table, such as what attributes are needed for each table, what primary keys are needed, and where the foreign keys will go.

Tables and Attributes

Using our example from Figure 7.10 as our blueprint, how many tables from the blueprint can we determine that we need to have for a normalized database to capture Joe's Ristoranté's Ordering and Bill Paying Process?

Hint: Do not count the same table twice!

Do you notice that Vendor is in our REA model twice? Do you also see that our internal agent is either Joe or an employee? Both the External Agent (Vendor) and the Internal Agent (Employees) would each be represented only once when we create our database. The REA model in Figure 7.10 repeats these entities to make it easier to read.

Hint: Where do we see that tables are modeled in Figure 7.10 with "many-to-many" maximum relationships?

Tables in the REA model that signify many-to-many relationships require normalization. Where we see a many-to-many relationship, it means we need one more table in our database to maintain entity integrity. Figure 7.10 has two of these relationships (Products to Order Products and Products to Receive Products).

Now that we understand how to read the REA model, how many tables from our REA model in Figure 7.10 are needed? The answer is nine. Add up the entities drawn on the REA model once: Product(s), Cash, Order Products(s), Receive Product(s), Pay Bill, Vendor, and Employees (this includes Joe, purchasing agents, receiving employees). This gets us to seven entities plus the two more we need from the many-to-many relationships to normalize the database giving us a total of nine tables.

data dictionary
Identifies structure and format of the database.

Now that we understand the number of tables, we can begin work on designing what information (attributes) we need for each table. We use a **data dictionary**, which will help us keep everything centralized about the data we want to collect, the format of the data, and to identify our primary keys and the related foreign keys for our database. Figure 7.11 shows an example of a data dictionary for all nine tables that we may want to consider when building our database.

FIGURE 7.11 Example of a Data Dictionary

Table Name: Products

Attribute	Data Type	Format	Description
Item #	Interger	6 Intergers	Unique number (PrimaryKey)
Description	Alpha	36 characters	Description of the inventory item

Table Name: Cash

Attribute	Data Type	Format	Description
Bank Account #	Interger	6 Intergers	Unique number (PrimaryKey)
Bank Name	Alpha	36 characters	Business name
Account Type	Alpha	36 characters	Type of account for business use

Order Products

Attribute	Data Type	Format	Description
Order #	Interger	6 Intergers	Unique number (PrimaryKey)
PO Date	Date	DD/MM/YYYY	Date from source document
Employee #	Interger	6 Intergers	Foreign Key
Vendor #	Interger	6 Intergers	Foreign Key

Order Products-Products

Attribute	Data Type	Format	Description
Order #	Interger	6 Intergers	Concatenated Key
Item #	Alpha	6 Intergers	Concatenated Key
Qty Ordered	Interger	6 Intergers	
Purchase Price	Dollars	6 Intergers	

Receive Products

Attribute	Data Type	Format	Description
Receiving #	Interger	6 Intergers	Unique number (PrimaryKey)
Date Received	Date	DD/MM/YYYY	Date from source document
Employee #	Interger	6 Intergers	Foreign Key
Vendor #	Interger	6 Intergers	Foreign Key

Receive Products-Products

Attribute	Data Type	Format	Description
Receiving #	Interger	6 Intergers	Concatenated Key
Item #	Interger	6 Intergers	Concatenated Key
Qty Received	Interger	6 Intergers	

Pay Bill

Attribute	Data Type	Format	Description
Check #	Interger	6 Intergers	Unique number (PrimaryKey)
Check Date	Date	DD/MM/YYYY	Date from source document
Check Amount	Dollars	6 Intergers	
Employee #	Interger	6 Intergers	Foreign Key
Vendor #	Interger	6 Intergers	Foreign Key

Vendor

Attribute	Data Type	Format	Description
Vendor #	Interger	6 Intergers	Unique number (PrimaryKey)
Vendor Name	Alpha	36 characters	
Vendor Address	Alphanumerio	36 characters	
Vendor Phone	Interger	10 Intergers	

Employee

Attribute	Data Type	Format	Description
Employee #	Interger	6 Intergers	Unique number (PrimaryKey)
Employee Name	Alpha	36 characters	
Employee Address	Alphanumerio	36 characters	
Employee Phone	Interger	10 Intergers	

Assigning Primary and Foreign Keys

Using our data dictionary from Figure 7.11 and understanding that we have nine tables that need to be related to one another, we first identify primary keys for each of the nine tables. Recall that the entity integrity rule requires that each table must have a primary key and that the primary key must be unique. Notice that we assigned each primary key in our database (see Figure 7.11) using the integer format. The sequential number will create a unique primary key for each of the respective tables, fulfilling the entity integrity rule.

Remember, however, that we need to consider one more rule to maintain integrity when we build our database: the referential integrity rule. This is why we now need to have the primary key from certain tables also be included as an attribute for another table in our database, which means they are called a foreign key. By having this foreign key, we can now physically link the two tables together when creating our database.

Let's see how that looks with just one portion of our tables from Figure 7.10, using the data dictionary in Figure 7.11, and reviewing the relationship between the two tables: Vendors to our Order Product(s) table. When we order the products, we want to know which vendor we are ordering from, thus we need to have our database be efficient and maintain data integrity and not violate entity integrity and referential integrity rules. We also know from Chapter 3 that data files can be master files or transaction files.

In looking at the Vendor and Order Product(s) tables, which one is a master file and which one is a transaction file? The Vendor table is the master file, and the Order Product(s) table is the transaction file. How would we want to physically connect these two tables together? We see from the data dictionary in Figure 7.11 that the Vendor table has Vendor # as the primary key and that the Order Product(s) table has Order # as its primary key. Which one of these two primary keys would need to become the foreign key to connect these two tables? We don't need each primary key to be the foreign key for the respective tables, just one that doesn't violate our rules.

Hint: Master file primary keys should be in the transaction file.

The primary key of Vendor # from the Vendor table (master file) should be the foreign key in the Order Product(s) table (transaction file). This is the only way that you will be able to capture the necessary transaction data and also maintain integrity in the database and not violate the rules.

Relationships and Cardinalities

As mentioned previously in Section Section 2, the relationships between two tables are depicted by cardinalities. In Figure 7.7, Figure 7.8, and Figure 7.9, the cardinalities are drawn showing the minimum and maximum relationships between the two entities. These are also named by the three different options of how two tables can be related to one another by their maximum cardinality: one-to-one, one-to-many, or many-to-many. Depending on which two tables are related, the cardinality needed for the data model would depict how the business transaction usually occurs.

For example, in Figure 7.10, we see that there is a one-to-one relationship between the Order Product(s) table and the Receive Product(s) table. There is also another one-to-one relationship that relates the Receive Product(s) table to the Pay Bills table. In addition, we also see that several of our "Agents" to "Events" tables have a one-to-many relationship, such as Vendors to Order Product(s). Further note that Figure 7.10 also has many-to-many cardinalities between two tables, which we already determined above: (Product(s) to Order Product(s); Product(s) to Receive Product(s). Cardinalities depicted on our REA model provide a means of how to interpret the business policies that are relevant for the business (e.g., Joe's Ristoranté) so that the database created will allow for you to capture those transactions.

7.4 How to Interpret Cardinalities for Business Process Design

Learning Objective

At the end of this section, students should be able to:

1. Explain the differences between one-to-one, one-to-many, and many-to-many cardinalities and interpret respective business policies based upon these cardinalities.

The REA model provides the duality of an event in business. Some events may be "give-get" (e.g., give products-get cash in the revenue cycle; others are "get-give" (e.g., get products-give cash in the expenditure cycle). The point is that there is an exchange when we are thinking about the event tables in our REA diagram. From our example of the Order goods to pay bills process of Joe's Ristorantè, the give-get duality is Get Products and Pay (Give) Cash. This is from the purchasing cycle doing business with vendors; we also have a give-get duality with the revenue cycle when we do business with our customers. This would be a duality of Give Product(s) and Receive (Get) Cash. When we look at the three different types of relationships among these types of events, we find it easy to interpret from the REA model the business policy as well as how to interpret the business policy to properly create our REA model. You probably didn't even notice that earlier in the chapter, when using the Joe's Ristorantè example, we provided you with this information on the business policy that was subsequently interpreted to create the cardinality:

Joe has more than one vendor and usually places orders for more than one product at a time. These vendors usually fill the orders in one shipment. When the items and a sales invoice are received at the restaurant from the vendor, Joe usually writes a check for the full amount when the bill is due.

One-to-One Relationship

cash on delivery (c.o.d.)

Payment is made when product or service is delivered.

When looking at the REA diagram, you can examine the cardinality between two tables to understand and interpret the business policy using the maximum cardinality. Let's examine the maximum cardinalities of one-to-one relationships from the give-get events for the revenue transaction cycle. A one-to-one maximum cardinality between the customer sales order and the give products tables indicates that the company has one sales order to one product shipment. This means that when the product is available to ship in the warehouse, the customer order will be completed and shipped all at once to the customer. This also means there are no backorders nor is there bundling of two or more sales orders to go in the one shipment. Now let's look at the one-to-one maximum cardinalities between the two events of give products and get cash. This is interpreted similar to a point of sale or **cash on delivery (c.o.d.)**; this also means that there are no deposits from the customer and no payment plans.

Similarly, from the expenditure cycle, these policies would be consistently interpreted between the order goods and the receive goods table from the vendor. In this case there are no back orders or bundled orders. The organization receives the goods from the vendor for each order. In addition, the payment for these goods received is interpreted as a point of sale or c.o.d. meaning the vendor is not requiring a deposit nor has the vendor given you credit to make payments on your purchase.

One-to-Many Relationship

One-to-many cardinalities between events may seem tricky; however, when you break it down to look at the relationship between the two event tables, you will see that the business policy is easy to interpret. From the perspective of the revenue cycle, we see that the maximum relationship between customer sales order and give products is a one-to-many. This indicates that there is one sales order to many give products and would be interpreted as a policy that allows you to ship the goods to the customer as they become available in the warehouse. Therefore, you may have a customer that orders two items and only one is available to ship in the warehouse today, but the other item is backordered until next week. There are two actual shipments; hence, the one-to-many relationship.

Let's now examine the two same events, customer sales order and give products, but now the relationship is many-to-one. How would we interpret this from a business policy perspective? It means that many customer sales orders can be bundled into one shipment. For example, an auto repair shop customer may make orders throughout the day because it keeps its inventory low; all of these orders would be bundled together with one delivery made in the middle of the day so the parts are delivered to get the cars repaired.

Again, examining the next sequence in the transaction of the events from give products to receive cash, we examine the one-to-many relationship, meaning that one invoice is related to many cash receipts. From this type of cardinality, the interpretation of the business policy implies that the organization either requires the customer to put down a deposit for the order or the organization allows the customer to make payments on the order similar to a layaway. If we continue with these two events of give products to cash receipts with a many-to-one relationship, that means many invoices are related to one cash receipt. The interpretation to a business policy is that the organization extends credit to the customer, allowing the customer to place orders throughout the month and then pay for all orders at the end of the month, similar to how a credit card may work. The same is true with the expenditure cycle, but the policies would be with the vendor.

Many-to-Many Relationship

We will continue examining the same revenue cycle events using the many-to-many scenarios between customer sales order and give products as well as the events of give products and receive cash. A many-to-many cardinality between customer sales order and give products means that many customer orders can be related to many give orders. If we go back to the interpretation from the one-to-many relationships, we are able to put the one-to-many and the many-to-one interpretations together. For purposes of this example then, the interpretation of the business policy means that the organization does both: ships the goods as they come available in the warehouse and bundles the orders together. Similarly, a many-to-many relationship between give products and receive cash is interpreted as the business policy for the organization is both: the organization requires a deposit, and the organization also has a policy for extending credit, allowing for customers to make payments. Figure 7.12 and Figure 7.13 summarize the interpretation of cardinalities to business policy for revenue and expenditure examples, respectively.

FIGURE 7.12 Revenue Cycle Example of Cardinality to Business Policy Interpretation

Revenue Cycle		
Cardinality Type	Event Transaction	Business Policy Interpretation
One - One (1:1)	Get Order-Give Products	A customer order is in one shipment (no backorders, no bundling of orders)
	Give Products-Get Cash	Customer cash receipts are 'point of sale' or 'cash on delivery'
One - Many (1:N)	Get Order-Give Products	Ship products to customer as it becomes available (includes backorders)
	Give Products-Get Cash	Customer can make payments on a order; Customer is required to make a deposit
Many - One (N:1)	Get Order-Give Products	Customer orders can be bundles into one shipment
	Give Products-Get Cash	Customer can make one payment at the end of the month for all orders
Many - Many (M:N)	Get Order-Give Products	Shipping customer products can include backorders and bundling of orders
	Give Products-Get Cash	Customer can make payments on an order or pay orders off at the end of the month

FIGURE 7.13 Expenditure Cycle Example of Cardinality to Business Policy Interpretation

Expenditure Cycle		
Cardinality Type	Event Transaction	Business Policy Interpretation
One - One (1:1)	Order Goods-Receive Goods	Goods ordered from a vendor is received in one shipment (no backorders, no bundling of orders)
	Receive Goods-Give Cash	Payments to vendors are 'point of sale' or 'cash on delivery'
One - Many (1:N)	Order Goods-Receive Goods	Goods ordered from a vendor are received as they become available, includes backorders
	Receive Goods-Give Cash	Vendor allows multiple payments in an order; Vendor requires a deposit
Many - One (N:1)	Order Goods-Receive Goods	Goods ordered from a vendor are bundled
	Receive Goods-Give Cash	Payment to vendor is at the end of the month for all orders
Many - Many (M:N)	Order Goods-Receive Goods	Goods ordered from a vendor can be backordered or bundled when received
	Receive Goods-Give Cash	Vendor allows multiple payments and payment of all orders at the end of the month

Key Takeaways

In this chapter we looked at databases from a designer's perspective. Two conceptual ways to visualize database design is through E-R and REA models. Database design needs to follow certain rules, and we examined the two important rules of database design: entity integrity and referential integrity. We learned how to put an REA model together for the expenditure cycle using the case of Joe's Ristoranté from Chapter 1. We further explored how cardinalities are used to interpret the different business policies.

Reference

- McCarthy, William E. "The REA accounting model: A generalized framework for accounting systems in a shared data environment." *Accounting Review* (1982): 554–578.

7.5 End-of-Chapter Exercises

Exercises

1. How are relational databases organized?
2. How are relational databases normally designed?
3. What type of anomalies can occur with relational databases? Give an example of each.
4. What is entity–relationship modeling?
5. What is REA modeling?
6. What is the purpose of the data dictionary?
7. List the three different types of cardinalities and provide an example of the business policies for each.
   a. for the revenue cycle
   b. for the expenditure cycle
8. Which of the following is a collection of records?
   a. file
   b. field
   c. database
   d. bits
9. Which of the following represents semi-permanent data, such as ledger accounts, customers, or inventory items, together with their balances in a master file?
   a. field
   b. file
   c. gigabyte
   d. chart of accounts
   e. None of the above
10. Which of the following is normally used to search and sort a database table?
    a. an entity relationship

b. the primary key
c. structured query language
d. an REA model

11. An insertion anomaly occurs when the database user cannot
    a. view data.
    b. add new data.
    c. delete data.
    d. modify data.
12. Entities in an REA model would include each of the following, except
    a. agents.
    b. relationships.
    c. events.
    d. resources.
13. When creating an REA diagram, economic events generally belong in/on the
    a. left.
    b. right.
    c. middle.
    d. None of the above
14. An REA diagram is different from an E-R diagram in which of the following ways?
    a. The shapes of the symbols are different.
    b. The relationships are different.
    c. The order in which the events are shown.
    d. There is no major difference between them.
15. Based on the REA diagram below, how should the order product-products relationship be described?
    a. a minimum of no products and a maximum of many products
    b. a minimum of one product and a maximum of one product
    c. a minimum of no products and a maximum of one product
    d. a minimum of one product and a maximum of many products

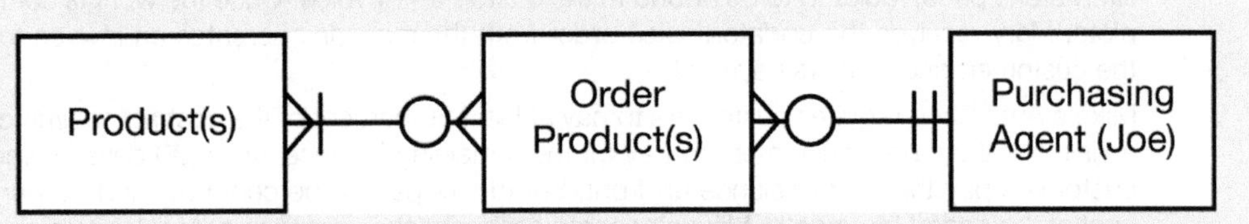

16. **NORMALIZATION:** Mountain Vineyards is a winery in California. Peter Herbert, the owner of the winery, has been happy with his success over the past 5 years. However, he has been having trouble tracking his data. He has asked you to assist him in creating a database. He currently keeps the following information in one large spreadsheet:

    Customer Name
    Customer Address
    Customer Phone
    Order #
    Order Date
    Wine Sku#
    Wine Description
    Quantity Ordered
    Unit Price
    Shipping Number

Quantity Shipped
Payment Date
Payment Amount

Required:

Assuming that a customer can buy more than one type of wine at a time, how would you normalize this information, meaning how many tables do you need?

17. **REA DIAGRAMMING: Joe's Ristoranté**

Joe's Ristoranté is a small restaurant near a college campus. It serves both lunch and dinner from a standard menu. It also has a salad bar. Staff take orders by writing down the orders on an order pad. The orders are then taken to the kitchen where the food is prepared. When the food is ready, the staff are notified and deliver the food to the customer's table. When the meal is finished, the staff provide customers with a bill, which has been prepared by hand. All sales must be paid by cash or credit card and entered into the cash register. Joe maintains one checking account for all sales receipts.

Required:

a. Create an REA diagram for Joe's order-taking and cash receipts process, including all relationships.
b. List the tables and attributes, including the primary key needed to implement the data model in a relational database.

18. **REA CASE: Auto Repair Shop**

Mike's Auto Shop is an automotive maintenance and repair shop located in Las Vegas, Nevada. The shop is owned by Mike, and he employs several ASE-certified mechanics as full-time employees. The shop's administrative functions are primarily run by Mike's wife, Mary, who is also an employee of the company.

When a new customer calls the shop or walks in to the office, Mary creates a customer file in the database and records pertinent information about the customer and the customer's vehicle(s). Each customer and each vehicle receive a unique identifier in the database.

Customers must schedule appointments with Mary to have their cars serviced. Mary schedules the appropriate amount of time needed, based on the customer's request for a specific service (e.g., brake repair, oil change, radiator replacement).

When the customer arrives, a mechanic receives the order from Mary and begins work to fill the request. The mechanics record any inventory used during the service (e.g., oil filter, brake pads, radiator) to be added to the customer's invoice. Once the work is complete, Mary receives the updated sales order from the mechanic, creates an invoice for the customer, and collects payment.

Mike's Auto Shop requires customers to pay at least 50 percent of the cost at the time of a visit, but they allow customers to pay off the remaining balance within 30 days. Some customers pay the entire balance up front, but others pay 50 percent now and 50 percent at the end of the month. Mike's accepts cash, checks, and Visa or MasterCard.

When a mechanic notices that the shop needs to order new parts or other inventory items, he sends a purchase requisition to Mary. She fills out a purchase order and sends it to one of three approved vendors. The vendors ship items as they are available, so it is possible for a single order to be spread across multiple shipments. The vendor does not, however, combine multiple orders in a single shipment.

Each of the approved vendors has agreed to allow Mike's Auto Shop to carry a monthly balance. Mike's Auto receives a monthly statement each month from the three vendors, and Mary submits payment in full each month to pay off the balances.

Required:

a. Create an REA diagram for the revenue cycle.
b. Create an REA diagram for the expenditure cycle.

19. **Reflective Learning**

a. What was this chapter about?
b. What was the most difficult part of the chapter for you? What questions do you have relating to this material?

CHAPTER 8

Enterprise Resource Planning Systems Implementation

Businesses evolve and so do their information needs. As we learned in Chapter 4 on emerging technologies, many organizations will want to update their enterprise resource planning (ERP) systems for the latest technology and replace legacy systems. This means that most businesses at some point in time will need to update and change their information systems. Indeed, it is estimated that up to 50 percent of companies will soon update to an ERP.[1] As an accountant, it is important to be involved in the ERP implementation because the software affects the organization's capabilities to produce financial information and reports. In addition, it is important for accountants to be aware of the costs involved from a budgeting perspective as well to help manage the costs of implementation.

8.1 What Are ERP Systems?

Learning Objective

At the end of this section, students should be able to:

1. Understand what is an ERP system and the business processes normally included in an ERP system.

Enterprise resource planning (ERP) systems are a collection of applications that integrate a company's business processes. Business processes are activities that get things done in an organization. ERP systems are modular applications that integrate together. ERP is built on relational database technology that contains both accounting and nonaccounting data. These business activities are combined, forming one integrated database for the organization, sometimes known as the "single source of truth." ERP systems are used by both manufacturing and service-based companies. While the modules integrated may differ among types of organizations, the fundamental goal is the same: Organizations want to manage their business in a connected and integrated manner that is the most efficient and effective.

enterprise resource planning (ERP) systems

A collection of applications that help integrate and streamline a company's business processes.

 What Is ERP Software?

This is a video that explains the basic concepts of ERP software.

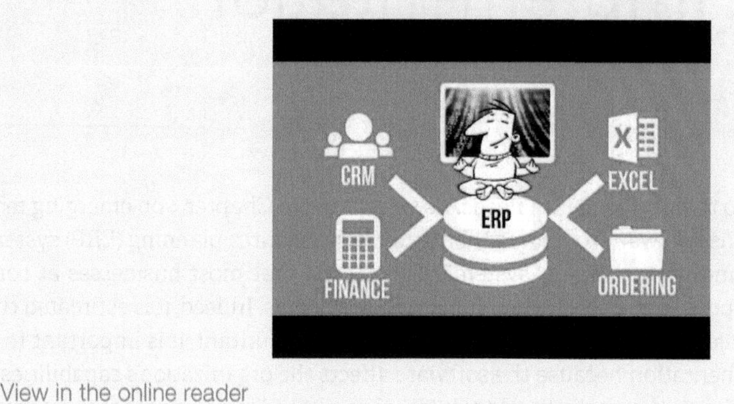

View in the online reader

Business Processes Normally Included in ERP Systems

ERP systems normally include several modules for the functions of accounting and finance, customer relations management, supply chain management, and human resources. Accounting and financial management includes capturing the transactions as well as the financial reporting and budgeting of the organization.

Customer relations management contains information on both existing and potential customers. Supply chain management contains the data necessary to manage production and inventory. Human resources contain data associated with employees, training, and annual reviews or information on disciplinary actions.

In addition to the functional modules that are included in an ERP system, many systems have the capability to do e-commerce. This allows an organization to have a web presence and the ability to provide up-to-date information on inventory using the internet browser (essentially connecting the front-end customer facing and the back-office functionality together). In addition to these modules, many ERP systems have analytics built in and the capability for organizations to do customized reporting.

Advantages of ERP Systems

The advantages to implementing ERP systems include streamlining processes by incorporating best practices (in the software), eliminating duplicate data, time lag, and data conflicts, and reducing errors and inefficiencies. When company management chooses an ERP package, they are effectively "buying into" the ERP vendor's view of best practices and will rely on the ERP system to support their efforts to embrace these practices. These features will vary from vendor to vendor. The largest vendors, such as SAP and Oracle, have literally thousands of best practices that are specific to the industry programmed into their software.

From the onset of desktop computing in business to the arrival of ERP systems, organizations typically created and maintained several sets of the data on customers and vendors in several different departmental databases. While these **closed databases** (separate databases that do not integrate information with other organizational databases) created inefficiencies involving duplicate data, they also created time lags as data moved from one department to another. Often this involved printing output from one system and passing it on to an employee in another department, who would read the printed output and enter the same data or parts of the data into that department's database. This created "stovepipes of information" as information was maintained and held in the functional areas and not all of the output transferred to the other departments. For example, the functional area of sales would have limited output of basic information on the customer and the order to the functional area of accounting (hence stovepipes in sales and accounting). With ERP systems, once the data are entered, they are available (with the proper system permissions) to potentially all users in all departments online and in real time, eliminating stovepipes of information in functional areas.

closed databases
Separate databases that do not integrate information with other organizational databases.

With ERP, the time lag that used to arise when documents sat inside "in-baskets" waiting to be rekeyed into another database is eliminated along with the paper documents themselves. The single point of entry also reduces the chance of inaccuracies in input, and employees spend less time checking and reconciling output from the different systems. Each time a rekeying requirement is eliminated, the likelihood of human error is reduced. ERP systems also provide organizations with a template to standardize business processes across an enterprise. As mentioned in Chapter 1, a business process is a collection of activities that together add value to an organization.

8.2 What Does Systems Implementation Involve?

Learning Objectives

At the end of this section, students should be able to:

1. Describe the principal steps involved in systems implementation.
2. Understand the criteria for selecting software.
3. Discuss the advantages and disadvantages of canned, custom, and modified software applications.
4. Discuss the four different types of system implementation methods.
5. Understand the advantages and disadvantages of implementing an accounting system in-house versus the cloud.
6. Understand the three types of cloud service models and deployment options.

As accounting technology continues to advance, we are now at a stage where organizations must either decide to implement a new or modified accounting system themselves or to host the application via cloud computing. Although change of any type involves some form of risk, having multiple factors and alternatives to choose from inevitably makes an implementation strategy decision more complex.

Companies that decide to implement a new or modified accounting system face the same principal step:

1. Deciding whether to handle it in-house or outsource it to a cloud vendor

If a company decides to handle the implementation in-house, it follows these steps:

2. Acquire the necessary computer software.
3. Acquire computer hardware that is capable of supporting the designated software.
4. Install and test the new hardware and software as well as train the employees so they will be competent in working with the new or modified system.
5. Convert to the new or modified system using the most appropriate implementation strategy (i.e., immediate, parallel, or incremental).

If the company decides to outsource the implementation, it follows these steps:

2. Weigh the advantages and disadvantages of the possible service models to ascertain which one is most appropriate in meeting the organization's needs (IaaS, PaaS, or SaaS).
3. Determine the most appropriate deployment method (public, private, community, or hybrid).
4. Select a vendor(s) from whom they will receive the service.
5. Train employees to use the cloud system.
6. Convert to the new system including migration of the data.

Regardless of in-house or cloud implementation, the organization should have a clear vision of how the system will support the organization's strategy and expected outcomes of success of an implementation.

Criteria for Selecting Software

Once an entity has decided to acquire the software itself, it must evaluate different options to ultimately select the one that is best suited to the business' needs. The following selection criteria are recommended:

1. Performance—meets requirements of the business' needs (e.g., key business processes with no need to customize application)
2. Ease of use—minimizes user frustration and increases user acceptance
3. Good documentation and support—facilitates training and use as well as minimizes downtime and user inconvenience
4. Cost—appropriate expense for perceived benefit
5. Compatibility with existing hardware, when already committed

The following steps are recommended for the process of software selection:

1. Review required features: usually defined during detailed design, e.g., key business processes, report layouts, chart of accounts capability, control features, network capability.
2. Identify available packages: consult professional publications that have conducted surveys or comparative reviews, hire consultants, etc.
3. Narrow the choices: eliminate packages not containing key required features that do not meet your needs or require customization for key business processes.
4. Perform detailed comparisons: evaluate feature strengths and weaknesses for each package.
5. Talk to users: obtain recommendations or references from users familiar with the packages under consideration.

6. Conduct your own tests: test drive the software on your computer with a demo package or see elsewhere to ensure that the software can accommodate your key business processes.
7. Select package: optimize based on net weight of strengths versus net weight of weaknesses.

When comparing and contrasting the three approaches to software acquisition, an enterprise must consider the advantages and disadvantages associated with each option. Organizations who choose to acquire software have three options to consider: canned, custom, and modified software applications.

Canned software: This type of software is available through retail stores, mail order, professional installers, and is also downloadable from the internet. Examples of canned software are Netsuite Accounting, Microsoft Great Plains, Sage, Quickbooks, etc.

canned software

Software that is purchased directly from a vendor that does not allow for customizations or modifications.

Advantages:

- Fully operational and "debugged"[2]
- Can be demonstrated before commitment is made
- Potential to be implemented immediately
- Usually well documented
- Substantially less expensive than custom programs

Disadvantages:

- Inflexibility (they are targeted at a hypothetical set of general requirements that may not meet all of an organization's needs)
- Unable to be modified unless a user can obtain access to the program's source code

Custom software: This type of software is programmed from scratch by in-house programmers, when a system development staff and programmers are available, or is programmed by an outside vendor, when staff are not available or capable.

custom software

Software that is programmed from scratch by in-house programmers.

Advantages:

- Fits "any" set of individual requirements

Disadvantages:

- High cost (often exceeding estimates)
- Long development time
- Risk that software will never work correctly
- Risk that it will not be adequately documented
- Risk that ongoing support will not be available

Modified software: A modified version of a canned package can be created when the software vendor is willing to make the source code available. However, most vendors are unwilling to do this, and the ones who are willing to provide source code may charge a lot of money for it. Modifying a package in-house can also void a warranty. One notable exception is "open source" software that has been created in accordance with the General Public License (GPL). Such software as Firefox and Open Office can be freely modified as long as the changes are made available to the open-source programming community.

modified software

The software vendor is willing to make the source code available to make modifications to the canned package.

Computer hardware should be selected to meet all general and software requirements specified in the design. In selecting hardware, the following should be considered:

1. Performance (minimum, expandability)
2. Compatibility (with existing/desired hardware/software)
3. Operation (ease, reliability—percentage of downtime)
4. Availability (lead time)
5. Vendor Support/Stability (service, reliability, financial status, and ethics)
6. Costs (basic, shipping, installation, maintenance, and operating)

Many companies today expect you to have a working knowledge of operating systems, familiarity with databases, and transferring data between programs. A basic understanding of these topics as well as understanding your business processes will allow you to be a good communicator with the software vendors and consultants helping you with your ERP implementation.

Approaches to System Conversion

System conversion is an anxious time for any organization or project team. The problems of conversion are real and are likely to occur to some degree in even the best-managed projects. The demands on people's time and energy are at a premium. Many individuals work long hours and are subject to unusual stress. Problems and delays are commonplace and often cause frustration. This scenario is familiar to anyone who has lived through the final stages of systems development. System conversion is a time where understanding your data is important as it involves making the decision of how much of the old data is going to get converted into the new system. This requires planning and an understanding of the data and if any data cleaning is needed.

direct changeover

The organization stops using the old system and now uses the new ERP system and all transactions from a beginning date are now in the new system.

parallel conversion

The new system is used at the same time for a given period with the old system to make sure results are compared and any issues are resolved with the new system before switching over.

phased conversion

Only one location may use the new system first to resolve issues before all locations of an enterprise convert over as this minimizes the system problems associated with system conversion.

pilot conversion

Allows an organization to implement the system for a department to see if it is successful with other departments adopting the system after the trial pilot.

An organization can plan its system conversion in several ways. The easiest is a **direct changeover**, which means the organization stops using the old system and now uses the new ERP system, and all transactions from a beginning date are now in the new system. For many small organizations, this may be the best means of conversion because it doesn't require transferring old data into the new system. The direct changeover would only have open items in the system such as Account Payable and Accounts Receivable detailed information as well as general ledger balance information.

A second approach is the **parallel conversion**, which means that the new system is used at the same time for a given period with the old system to make sure results are compared and any issues are resolved with the new system before switching over. This requires additional effort from the employees because it is double work as well as reconciling both systems. A third approach is an incremental (**phased conversion**), which means that only one location may use the new system first to resolve issues before all locations of an enterprise convert over. This approach minimizes the system problems associated with system conversion. And lastly, a **pilot conversion** allows an organization to implement the system for a department to see if it is successful, with other departments adopting the system after the trial pilot. View a video here on the four methods of system conversions that an organization can select.

Project Management: Implementation Methods

This is a video that describes the implementation methods for information system conversions.

Phased Conversion

The gradual implementation of the new system.

Old System

New System

View in the online reader

Critical Success Factors of Systems Implementation

The press is full of stories where systems implementations have exceeded budgets and did not live up to the promises of management. Understanding basic ways to approach a system implementation that will set your organization up for success brings us back to the simple way we understood systems from Chapter 1: people, process, and systems.

From a process and systems perspective, the organization needs to have a detailed business case prior to doing the implementation. Hence, they should understand how they are defining success in the beginning so as to measure the success of the implementation throughout the project. In addition, the organization needs to understand how the system implementation changes the business processes for improvement, what data are needed, how they are cleaned to migrate to the new system, and be assured that the IT infrastructure is able to support the new ERP software.

In-House Implementation versus "The Cloud"

ERP implementation has two approaches: in-house implementation, where the organization acquires the software, and cloud implementation, where the organization subscribes to the software. This decision depends on whether the entity already has the software it will need and if it prefers to continue maintaining it. It also depends on whether the entity must have control over specific performance requirements or risks of downtime. For example, if the customer must configure a database or server to maximize throughput or build redundant services over multiple physical or virtual data centers to minimize downtime, then the entity will need to choose to install its software on the cloud provider's infrastructure.

In the more likely case, when a customer is able to give a cloud service provider total control over the infrastructure, performance, security, scalability, and privacy, they are more likely to choose the software as a service (SaaS) approach. SaaS is particularly well suited to accounting since most companies are not capable of developing their own accounting applications. Therefore, many companies will choose a cloud service provider's accounting software, such as NetSuite, Xero, QuickBooks Online, or Microsoft Dynamics, assuming it meets their needs and is affordable. Each of these services has its own set of supported features and costs that need to be compared and contrasted. For many companies, especially smaller ones, it may not be feasible to buy or develop accounting software and servers, manage the servers, and pay people to secure and provide other non-value-added tasks to keep the services running. SaaS is also well suited for payroll and customer relations management.

In the more unique case, an organization may have a set of industry requirements that cannot be adequately met by existing service providers. In these cases, organizations will opt to develop their own accounting applications with the software languages and tools offered on a cloud provider's platform as a service (PaaS). The PaaS option provides both the needed hardware (e.g., servers and storage) and software development tools. These tools include operating systems (e.g., UNIX, Windows, OS X), programming languages (e.g., JAVA, Python, PERL, C++), and tools (e.g., cloud management, cloud cost analytics, cloud optimization, cloud integration).

In addition to choosing a cloud service model, an organization must decide how it wants to deploy its accounting system. An organization can opt to use a public cloud where any company is free to choose that vendor; a private cloud, where the organization maintains its own service model, but usually outsources its maintenance to a third party; a community cloud where an infrastructure is shared by several organizations with common concerns; or a hybrid cloud, which is a combination of two or more of the other cloud models.

Once the organization chooses its preferred service model and deployment approach, it needs to select a vendor. Some issues should be considered:

1. How will you be charged (e.g., amount of storage used, processor or software usage time, bandwidth used, or number of active user accounts)?
2. How are data migrations handled?
3. How hard would it be to move to a new provider, if necessary?
4. Can any downtime be expected? When will the service provider schedule maintenance?
5. How transparent will the vendor be with performance and billing metrics?

The vendor may then assist with any needed training; the organization can select an outside training firm or coordinate it themselves. Finally, the organization's data need to be migrated to the cloud servers, and the applications need to be tested to ensure that they are generating expected results.

8.3 Risks of Implementation

Learning Objectives

At the end of this section, students should be able to:

1. Understand the three different types of implementation risks.

Although an ERP system has many potential benefits, ERP implementation has several risks. For example, because many ERP systems are available for various types of organizations and sizes, it is possible to choose the wrong ERP system. Some ERP packages are designed for manufacturing firms. These ERP systems may, therefore, not be suited for service-oriented organizations, such as educational institutions, or companies with specialized products, such as insurance companies. According to Scott and Vessey (2002), implementation risks are organizational, information systems, and project management risks. In addition, the organizational risks are much more difficult to resolve whereas the project management risks are more specific and less difficult for organizations to resolve.

Organizational Risks

Organizational risks include a lack of strategy and understanding how the new ERP system supports that strategy. This is because choosing and implementing an ERP package does not occur frequently for an organization and implementation is very complex. Since the necessary expertise normally does not exist in-house, outside consultants are almost always retained. Thus, not having enough skills to implement an ERP system is an organizational risk. Unfortunately, qualified ERP system consultants are in short supply, and so it is "possible" that the really talented persuasive ones who make the initial presentations are not the ones who are actually assigned to the job. There is also a chance that the consultants may not clearly understand the needs of the organization or will promise more than they can deliver, which increases costs and may take more time. There is also the possibility, when the ERP consulting contracts are too open ended, that the consultants may extend the project time.

To minimize these potential problems, management needs to ensure that their consulting contract specifies who is going to provide the services, the level of expected performance and deadline, and any penalties if performance levels and deadlines are not meet.

Finally, because ERP implementations are so significant in scale and complex, it is possible that organizations would implement the wrong strategy. ERP implementation failures can occur when too much is attempted in too short a time span. Either the systems end up not being properly configured and tested or the employees are not sufficiently trained or accustomed to the new business processes.

Information Systems Risks

Even when management chooses an ERP implementation strategy that is a "fit" for the organization, it is still possible for the ERP software to be improperly customized. No ERP system is likely to meet every information need of an organization and so customizations are often performed. Unfortunately, in some cases, too many customizations are performed, or they are not programmed properly. Consequently, they can cause system slow down or down time.

It is also important to understand that ERP system implementations are expensive and cost organizations hundreds of thousands or up to millions of dollars. Cost overruns often occur because it is difficult to estimate all of the costs. It is, therefore, possible to underestimate the total cost of training, system testing and integration, database conversion, and consulting fees. These risks may be due to poor support from top management.

In addition, poor data conversion management is also considered an information system risk. We have all heard of "garbage in—garbage out," which means if bad data are converted into the new system, you will still have bad data. It is important for organizations to understand the data needed and how to make sure that all data used in the conversion are considered "clean." Therefore, data need to be useful and reliable.

Project Management Risks

Project management risks are directly involved with the management of the project itself. Again, considering people, process, technology, and controls from Chapter 1 is an important means to frame these risks. Poor project management leadership and communication means that the entire implementation can go sideways. Before it does, a project manager will need to maintain budgets and communicate both upward to top management as well as downward to the employees continuously as to project progress and issue resolution. This includes determining how to use the outside consultants and how to bring in employees throughout the implementation. A common risk is that outside consultants implement the system and then leave; meanwhile, the employees have no support on how to use the system nor understand why customization decisions were made.

Another project risk is that the project can easily lose its scope and result in budget overruns. Managing the project is important so as to not lose scope of the project and requires that a detailed business case be created. For example, a system scope can go awry when customizations are involved. Customizations require changing the software code, which means more testing is needed to resolve errors before the system is placed into the operating environment.

Once the ERP system is operating and because the ERP system is so integrated, a number of access and authorization issues can arise. It is, therefore, critical that the access control list be properly established so that only authorized individuals can see certain data and initiate authorized transactions.

8.4 Why Is Change Hard?

Learning Objectives

At the end of this section, students should be able to:

1. Recognize why change is hard and resistance to change happens.
2. Recognize the need for staff training.

Change is hard for most everyone. We have all heard "that the only thing that stays the same is change," wisdom from the Greek philosopher, Heraclitus. It is because we are human and psychology and behavior makes it hard for most of us to change. From an ERP systems implementation perspective, management may face negative attitudes from employees regarding the new system. This can lead to system rejection and nonuse with employees finding work-arounds and not accepting the new system. It is important for management to be proactive and anticipate that some employees may have negative feelings surrounding the new implementation. The employee resistance to change can be moderated by employing change management techniques.

Managing Behavior During Systems Implementation

A proactive approach to managing behavior during systems implementation is necessary and helps employees feel that they are supported by management. Top management support provides critical leadership as well as necessary communication. Top management support means that leadership is required as well as communicating to employees the benefits of implementing to the new system.

In addition, communication is crucial throughout the entire project (before, during, and after). While top management is (usually) good at communication, it may get lost with middle management, and the message does not clearly reach down to the employees. The best way to manage behavior and proactively deal with resistance to change is to communicate, communicate, communicate. Communication also requires listening. Listening to employees can identify issues early on, such as the need for more employee input and training.

During the planning stages of an ERP implementation, it is important to involve employees. Employee involvement includes listening to their concerns and problems (before, during, and after implementation), but it also includes involving some employees in the decision-making.

Implementation Challenges: Change Management

This is a video on implementation challenges and change management.

View in the online reader

Importance of Training

System implementations can have a significant impact on many people. There is almost always a need to provide training to the existing staff. In addition, new people may need to be recruited and trained while others may even be laid off. Training can be provided by software vendors, vendors specializing in training, and programs established by the entity itself. Because change is hard for everyone, organizations need to include an adequate budget for training.

No matter how well you implemented the new ERP software, if you do not have properly trained employees to use the software, all efficiencies of a new application will go away. For example, a new ERP system is projected to reduce month-end close to 5 days from 15 days, saving 10 days of employee time in the accounting department. However, due to poor planning, the training budget was limited, and the employees received 1 day of training. The first month-end close did not happen in 5 days. Why? This was the first time the employees encountered closing month-end with the new system, and they did not feel confident using the new system. Management needs to understand that to get the successful end results with a new system, the return on investment may take time, depending on how much support and training that you have considered in the implementation budget. A rule of thumb is to expect around 30 percent of your cost should be in training and post-implementation support.

Key Takeaways

In this chapter, we learned about the main steps involved in implementing a new or modified ERP system. Next, we examined the approaches an organization may use to acquire its software and hardware when implementing a new or modified system itself. We discussed the different approaches to system conversion. We looked at the different types of cloud computing service models and deployment options and how they can be used to speed up implementation, lower operating and software development costs, and easily scale to an entity's growing needs. We saw that cloud computing can also have some issues with security and estimating costs. Finally, we discussed implementation risks using a framework of organizational, information systems, and project management risks. We learned that change is hard for employees and they are likely to resist that change and learned what management can do to manage the change.

Now that we have learned how to implement an accounting system that addresses an entity's needs, we need will move to the last section of the textbook, understanding accounting information systems from a risk management perspective.

Reference

- Scott, Judy E., and Iris Vessey. "Managing risks in enterprise systems implementations." *Communications of the ACM* 45, no. 4 (2002): 74–81.

8.5 End-of-Chapter Exercises

Exercises

1. What are the principal steps in systems implementation, and why do they vary? Do they vary in risk?
2. What factors should be considered when assessing the advantages and disadvantages of cloud computing?
3. Compare (explain what is similar) and contrast (explain the difference) between IaaS, PaaS, and SaaS. What would be a good example for each of these service models? Explain.
4. How many ways can cloud computing be deployed? Provide an example of each way.
5. What are the three main approaches to in-house software acquisition?
6. What criteria should be used for selecting software?
7. What are the seven steps for acquiring in-house software? Provide an example for each step.
8. What do companies expect you to know about software in the current work environment?
9. What criteria should be employed in deciding what hardware to purchase?
10. What are the main issues involved in system conversion, and how can they be mitigated?
11. If an entity chooses to implement its accounting system in the cloud, what strategies must be considered?
12. Why don't accountants just leave systems implementation to the management information systems professionals?
13. Describe the three main categories of implementation risks?

14. Which of the following is not an advantage to using canned software?
    a. well documented
    b. less expensive
    c. generally meets all of the needs
    d. easily demonstrated prior to commitment
15. Modifying software as a software acquisition strategy is only technically and operationally feasible when
    a. the source code is available.
    b. the cost is less than customization.
    c. a cloud alternative is not available.
    d. programmers can get the job done faster than consultants.
16. When the risk of unexpected implementation issues is high, which of the following approaches to system conversion would most likely be best?
    a. immediate
    b. incremental
    c. parallel
    d. delayed
17. When the required features of software cannot be met with existing packages, it is often necessary to use which of the following?
    a. canned software
    b. modified software
    c. custom software
    d. modified or custom software
18. Which of the following criteria is normally most important in selecting accounting system software?
    a. cost
    b. ease of use
    c. meeting the required features
    d. documentation
19. Which of the following is not a main risk of end-user computing?
    a. poorly controlled systems
    b. poorly documented systems
    c. purchase of unnecessary software and/or hardware
    d. None of the above
20. When an enterprise wishes to continue developing its own software applications, but no longer wishes to maintain its IT infrastructure, it should choose which of the following cloud service models?
    a. SaaS
    b. IaaS
    c. PaaS
    d. either Paas or SaaS
21. **PROBLEM-SOLVING IN THE REAL WORLD: Thinking and Generating Solutions that Answer Questions and Improve Profits**

    Each of the following scenarios below describes an ERP system implementation.

    - In 1996, Hershey Foods decided to upgrade its legacy IT systems and implement a new integrated ERP system using SAP R/3, Manugistic's supply chain management software and Seibel's customer relationship management (CRM) software. Although SAP R/3 is the world's leading ERP system based on sales, it is one of the most complex to understand and implement. In this case, 48 months was recommended, but management wanted it done in 30–36 months so it would be Year 2000 (Y2K) ready. Hershey started the project in 1996 with the objective of solving its expected Y2K problem and having better coordinated deliveries to retailers. With the new ERP system, Hershey would continue its tradition of innovation, reorganize its business processes using embedded best practices, and be ready to implement by mid-1999.

By July 1999, a number of modules were 3 months behind schedule, and the Y2K problem was looming large. This was also one of Hershey's busiest times, when it would receive the bulk of its Halloween and Christmas orders. As a result of the delays, Hershey fell increasingly behind its normal 5-day delivery schedule to retailers. By August 1999, it was 15 days behind its regular order schedule. To remedy the problem, general management ordered the full rollout of the system, a so-called "big bang" approach. Hershey did not have a Chief Information Officer (CIO) or board members with IT competence. Unfortunately, its employees were not adequately trained in the new procedures, it was an increasingly busy time of the year, and too many unforeseen issues made it impossible to process more than $100 million in orders.

Consequently, the company lost credibility with its retailers for failing to supply products on time and lost market share as its retailers looked for more reliable alternatives, resulting in a 19 percent drop in its quarterly profits and an 8 percent drop in its stock price. By September 2000, the company's inventory was 25 percent higher than in previous years. Although at the time it was not clear to management what was going wrong, they ultimately realized that the problem involved the inventory database and a lack of coordination between technical personnel and the people involved in operations who did not update the inventory data properly. With such a complicated system, however, such unplanned occurrences are common.

- In 2000, Nike, the world-renowned athletic shoe and clothing manufacturer, planned a $400 million upgrade to its ERP, supply chain, and CRM systems. In the process of trying to integrate these systems, it lost $100 million in sales, saw a 20 percent dip in its stock, and acquired a collection of class-action lawsuits.
- Another epic tale of ERP implementation involves an ERP centralization project. In 2004, Hewlett-Packard (HP) attempted to bring its disparate North American ERP systems together. The project eventually cost HP $160 million in order backlogs and lost revenue—more than five times the project's estimated cost. Although its CIO claimed to be aware of the numerous implementation issues that could occur all the way, he was presumably surprised by how many could actually occur at one time.
- In 2004, another ERP implementation took its toll at the University of Massachusetts. In this instance, the computer problems resulted in 27,000 students either not being able to obtain their class schedules or their financial aid checks.
- In 2005, Waste Management, the large garbage disposal company, began what was supposed to be an 18-month implementation of the SAP ERP system. By the first quarter of 2008, the system was still not implemented, so Waste Management sued SAP for more than $100 million, claiming that SAP executives participated in a fraudulent sales scheme that resulted in a massive failure. According to CIO magazine, SAP retaliated several months later, claiming that Waste Management allegedly violated its contractual agreement with SAP in several ways, including by "failing to timely and accurately define its business requirements" and not providing "sufficient, knowledgeable, decision empowered users and managers" to work on the project.
- In 2008, *CIO* magazine surveyed 400 IT managers about their ERP systems. In that survey, fewer than 10 percent of the CIOs indicated any willingness to store sensitive data (including accounting, human resources, and supply chain) in another company's data center (cloud).

Required:

a. Analyze each and indicate whether you think that any common problems exist across these scenarios (and why).

b. If the CIO survey discussed in the final bullet point were conducted again today, what do you think the results would be? What do you think the results should be?

22.

Implementing an ERP System at Samsonite

Company Background

Samsonite International S.A. is the world's largest travel luggage company by retail sales value and is headquartered in Mansfield, Massachusetts. The company was founded in 1910 in Denver, Colorado, and began business as a trunk manufacturing company. Samsonite became a public company in 2010 and is traded on the Hong Kong Stock Exchange. Over the last century, it has developed and widely commercialized numerous innovations in luggage, established key industry trends, and adapted to evolving consumer needs. Samsonite is engaged in the design, marketing, and sales of travel, business, and casual luggage as well as travel accessories. Its products are sold in more than 100 countries through a variety of wholesale and retail distribution channels.

The company's core brand, Samsonite®, is one of the most well-known travel luggage brands in the world and has been central to the growth and success of its business since the brand was first introduced in 1941. In 1993, the company acquired American Tourister, Inc., based in Providence, Rhode Island. This acquisition enabled Samsonite to market products under two of the most well-known and respected brands in the luggage market. Samsonite's market-leading position results from its strong international brand presence, significant scale, robust investment on advertising and product innovation, scalable distribution and sourcing ability, as well as its market-leading, high-quality products. Its operating philosophy emphasizes lean and flexible business processes, and so it tends to prefer outsourcing when it makes business sense.

Product Sales

For the year ended December 31, 2012, Samsonite had worldwide sales approximating $1.8 billion through three distinct sales channels: wholesale, retail, and e-commerce. Its customers include department and specialty retail stores, mass merchants, catalog showrooms, and warehouse clubs as well as individual retail customers. Samsonite sells its products in Asia, Europe, North America, and South America. As of December 31, 2012, the company's products were sold at more than 45,000 points of sale in more than 100 countries. For the year ended 2012, its sales breakdown in millions was as follows: Asia $684, Europe $465, North America $500, and South America $113. Its four principal product categories are Travel 76.6 percent, Business 10.7 percent, Casual 6.2 percent, and Accessories 4.5 percent. Sales breakdown by distribution channel is wholesale 80.5 percent and Retail and E-Commerce 19.5 percent. Most of Samsonite's products are designed at their corporate headquarters in Mansfield and manufactured in China.

The Accounting System

After moving the corporate headquarters from Denver to Mansfield in 2005, Samsonite was using JD Edwards software on an IBM AS400 mainframe computer to do its accounting. The company was private but was considering a change in ownership. Moreover, transaction volume was increasing, and there was a push to globalize the accounting system by combining several separate installations. A worldwide system would also need to support multiple currencies and have a more robust database and chart of accounts. At the time, the company had a small IT function with no CIO, and consequently, the chief executive officer (CEO) ended up making the decision to implement SAP R/3. SAP R/3 is a client-server ERP system. The CEO also decided to hire a consultant to act as the CIO and run the SAP implementation project.

To handle the details of the implementation, the new CIO consultant hired additional consultants. Since the IT function was small in Mansfield, the consultants decided to purchase SAP as a hosted application from SAP and have it hosted at a SAP facility in Germany. To access SAP, they also purchased dedicated network capacity from AT&T, which had essentially constructed a large-scale proprietary network and then rented out parts of it to dedicated clients. The bandwidth of the AT&T network was roughly 54 mbps. The implementation was then done incrementally by region, starting with North America, Asia, and then Europe. South America and India, however, remained on JD Edwards. To input data to the hosted SAP software in Germany, users at the local offices of Samsonite used a client-based application called SAP Front End and SAP Login. This enabled users to log into the SAP server and run the app as though it were installed on their desktop computer. At the host facility in Germany, SAP was running on SAP-owned servers using Microsoft SQL Server database to store the data.

As part of the implementation, the consultants decided to add a number of customizations. Customizations help to meet specific needs, but they take more time and can be costly to implement. As the new SAP modules came online, users began to complain about performance and down time. The consultants attempted to address the problems, but because the customizations added complexity, attempts to identify and remove the source of the problems were difficult. Then the company was purchased by CVC Capital, and after a short period of time, both the CEO and chief financial officer (CFO) left. The board of directors then conducted a search and hired a new CEO and promoted someone from within to CFO. Soon thereafter, the new CFO recommended that the CIO consultant be replaced by a full-time in-house CIO. They also decided to replace all of the outside consultants with a full-time IT director.

Under the direction of the new CIO and CFO, the IT director worked with a team of in-house SAP experts to remove the customizations to stabilize and reconfigure the system. In the process, SAP decided to discontinue hosting its application in Germany. The new IT Department then decided to outsource the servers to a hosting service run by Hewlett Packard (HP). Under this arrangement, Samsonite purchased the new business-class servers, and HP administered the hardware at a datacenter they (leased or owned?) located in Swindon, United Kingdom.

At the Swindon data center, SAP was installed on four servers and was maintained by the HP service staff. The servers were setup in three tiers: (1) development, (2) quality control, and (3) production. The development server ran SAP on a four-core HP business-class server running the UNIX operating system and the Oracle database. The development server was used to experiment with new features and upgrades. The quality control server was also running SAP on a four-core business class server with UNIX and Oracle. The quality-control server was used to test upgrades and maintenance changes with data to ensure that the software would function as expected. The production server was then used to run the final versions and used a twenty-core HP business-class server running UNIX and Oracle. To provide redundancy in case something caused the main production server to malfunction, Samsonite had HP maintain a second twenty-core production server with identical specifications. After the move and maintenance fixes were implemented by the new IT director, they were able to stabilize the system and users were now satisfied.

The SAP R/3 ERP system that Samsonite ultimately installed includes a number of modules in addition to the Accounting and Finance Module that maintains the general ledger. The additional modules include Supply Chain for purchasing, Warehouse Management for inventory, Sales and Distribution for billing and accounts receivable, EDI for accepting orders from business partners such as Walmart, and Business Intelligence for self-service analytics and a graphical reporting tool. The corporate office also uses Business Objects for custom reports. In addition, the company uses a separate software application called Hyperion for consolidation of subsidiary data and ADP for payroll and benefits administration.

SAP R/3 is a powerful enterprise-class suite of applications that integrates and helps streamline business processes using the Oracle database. In addition to the nonaccounting business processes it tracks, SAP includes a robust chart of accounts with a capacity of up to ten digits for block codes and ten digits for any group codes. Sam-

sonite's chart uses a six-digit block code and a seven-digit group code. To appreciate the scale of a real public company, it is worthy to note that their chart contains 3,824 accounts, 70 percent of which are currently used, and 4,889 group codes, which SAP refers to as cost centers. The cost center feature adds dimensionality to the chart and allows it to produce information by region, product, etc.

In addition to implementing the new enterprise accounting system, Samsonite had an IPO in 2010. As a result of listing its shares on the Hong Kong stock exchange, the company had to convert its financial statements to International Financial Reporting Standards (IFRS). To facilitate this process its staff was trained by KPMG consultants. Fortunately, the new SAP system supports IFRS, and so the transition was not difficult. Also, due to listing its shares oversees, the company is not required to file XBRL instance documents with the U.S. Securities and Exchange Commission or comply with section 404 of Sarbanes-Oxley. All in all, the new personnel at Samsonite were able to stabilize the new SAP system and overall company profitability has increased by more than 50 percent over the last three years.

Required:

a. Was the ERP implementation at Samsonite a success or a failure? Explain, including what went right and what went wrong.
b. Did Samsonite follow the steps for implementing an accounting system discussed in the chapter? What were the implications of its approach?
c. What are the advantages and disadvantages of outsourcing IT services? Did Samsonite take advantage of this approach?
d. What are the advantages and disadvantages of using SAP as a company's ERP system?
e. What is SAP's chart of accounts capability and what are the dimensions of Samsonite's chart? What implications does this have for the information the system can produce?
f. Should a company use internal IT personnel or consultants to implement an ERP system, including training?
g. Should a company consider using a VPN to connect to its accounting system instead of a private network?
h. What are the advantages and disadvantages of using another company such as Amazon.com to warehouse your products and maintain your e-commerce website?
i. Do companies listed on the Hong Kong stock exchange have a requirement similar to SOX 404? If so, what is it?
j. What is business process reengineering? Do ERP systems facilitate or conflict with these principles?
k. How would you describe the design of Samsonite's chart of accounts? What do you believe are its advantages and disadvantages?

Endnotes

1. https://www3.technologyevaluation.com/research/article/erp-software-facts-stats-and-lessons-learned.html
2. There is no such thing as a fully debugged computer problem. Every program in the real world has some programming or compatibility issues.

PART 3

The Control Perspective

CHAPTER 9

Internal Control Environment

Starting with Chapter 9, we begin the third and final section of the book. This last section takes on the perspective of risk management. Chapter 9 focuses on the internal control environment from a risk management perspective. Internal control is an integral part of any effective accounting system. Accounting systems are complex, and therefore the likelihood of something going wrong is always a concern. Although we can define the concept of internal control, ensuring that it is effective is not that simple. Control problems can occur as a result of unintentional errors or, in a worst-case scenario, intentional fraud. Anticipating what can go wrong and taking the necessary steps to prevent, detect, or correct these problems will vary from one organization to the next. How to respond to potential problems can also take many different forms, and therefore a systems approach must be taken to ensure that internal controls will be effective. To obtain the needed system perspective, this chapter covers a recommended framework that is used to help us understand what an effective internal control system should entail and how the various parts must work together. We also discuss principles that are used within the framework to evaluate an internal control system as well as management's responsibility for designing and maintaining it. Finally, we look at the importance of documenting a control system, recognizing its limitations, and assessing its costs and benefits.

9.1 Internal Control Frameworks Used in Accounting

Learning Objectives

At the end of this section, students should be able to:

1. Understand what internal control is and why it is important.
2. Name and discuss the five components of the COSO integrated framework.
3. Identify the seventeen principles that COSO added to its internal control framework in 2013. Understand how companies will map these principles to their controls to identify any gaps in the design or operating effectiveness that need to be addressed.

An organization implements internal controls to minimize risks. Internal controls involve implementing procedures and policies so the organization's objectives can be achieved. In financial reporting, the things that can go wrong include errors and irregularities. Errors are unintentional mistakes (resulting from such things as fatigue or misunderstanding instructions). However, irregularities are intentional and result in either deliberate misstatement of the financials or the unauthorized removal of an asset. Because an organization's management prepares financial statements for internal, as well as external stakeholders, it is important for all of these stakeholders to rely on the accuracy of the financial statements. Internal controls help management minimize errors and irregularities.

A clear understanding of internal controls helps to ensure the following:

- Reliability of information—accurate, complete, and timely
- Safeguarding of assets—against unauthorized acquisition, use, or disposition
- Compliance with applicable laws and regulations
- Efficiency of operations

The quality of an organization's internal control affects not only the reliability of its financial information, but also the ability of the organization to make good decisions and remain in business. According to AICPA standards,[1] CPAs are also required to understand and evaluate their client's control structure since deficiencies directly affect the types of errors that may occur and go undetected in the financial statements. The auditor must then plan appropriate audit tests to detect these problems. Overall, internal control has become an integral part of an organization's governance and enterprise-risk management. A key guiding framework that organizations use for internal control evaluation is the COSO (2013) framework. Organizations that want to focus on risk throughout the enterprise can use the COSO-ERM (2017) framework, which includes the COSO principles and expands risk management.

COSO

Currently there are numerous frameworks internationally, but the COSO Integrated Framework (2013) is widely accepted in the United States. COSO is the Committee of Sponsoring Organizations of the Treadway Commission and is sponsored by five professional organizations. The American Accounting Association (AAA) is a professional organization for accounting academics. The remaining four organizations are for practitioners and include the American Institute of Certified Public Accountants (AICPA), Financial Executives International (FEI), the Institute of Internal Auditors (IIA), and the Institute of Management Accountants (IMA), which commissioned the study.

According to COSO (2013),[2] internal control is made up of five components:

1. Control environment
2. Risk assessment
3. Existing control activities
4. Information and communication
5. Monitoring activities

Briefly, COSO (2013) describes the control environment as the organization's attitude toward internal control. Risk assessment is the process of thinking about what can go wrong. Control activities help reduce the risks. Information and communication ensure that everyone understands the policies and procedures relating to internal controls. Monitoring is the continuing assessment of internal controls.

Five Components of Internal Control: Understanding the COSO Framework and C.R.I.M.E.

This is a video that uses a helpful acronym to remember the five COSO components of internal control.

View in the online reader

The control environment, risk assessment, information and communication, and monitoring are referred to as entity-level controls because they apply to the entire organization. Transaction cycle controls are known as "control activities" since they apply to the specific cycle (e.g., expenditure cycle). Together all of these components should operate as a system and are structured around seventeen guiding principles (COSO 2013), as shown in Table 9.1 and which we will discuss further in the chapter.

TABLE 9.1 Seventeen Principles of Internal Control (COSO 2013)

Control Environment
1. The organization demonstrates a commitment to integrity and ethical values.
2. The board of directors demonstrates independence of management and exercises oversight for the development and performance of internal controls.
3. Management establishes, with board oversight structures, reporting lines, and appropriate authorities and responsibilities in the pursuit of objectives.
4. The organization demonstrates a commitment to attract, develop, and retain competent individuals in alignment with objectives.
5. The organization holds individuals accountable for their internal control responsibilities in the pursuit of objectives.
Risk Assessment
6. The organization specifies objectives with sufficient clarity t enable the identification and assessment of risks relating to objectives.
7. The organization identifies risks to the achievement of its objectives across the entity and analyzes risk as a basis for determining how the risks should be managed.
8. The organization considers the potential for fraud in assessing risks to the achievement of objectives.
9. The organization identifies and assesses changes that could significantly impact the system of internal control.
Control Activities
10. The organizations selects and develops control activities that contribute to the mitigation of risks to the achievement of objectives to acceptable levels.
11. The organization selects and develops general control activities over technology to support the achievement of objectives.
12. The organization deploys control activities as manifested in policies that establish what is expected and in relevant procedures to affect the policies.
Informations and Communication
13. The organization obtains or generates and uses relevant, quality information to support the functioning of the other components of internal control.
14. The organization internally communicates information, including objectives and responsibilities for internal control, necessary to support the functioning of other components of internal control.
15. The organization communicates with external parties regarding matter affecting the functioning of other components of internal control.
Monitoring Activities
16. The organization selects, develops, and performs ongoing and/or separate evaluations to ascertain whether the components of internal control are present and functioning.
17. The organization evaluates and communicates internal control deficiencies in a timely manner to those parties responsible for taking corrective actions, including senior management and the board of directors, as appropriate.

COSO-ERM

COSO-ERM (2017) is also a framework that was issued by the Committee of Sponsoring Organizations of the Treadway Commission. Originally issued in 2004, the purpose of this framework is to help organizations implement risk management throughout the enterprise. This framework was recently updated to respond to the complexity of conducting business in today's environment. The COSO-ERM (2017) framework uses twenty guiding principles centered around five components:

1. Governance and Culture
2. Strategy and Objective-Setting
3. Performance
4. Review and Revision
5. Information, Communication, and Reporting

While many of the concepts found in the COSO-ERM (2017) framework are consistent with the COSO (2013) framework, the COSO-ERM (2017) framework is not only focused on internal control risk, but also the challenges of managing risk throughout the enterprise, such as global business risks, technology and data risks, and strategic alignment. Within the last 10 years, we have seen disruptions in worldwide economies and capital markets due to recessions and pandemics. For purposes of this book, it is important for accountants to understand that their role may be at a broader management level and require basic awareness of a more extensive framework from which to evaluate and apply risk management enterprise-wide. However, all accountants are expected to have a solid working knowledge of internal controls, and the remaining portion of this chapter is devoted to the components and concepts of the COSO (2013) framework.

9.2 Governance and the Control Environment

Learning Objectives

At the end of this section, students should be able to:

1. Understand management's responsibilities under the Sarbanes-Oxley Act.
2. Understand the role of the board of directors.
3. Understand the role of an audit committee.

An organization requires proper governance oversight by the board as well as an adequate control environment to be established by management. Together the board and management establish attitudes and create standards of conducting business, often referred to as the "tone at the top," which is communicated to the rest of the organization through their words, actions, and beliefs. View a video here about why "tone at the top" is so important.

What Is Tone at the Top?

This is a video explaining "tone at the top" for organizations.

View in the online reader

According to COSO (2013), the control environment is influenced by the following: ethical values, the board of directors, management's style and philosophy, the organizational structure, the assignment of authority, and the commitment to ensuring employee competence. Figure 9.1, which depicts the control environment, indicates how these factors can be viewed as parts of a system beginning with ethical values.

FIGURE 9.1 Factors Influencing the Control Environment

Ethical Values
Board of Directors Influence
Management's Style & Philosohpy
Organization Structure Influence
Assigning Authority Influence
Commitment to Competence

An organization needs a positive control environment to ensure that everyone takes their control responsibilities seriously. Without it, even a well-designed set of controls will likely be diminished or not followed at all. The control environment is important because many accountants have been fooled by a set of control procedures that look good on the surface but were never followed because employees failed to take them seriously or upper management decided to ignore or override them. According to COSO (2013), five principles must be present for the control environment to be effective. These principles require both management and the board to be responsible for an organization's control environment.

What Is Management's Responsibility?

Managerial integrity requires a commitment to doing the right thing. When people in the organization know that ethical standards will be enforced, the likelihood that employees will engage in improper or illegal activities is lower. They will also be more careful in their dealings with customers and vendors, which consequently reduces the risk of financial loss and conflict. Therefore, having high ethical standards is an integral part of creating a positive attitude toward internal control.

Managers tend to be role models for their employees. Therefore, their approach to business risk can undermine controls if it is too aggressive. Their attitude toward the accounting function can also be a problem when they are more concerned with meeting targets and analyst's expectations than providing reliable information for decision-makers. When assessing management's philosophy, it is always important to determine if they are aware and concerned about internal controls or if they are primarily concerned about making money.

In addition, management should hire competent individuals. When companies try to hire the best people, provide them with the best training, and give them fair compensation, employees will be more committed to implementing controls in an effective manner. Moreover, caring, competent, trustworthy employees can contribute more to the achievement of internal controls than any other factor (conversely, dishonest or incompetent employees can be a serious problem). Personnel policies should emphasize hiring the "right" people as well as properly training, evaluating, compensating, and promoting them. Unwillingness to pay what the market requires an over-reliance on interns or part-time employees are examples that contribute to a negative control attitude.

The organizational structure of an enterprise creates order or chaos depending on whether or not it is properly aligned. For example, if an organization is large and deals with complicated products that require decisions to be made by those closest to the problem (i.e., decentralized) but all of the decisions are actually made by the president (i.e., centralized), then lower-level managers will likely not take their jobs or the controls they are responsible for seriously. Conversely, if an organization is small or expects an authority figure (i.e., centralized direction) and those in charge keep delegating responsibilities to lower levels (i.e., in a decentralized manner), confusion about who is responsible for implementing internal control could occur and deter people from doing their jobs. Hence, the key to alignment is whether the organization structure matches the business environment (or not).

When the organization structure is ambiguous or inappropriate, chaos often occurs, and attitudes become negative. In organizations that require decentralization, centralization can lead to demoralization and employee inefficiency. In organizations that expect or need centralization, decentralization can cause confusion or deepen employee skepticism.

Clearly assigning authority and responsibility reduces the risk that employees will either take their responsibilities lightly or overstep their authority. Clear assignment allows people to understand what they should do (or not do) when carrying out their job responsibilities. When evaluating clear assignment of authority and responsibility, the following question is highly relevant: Are people aware of their code of ethics, job descriptions, and procedures manuals? When the answer is yes, then they are more likely aware of good business practices, which contribute to a positive control environment. If people are unaware or confused about what they are supposed to do, then this will diminish the control environment.

Assigning responsibility also requires accountability. Holding people accountable in a business organization is often necessary or they may not take their responsibilities seriously. The chief executive officer (CEO) and chief financial officer (CFO) are responsible for creating and maintaining proper internal controls and to have accountability throughout the organization. The board of directors hold the CEO accountable for internal control in achieving the organization's objectives. Both management and the board establish measures of performance to manage the organization for the short and long term.

What Is the Role of the Board?

The board of directors are independent of management and, at a high level, oversee internal control. An active board comprised of experienced and independent directors is best equipped to critically examine management's actions. Independent directors are more apt to recall that they can be held legally liable for corporate malfeasance and, as a result, will likely influence the organization in a more appropriate manner. View a video here on corporate culture and the board.

Corporate Culture and the Board of Directors

This is a video that discusses how the board of directors understand culture throughout the organization.

View in the online reader

The board forms subcommittees for oversight in areas of specific expertise, such as the audit committee, which is responsible for making the following recommendations:

1. Selecting the external auditors
2. Overseeing the effectiveness of the internal control structure
3. Conducting investigations of possible fraud or management irregularities
4. Serving as a communications link to the internal and external auditors

An active audit committee will normally cause an organization to pay more attention to its internal control. Effective internal control begins with the tone (i.e., attitudes) set by upper-level management with oversight by the board of directors.

The Audit Committee

This is a video that explains what an audit committee does in an organization.

View in the online reader

9.3 Risk Analysis

Learning Objective

At the end of this section, students should be able to:

1. Describe the four types of risk responses an organization has to a specific risk.

Just like a coin, risk has two sides: What could go wrong, and what is to be gained? What can go wrong in a business is the negative side of risk, which would reduce business value. What can be gained from business actions, however, is the positive side of risk and would increase business value. Risk analysis includes the four COSO principles of risk assessment as well as an understanding of how organizations can respond to risk. Risk assessment is the process of thinking about what might go wrong. Risk response is how the organization plans on dealing with each risk.

Risk Assessment

For an organization to assess its risk, it must clearly understand its business objectives and goals as it relates to operations, reporting, and compliance. For example, COSO (2013) suggested the following might be used by a retailer as operations objectives:

- Beat the competition on product price
- Increase inventory turnover to be efficient in the sales cycle
- Lower CO_2 emissions and recycle packaging material to reduce the carbon footprint of the organization

Reporting objectives are often driven by regulations and standards, but they are also important for providing complete information for managing an organization. Examples of reporting objectives include the following:

- Prepare accurate and complete financial reports for all important stakeholder groups
- Recognize revenue only after goods have been shipped, a price is determinable, and collection is reasonably assured
- Ensure that balanced scorecards and performance dashboards provide complete and accurate information for managing the organization

COSO (2013) states that compliance objectives may relate to government or industry, such as taxes, environment, or trade. Example compliance objectives might include the following:

- Prevent and detect criminal conduct and other wrongdoing
- File tax returns accurately and on time
- Provide nutritional information on food packaging

The possibility that an event will occur and negatively affect the organization from achieving its goals is what COSO (2013) defines as risk. Once an organization is clear on its objectives and goals, the organization should identify risks that would prohibit the organization from reaching those specific goals. Risk assessment is necessary to identify potential events that may affect the organization. Once the organization knows the risks it faces, management can initiate plans, programs, or controls to mitigate these risks. For example, management identifies that the accountants may make mistakes in estimating the company's bad debts. After looking at both the likelihood and magnitude of this mistake, management may decide to accept the risk, or they could decide to hire more qualified personnel. Alternatively, or in addition, they could spend more money on training, bonuses, or other people to check the work.

Management may also identify the risk that their computer system could be damaged and cause them to lose important accounting information. One response to this is to purchase insurance (a form of corrective control). Alternatively, the company could increase its physical security or develop a disaster recovery plan that includes regular backup of computer files and offsite storage (which are forms of preventative and corrective control). Or management could choose to outsource the company's computer operations to a cloud service provider and thus, theoretically, avoid some portion of their computer-related risks (assuming that they have chosen the cloud service provider wisely).

The assessment of risk involves two parts:

1. Estimating the potential loss or exposure from the problem
2. The probability or likelihood of occurrence

expected loss

Expected loss = Exposure x Probability of Occurrence

The product of these two factors is equal to the **expected loss**:

Expected loss = Exposure × Probability of Occurrence

For example, the potential loss from having an organization's customer credit card accounts stolen could be $100 million. The probability of this happening might be estimated at 1 percent. The expected loss from this problem would therefore be ($100,000,000 x 0.01) or $1 million. Managers should then design controls to reduce the expected loss in a way that does not exceed the expected loss amount.

Consequences (i.e., effects) occur as a result of inadequately controlled risks (i.e., causes) and may include the following:

- Critical information is unavailable
- Bad decisions are based on faulty data
- Resources are lost, wasted, or abused
- Management spends unnecessary time dealing with problems
- Public credibility is tarnished
- Employee and management turnover increases
- Litigation against the company occurs
- Investors and creditors become unwilling to provide financing
- The company files for bankruptcy

Organizations need to understand the risk of fraud. When the original COSO framework was released in 1992, fraud risk was not explicitly considered by many companies and their external auditors. It was almost as though they pretended or did not want to admit that this could be a real problem. To address this issue, a new group of professionals called Certified Fraud Examiners (CFE) was created in 1988. However, after growing accounting scandals hit the financial markets in the early part of the twenty-first century, the Sarbanes-Oxley Act of 2002 was passed by the federal government. The consideration of fraud in an accounting system is now an explicit principle in the revised COSO (2013) framework.

As part of the risk assessment process, companies need to identify the various ways that fraud can occur. This process includes the judgment used to prepare external reports, ensuring incentives do not create a motivation for fraudulent behavior, and reducing vulnerability of management override to existing internal control.

The fourth principle under risk assessment involves an organization's ability to identify and assess changes that could significantly impact the system of internal control. When performing risk assessment, companies should identify significant changes to any of their systems, the economy, and any laws or regulations. Errors or irregularities can occur when the business environment changes and the enterprise is not ready for it. For example, what if the Federal Reserve Board increased interest rates that caused an unexpected recession and an organization was caught with excess inventory and uncollectible accounts receivables? What if certain states passed laws requiring the collection of sales taxes on internet-based transactions, and a company failed to build this change into their system? What if transaction volume on a company's website increased dramatically, and the site crashed? Such surprises can be costly, and therefore companies should identify possible changes and build controls into their systems to reduce any expected loss.

Risk Response

Once organizations assess and identify specific risks of "what could go wrong," the organization should plan on how to respond to each risk. There are four ways for an organization to respond to a specific risk:

- Avoid the risk
- Accept the risk
- Mitigate the risk
- Share the risk

Avoidance and acceptance are at opposite ends of the spectrum. An organization may decide after evaluating all the options and understanding its risk appetite that the risk is too great and avoid engaging in the activity that produces the risk in the first place. On the other end of the spectrum, an organization may do nothing and accept the likelihood of the risk and engage in the activity that produces the risk.

Organizations mitigate risk by reducing the likelihood of the risk and choosing to implement internal controls. Sharing the risk requires the organization to use different options that reduce its exposure to a risk that results from engaging in a business activity. This can be done by buying insurance, hedging, or outsourcing. An example of risk an organization may encounter is the risk of lawsuits from data hacks; organizations can share the negative impact of this risk by buying insurance to cover the costs of data hacking on their information systems. Airlines often share the risk of price volatility of jet fuel and will implement price hedging contracts. Other business risks relating to business processes are shared through outsourcing contracts.

It is important to understand that all organizations face **inherent risk**, which is the risk that is faced prior to taking action. However, an organization may take action by implementing controls, but risk will not be entirely eliminated, and this leaves what is known as **residual risk**. Residual risk is what remains after management takes action to respond to the risks threats and implements counteractions.

inherent risk

Risk that is faced prior to taking action.

residual risk

Risk that remains after management takes action to respond to the risks threats and implements counteractions.

9.4 Control Activities

Learning Objectives

At the end of this section, students should be able to:

1. Describe how the internal control process works, what must be documented, and why documentation is important.
2. Understand fraud and explain the consequences of inadequately controlled risks.
3. Explain the three accounting functions that need to be separated and why, providing an example.

Control activities are used in addition to the control environment to achieve objectives at the accounting application level. The control environment provides general influence, while control activities assume that the environment may not always work. Control activities are specific things you do to reduce the likelihood of accounting problems to achieve your objectives (i.e., the accuracy of accounting records and safeguarding of assets). Moreover, the control environment is attitudinal, whereas control activities are procedural.

Examples of control activities include the following:

- Reconciling the bank account
- Comparing the physical inventory to the system inventory records
- Completeness check in a web form to ensure that all required fields are completed before a customer clicks the submit button
- Credit checking a new customer before approving a sales order
- Approving a journal voucher

Internal Controls Overview

A video on the importance of internal controls.

View in the online reader

Management must document control activities. Paragraph 42 of PCAOB Standard No. 5 requires public companies to document the design of controls over all significant financial accounts and disclosures. The documentation should include both entity-level and activity-level controls. Entity-level control is important because it is intended to reduce risk across the entire organization. Entity-level controls affect the entire accounting system, while activity-level controls affect specific accounting cycles and functions.

In addition, management must document the findings of its review, whether any control deficiencies were noted, and if so, what corrective action was taken. Documentation can be in written or electronic form. It can include a policy and procedure manuals, flowcharts, job descriptions, and internal control questionnaires. Additionally, by documenting what should be performed, when, and for what purpose makes it easier to evaluate, eliminate weaknesses, and improve system effectiveness.

No internal control system can provide foolproof protection. In fact, it is practically impossible to create a perfect control system. Limitations exist no matter how good the control system is and are called inherent limitations. Inherent limitations include the following:

Fatigue: For example, a company can have a "perfect" control procedure that is not followed because an employee just got tired and made a mistake.

Misunderstanding or not following instructions: Even when a company places job responsibilities in writing and communicates them clearly, it is still possible for someone to misunderstand them or not follow them because they were rushed to meet a deadline.

Collusion: A company could assign one person to oversee another or to maintain records on someone else's activities (supposedly segregating incompatible duties) only to find out later that the two employees worked together to defeat the system.

collusion
When two employees worked together to defeat the system to commit fraud.

Management override: A "perfectly" good system can be ignored by someone in authority by simply telling an employee to suspend or disregard a procedure for some supposedly "good" reason or by just deciding to override the control themselves.

The goal of internal control should be to provide reasonable assurance. That means that no control structure is perfect because of its inherent limitations and that the costs should not exceed the benefits. One of the more common ways of selecting control activities is to create a matrix of risks associated with various transaction processes and then map them to various internal controls that may be effective in mitigating them. They are also developed by identifying incompatible functions and considering alternative ways of controlling these activities. Specific control activities will be examined in further detail in Chapter 11 through Chapter 14 in connection with the related transactions cycles.

What Is Fraud?

Fraud is when there is intent to deceive for personal gain. Accountants must be aware of two potential types of fraud:

1. Misappropriation of assets
2. Financial statement fraud

Misappropriation of assets are related to theft of an organization's assets, such as cash or inventory. For example, in a retail environment, theft of inventory from the store by employees is considered misappropriation of assets. Similarly, embezzlement, which is where bookkeepers write checks to themselves for fictitious business expenses, is also a misappropriation of assets.

Financial statement fraud is where management misrepresents the financial statements. This can be done in many ways; however, financial statement fraud may show that assets or revenues are represented at higher values than they actually are or liabilities and expenses are represented at lower levels than they actually are.

Fraudulent Financial Reporting

This is a video that discusses the most common fraudulent financial reporting schemes.

View in the online reader

For fraud to occur, there must first be a motive or **pressure** to commit the fraud. Second, an **opportunity** to commit the fraud must exist. Finally, there is a **rationalization** to commit the fraud. Together, this is called the **fraud triangle**.

pressure

Element of the fraud triangle that is the motive to commit the fraud.

opportunity

Element of the fraud triangle that is the availability to commit the fraud.

rationalization

Element of the fraud triangle that is the reasoning to commit the fraud.

fraud triangle

Requires all three elements, pressure, opportunity, and rationalization, to commit fraud.

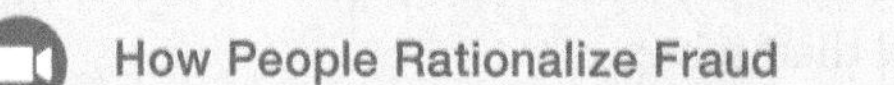

How People Rationalize Fraud

This video explains the fraud triangle and provides examples.

View in the online reader

Segregation of Duties

To minimize the threat of fraud, **segregation of accounting duties** is needed. An appropriate segregation of duties means that the three major functions involved in a transaction (i.e., approval, recordkeeping, and custody of the related assets) are segregated to different people to minimize error or fraud. For example, warehouse employees should not be maintaining the inventory records, or they could ignore or cover up a shortage. Employees who open the mail and have access to cash receipts should not be able to approve write-offs of bad debts or allowances to customer accounts, or they could divert cash receipts and cover up the embezzlements by approving offsetting journal entries.

segregation of accounting duties

Used to minimize errors and fraud; different individuals should be responsible for each of the three major activities of a transaction: approval, recordkeeping, and custody.

For the revenue cycle, three major functions (and tasks within these functions) require segregation:

Approval function

- Receiving orders for sales
- Granting credit

Recordkeeping function

- Billing customers and recording sales
- Maintaining inventory records
- Maintaining general ledger accounting records
- Maintaining detailed accounts receivable records

Custody function

- Shipping goods
- Processing cash receipts

For the expenditure cycle, three major functions also require segregation:

Approval function

- Purchase orders
- Vendor payments

Recordkeeping function

- Record vendor invoice
- Maintain inventory records
- Maintain general ledger accounting records
- Maintain detailed accounts payable records

Custody function

- Receiving goods
- Processing cash payments

Sometimes in smaller organizations, it is difficult to assign separate people for the different accounting functions. If this is the case, it is the responsibility of the business owner to be more involved.

Role of Information and Communication

Information and communication allow management to take effective and timely corrective action. Examples include timely financial reports, budgets, and other performance reports, balanced scorecards that map goals to metrics and to actual results, surveys, hotlines, presentations, training, and periodic news reports via email or other media.

Internal communication begins with clearly communicating objectives. The organization is expected to communicate significant issues that relate to internal control, which includes noncompliance to policies and procedures and discovery of internal control weaknesses.

Communication should also occur with those outside the organization. An open two-way process with trading partners may identify potential issues that could affect the achievement of objectives. For example, customer or supplier complaints relating to problems with shipping or billing may indicate fraudulent activities or other potential control-related problems.

Role of Monitoring

Monitoring can be done in three ways: (1) ongoing evaluations, (2) separate evaluation, (3) combination.

Ongoing monitoring activities are usually part of ongoing processes, such as management supervision or budget variance analysis, or may be built into the software of business processes, including some form of business analytics or continuous auditing modules. Budgets can be used to influence the organization by identifying problem areas and focusing attention. When employees realize that management takes budget variances seriously, the employees will usually take more care in what they do.

Separate monitoring activities often include internal auditing or the use of external systems consultants. Internal auditors are responsible for assisting management in ensuring the adequacy of the control structure and are often a critical part of monitoring activities. They also assist in communicating management's policies and procedures, reporting on the reliability of financial information, and ensuring the proper use of an organization's assets. Internal auditors can influence activities in a positive way. Everyone tends to take controls more seriously when they know that internal auditors may be monitoring their work. The internal audit function should develop a plan of projects that are selected on the basis of risk to ensure that key controls are operating effectively. For organizations that do not have an internal audit group or when management is interested in a more independent point of view, they may use outside consultants to assist in evaluating the design and operation of their internal controls.

Regardless of how an organization chooses to monitor its internal controls, deficiencies should be reported to senior management and the board of directors. These should be reported on a timely basis for management to implement corrective action.

Key Takeaways

In this chapter, we discussed the importance of internal control and why an in-depth understanding of the concept is essential for anyone studying accounting. We examined the COSO (2013) framework, which provides a model for companies to see what an ideal system of internal control might look like. We learned that it is important for organizations to have an ethical culture and looked at the role of the board of directors as well as the role of the audit committee. We discussed the key components and underlying principles of internal control that must be present and functioning for a system of internal control to be considered effective. Finally, we learned about risk assessment, what response options organizations have to specific risks, and how it is important to understand the risk assessment of fraud. We learned about the two types of fraud and the fraud triangle. We learned how segregation of duties is important in preventing fraud.

References

- Committee of Sponsoring Organizations of the Treadway Commission. *Enterprise Risk Management-Integrated Framework*. Committee of Sponsoring Organizations of the Treadway Commission, 2017.
- Committee of Sponsoring Organizations of the Treadway Commission. *Internal Control-Integrated Framework*. Committee of Sponsoring Organizations of the Treadway Commission, 2013.

9.5 End-of-Chapter Exercises

Exercises

1. Why is an understanding of internal control important? (Hint: There are many reasons, but be sure to include the benefits of the control objectives.)
2. What are internal controls? How does the Sarbanes-Oxley 404 view of internal control over financial reporting differ in any way?
3. How does an error compare and contrast to an irregularity in financial reporting?
4. What is the COSO (2013) framework? What is it used for? What are the components? Give an example for each component. How do the seventeen new principles change the framework?
5. What are the purposes of the principles and points of focus? How are they similar (compare), and how are they different (contrast)? Are they required?
6. Is there a process to internal control that could be described hierarchically or by flow? Can internal control be viewed as a system (explain)? If so, could there be problems with the system? If so, what would they be classified as according to SEC rules?
7. Compare and contrast control activities to the control environment. How are they similar? How are they different?
8. Provide three examples of control activities. What activities should be segregated?
9. Explain how the control environment may augment or diminish the effectiveness of control activities.
10. What are the primary factors that contribute to a company's control environment? Give one example of how each factor contributes positively and one example of how it contributes negatively.
11. Assume that you have been asked to evaluate a company's internal control using the COSO (2013) framework and have found the following deficiencies, which you estimate could have the following impact on their financial statements. The first two you consider to be inconsequential, and the remaining four you consider to be significant. Although none of the deficiencies were considered to be material on their own, how should management eval-

uate the effectiveness of its internal control given that its reported income before taxes is expected to be approximately $2,165,000?

Deficiency	Potential Impact
def 1	< $1,000
def 2	< $800
def 3	$25,000
def 4	$38,000
def 5	$51,000
def 6	$44,500

12. How do ethical values affect internal control over financial reporting? To what extent does the SEC care about this issue? Can ethical values in an organization be measured?
13. What is risk assessment, and how does it relate to the COSO (2013) framework of internal control?
14. What is monitoring, and how does it relate to the COSO (2013) framework of internal control? How is monitoring similar to and different from control activities?
15. What are management's responsibilities under Section 404 of the Sarbanes-Oxley Act?
16. Is the Sarbanes-Oxley Act of 2002 really necessary? Can't the free market be effective in regulating corporate malfeasance?
17. Documentation of internal control may vary according to whether a company is public or private. To what extent must the nature of internal controls used by a public company be documented and tested for operating effectiveness? Are the requirements the same for private companies? If they are different, explain how and why.
18. What are the inherent limitations to a "perfectly" designed internal control system?
19. How would management determine the ROI of documenting its internal control system? Could it be important to do so? Provide an example of how.
20. Understanding internal control is critical because it helps ensure
    a. quality of information.
    b. efficient operations.
    c. security over the assets.
    d. compliance with regulation.
    e. All of the above
21. Which of the following statements about the COSO Integrated Framework of Internal Control is true?
    a. The Committee of Sponsoring Organizations issued their first recommended framework for internal control in 1992.
    b. The environment in which controls operate has changed due to technology, globalization, and wealth inequality.
    c. As a result of the COSO framework and efforts of the SEC, fraud has begun to decrease.
    d. To improve internal control, COSO decided to adopt a new rules-based approach.
22. Which of the following is not a factor within the control environment?
    a. management's style and philosophy
    b. influence of the board of directors and its committees
    c. personnel policies, which reflect a commitment to competence
    d. methods of assigning authority and responsibility
    e. None of the above
23. Which of the following is not a control procedure/control environment combination, respectively?
    a. reconciliation/management doesn't like controls

b. second signatures on checks/concern about being audited
c. double checking the daily cash deposit/a board of directors that demands results
d. not knowing who's in charge of what/locking up the gift certificates
e. marking an invoice paid/concern about a surprise internal audit

24. Which of the following is not one of the principles of internal control?
    a. The organization demonstrates a commitment to integrity and ethical values.
    b. The organization considers the potential for fraud in assessing risks to the achievement of objectives.
    c. The organization evaluates and communicates internal control deficiencies in a timely manner to those parties responsible for taking corrective actions, including senior management and the board of directors.
    d. The organization selects and develops general control activities over technology to provide the information it needs to support the functioning of other components of internal control.
25. Which of the following is not one of the four key concepts relating to the risk assessment principles contained in COSO?
    a. The organization specifies objectives with sufficient clarity to enable the identification and assessment of risks relating to its objectives.
    b. The enterprise considers the potential for fraud in assessing risks to the achievement of objectives.
    c. The organization identifies risks to the achievement of its objectives related to financial reporting and analyzes those risks as a basis for determining how the risks should be managed.
    d. The organization identifies and assesses changes that could significantly affect the performance of its internal controls.
26. Which of the following is false regarding the principle of internal control that addresses external communications?
    a. An enterprise should establish and implement policies and procedures that facilitate external communication.
    b. Information resulting from external assessments about the enterprise's activities that relate to internal control should be evaluated by management.
    c. Communication to external parties allows them to understand events, activities, and other circumstances that may affect how they should interact with an entity.
    d. An organization's culture and values are proprietary and, therefore, should not be shared with customers and suppliers.
27. Which of the following is not one of the principles pertaining to the control environment of the COSO internal control framework?
    a. The board of directors demonstrates independence from management and exercises oversight of the development and performance of internal control.
    b. The organization evaluates and communicates internal control deficiencies in a timely manner to those parties responsible for taking corrective actions, including senior management and the board of directors, as appropriate.
    c. The organization demonstrates a commitment to attract, develop, and retain competent individuals in alignment with objectives.
    d. Management establishes, with board oversight, structures, reporting lines, and appropriate authorities and responsibilities in the pursuit of objectives.
28. After a study by internal auditors, the accounting system for collecting revenues at your retail store is determined to be 90 percent reliable. A major threat like the one that occurred at Target stores has been identified and could cost the company $5,000,000. To minimize this potential loss, the internal auditors have recommended adding two possible control procedures. The first control would cost approximately $210,000 to implement and reduce the likelihood of loss to about 5 percent. The second control would cost about $380,000 and reduce the likelihood to 3 percent. Based on the costs and benefits, which of the following would you recommend to management?

a. recommend the first control only
b. recommend the second control only
c. recommend both controls
d. recommend neither of the two controls

29. Conducting ongoing and separate evaluations is best associated with which of the following elements of internal control?
a. risk assessment
b. the control environment
c. monitoring activities
d. control activities

30. **DIAMOND FOODS: Errors versus Irregularities**

In this chapter, it was noted that internal controls are used to prevent system problems in financial reporting, such as errors and irregularities. In 2010, Diamond Foods, one of the world's largest distributors of snack foods, found itself in a bind. One of the company's significant lines of business involved buying walnuts from its growers and selling them to retailers. With sharp increases in walnut prices in 2010, Diamond encountered a situation where it needed to pay more to its growers in order to maintain longstanding relationships with them. However, Diamond felt that it could not increase the amounts paid to growers for walnuts, which was its largest commodity cost, without also decreasing the net income that Diamond would report to the investing public. To fix this problem, Diamond worked out an arrangement with its growers to split up a shipment of walnuts into two bills, where one would be coded as purchases and the other as advances on crops that had not yet been delivered. Through this accounting, Diamond was able to hit quarterly targets for earnings per share (EPS) and exceed analyst's estimates. After restating its earnings for 2010 and 2011 in November 2012 at the recommendation of its board to reflect the cost of its walnuts, its stock dropped to $17 from a high of $90 in 2011. Diamond's CFO, however, argued that the accounting treatment was justified because it was approved by its external auditor. Please answer the following questions:

a. Explain using the facts of this short case and anything you can learn through research on the internet whether there is a system problem and whether you would classify it as an error or an irregularity.
b. Can you think of any internal controls that a company could use to prevent or detect this type of problem?

31. **SEGREGATION OF DUTIES**

In this chapter, we noted that allowing one person to have more than one of the key responsibilities in processing a transaction can increase the risk of errors or irregularities. Analyze each of the following scenarios and explain how the principle of segregation of incompatible duties was violated.

a. A supervisor in a manufacturing department who is responsible for approving employee time cards in that department and distributing the payroll checks decides to fire an employee and neglects to report the termination to the payroll department. The following week a payroll check comes for the terminated employee, and so the supervisor decides to endorse it in the employee's name and deposits it in his account.
b. An accounts receivable clerk cashed a check from customer A that was a payment toward accounts receivable. The clerk was able to endorse and deposit the check made out to the company in his own account by opening an anonymous savings account in the Bahamas. The clerk later covered customer A's remittance by posting a check received from customer B to customer A's account.
c. In Company A, warehouse employees are assigned the responsibility of pulling goods from the shelves to fill orders based on approved sales orders. During the peak holiday season, to save on labor costs, Company A decided to have warehouse employees reduce inventory quantities on the computer after goods were shipped instead of hiring an extra data entry clerk. For some reason, the financial statements showed a significant decrease in Company A's gross profit, but after the year-end physical inventory, which compares the goods on hand to the perpetual inventory maintained on the computer, no unusual shortages were found.

32. **APPLYING THE COSO PRINCIPLES OF INTERNAL CONTROL**

    Each of the following describes an internal control problem. Based on your analysis of each situation, explain which of the seventeen principles of internal control is most likely not present:

    a. After conducting a survey, you find out that employees feel underpaid and that their company is against collective bargaining.

    b. You meet with the company's audit committee that is made up of a retired Big 4 partner, an SEC lawyer, a member of another company's board who serves on their audit committee as a financial expert, and the company's controller.

    c. After holding a focus group with some employees, you find out that they feel that the company's code of ethics is a very effective public relations document.

    d. Sweet Donuts Company hires a former Big 4 senior manager to head up a new internal audit department at the recommendation of its private equity investors in anticipation of it going public. After going public, the company fires all of its internal auditors and replaces them with an outsourced internal audit service that only has two unqualified employees.

    e. A company's computer system gets hacked, and one million credit card accounts get stolen, including the three-digit security codes from the back of the cards. The company didn't find out about the theft until several of their customer's credit cards were charged for thousands of dollars of unordered merchandise.

    f. A company decides to diversify its product line based on a competitor's actions and ends up losing a lot of money but is totally surprised by the outcome.

    g. A company allows a trader to use a hedging scheme to offset possible losses on decreases in commodity prices only to find out 6 months after the employee quit that the trader was using company funds to speculate on the trader's behalf and was about to lose several million dollars when a number of the futures trades were to close.

    h. A company's accounting department significantly underestimates the level of bad debts for the quarter.

    i. The internal audit staff at a publicly traded company is aware of a weakness that could be material but fails to report it to upper management because of concern that the deficiency involves upper management and that there might be retaliation.

    j. Employees seem skeptical and even confused at times about how best to perform their jobs because of the amount of autonomy they have been given.

33. Assume that management is testing the effectiveness of its internal control over revenue recognition and accounts receivable evaluation. The company is a manufacturer, and all sales over $10,000 require a computer check of outstanding balances to determine if approved credit limits have been exceeded. Management tested sales throughout the year with a sample size of thirty transactions. Only three failures were found, all in the last quarter, but the sales manager approved all of them. Based on the test results, should management conclude that the control is effective, or is there a control deficiency? If so, is it a significant deficiency or a material weakness?

34. Assume that you have been placed in charge of your college's effort to control dorm damage. Using each component of the COSO framework, provide an example of the process you would use to do it. Consider dorm rooms, common areas, and college-wide damage.

Endnotes

1. American Institute of Certified Public Accountants. "Code of Professional Conduct and Bylaws (as of June 1, 2013)."
2. Committee of Sponsoring Organizations of the Treadway Commission. "Internal control-integrated framework."

CHAPTER 10
IT Security and Controls

You may be thinking right now, "Why do I need to understand IT security and controls when I plan to be an accountant after I graduate?" That is a good question, and the answer stems from one that has been evolving in the accounting profession for some time and is becoming more of a reality with the new CPA exam and licensing model effective January 2024. Here's a video that explains more on this new model and why understanding IT risks and controls are important knowledge for an accountant.

CPA Evolution: New CPA Licensure Model Coming in 2024

This is a video that explains the new CPA exam and licensing.

View in the online reader

10.1 Why Do We Need IT Controls?

Learning Objectives

At the end of this section, students should be able to:

1. Understand the threats to an organization's information and the need for IT security controls.
2. Understand the regulatory expectations from the Security and Exchange Commission and Public Company Accounting Oversight Board as it relates to IT security and controls.
3. Recognize that more than one IT control framework exists.

An organization's information faces many threats. Some threats are unintentional, while others are intentional. Unintentional threats include mistakes made by employees, such as clicking on a malicious link in an email that downloads a virus or deleting files by mistake. In addition, acts of nature can cause power outages or flooding. Intentional threats are security threats to the IT system, such as outsiders (or inside employees) hacking into the system and gaining access to unauthorized files.

While most large organizations have separate IT and security departments, and department personnel have specific expertise in this area, it is important for accountants to understand how the IT risks have an impact on producing financial information and the controls to mitigate those risks. To summarize, the following are some of the risks to computer-based accounting systems:

- Inadequate training and supervision
- Unauthorized transactions
- Mistakes in data entry or in storage
- Hardware failure
- System inability to meet the users' needs
- Theft of the assets
- Computer abuse (e.g., sabotage, hacking, or denial of service)
- Fraudulent financial reporting (management fraud)

Role of the Security and Exchange Commission and of the Public Company Accounting Oversight Board

Both the Security and Exchange Commission (SEC) and the Public Company Accounting Oversight Board (PCAOB) offer guidance for accountants on information security. The SEC is concerned about keeping investors informed about cybersecurity and providing guidance for publicly held companies by discussing threats and disclosing material events impacted by cybersecurity. While the SEC first recognized cybersecurity as an issue in 2011, the landscape continues to evolve on how organizations should best grapple with these issues. The latest guidance is from 2018, where the SEC continues to emphasize that organizations discuss risks from cybersecurity in the Management, Discussion, and Analysis (MDA) section of the annual 10K. If there is a material event, such as a cybersecurity event that materially affects the organization, it must be disclosed on the 8-K report. These disclosures are important because investors need to be aware of the risk and probability of a cybersecurity risk affecting costs. For example, in 2017, Equifax had a data breach that affected more than 100 million people and cost the company in excess of $1.5 billion. In fact, the CEO and chair of the board had to testify before Congress. The SEC does have the right to issue an enforcement action against a company for failure to protect customer data. One of the first companies receiving an SEC enforcement action was Voya Financial in 2018.

The PCAOB regulates auditors and has given guidance that auditors need to consider cybersecurity risks as it relates to the financial reporting risk of the companies they audit. This means that auditors need to understand the reliability of the data used for financial reporting. From the function of cybersecurity, the auditor's role is limited, but important. While the role of accountants is not a specific function of cybersecurity, the expectation is that accountants will understand basics of cybersecurity that can protect organizations and minimize the damage. These basics include policies and control procedures that protect the processing of information, known as application controls and general IT controls.

IT Control Frameworks

An organization may choose from many different IT security control frameworks; however, the two most common that accountants should be aware of are COBIT and NIST. COBIT was created by the Information Systems Audit and Control Association (ISACA) and the IT Governance Institute

(ITGI). COBIT[1] provides a structure for developing appropriate IT governance and control in a company to manage risk as well as to optimize IT resources. Updated in 2019, the COBIT framework is enterprise-wide and has forty high-level governance and management objectives that cover control objectives categorized within these core domains:

Governance Objectives

1. Evaluate, Direct, and Monitor

Management Objectives

1. Align, Plan, and Organize
2. Build, Acquire, and Implement
3. Deliver, Service, and Support
4. Monitor, Evaluate, and Access

Briefly, the governance objective of Evaluate, Direct, and Monitor is focused on evaluating strategy with executive management and monitoring strategy performance. The management objective of Align, Plan, and Organize addresses the need for a technology strategic plan and organization of the IT function. Build, Acquire, and Implement deals with the need for sound practices in acquiring and implementing new hardware and software. Deliver, Service, and Support addresses the need for a clear definition of the IT services provided and the availability of training and help. Monitor, Evaluate, and Access is the process for making sure that the IT governance and control practices established are working properly. The framework is extensive and detailed; ISACA.org provides guides and toolkits for IT professionals to use for designing effective IT controls.

The National Institute of Standards and Technology (NIST)[2] created a specific cybersecurity framework for organizations. The framework is organized around five functions: identify, protect, detect, respond, and recover. Briefly, *identify* addresses understanding and assessing cybersecurity risk; *protect* involves implementing controls to mitigate the risks; *detect* is the ability to discover events on a timely basis; *respond* is centered around actions to take once an event is detected; and *recover* addresses getting back to normal operating capabilities after an event occurs. Organizations often use the NIST cybersecurity framework in conjunction with other enterprise-wide frameworks, such as COBIT or COSO-ERM.

The Cybersecurity Framework

This is a video that explains the NIST cybersecurity framework.

View in the online reader

10.2 Application Controls

Learning Objectives

At the end of this section, students should be able to:

1. Understand the need for and nature of application controls.
2. Recognize and describe input controls, processing controls, and output controls and identify examples.

application controls

Controls concerned with processing transactions that are specific to the software application.

general IT controls

Entity-wide IT risks that affect the entire computer system.

Application controls are the policies and procedures used to prevent, detect, and correct errors and irregularities in processing transactions. These controls are therefore concerned with specific applications, such as order processing, cash receipts, and cash disbursements. Application controls are different in scope than general IT controls. **General IT controls** are concerned with entity-wide IT risks that affect the entire computer system, whereas application controls are embedded in specific application input, processing, and output.

Application Testing: Not Just for IT Auditors, Pt 1

This is a video that explains the importance of application controls.

View in the online reader

Input Controls

input controls

Application control that relates to data input to ensure accuracy, validity, and completeness of the data.

validity check

Input control that ensures an account number exists.

In this stage of transaction processing, data must be entered into the application. **Input controls** to edit data input must therefore be performed to ensure the validity, accuracy, and completeness of all data. These input controls include a validity check, consistency check, check digit, limit check, completeness check, and field check.

A **validity check** is an application control designed to ensure that account numbers or individual customers exist. For example, if C1002356 were input as a customer ID into the order processing application of the revenue cycle, a validity check would ensure that customer C1002356 exists in the customer file before that transaction could be processed. This mitigates the risk of creating a transaction for a nonexistent customer.

A **consistency check** ensures that data entered into fields make sense in relation to other data or in a situational context. A consistency check would be appropriate if a system designer needed to prevent an employee from setting a due date as a date that had already passed or a user from entering data into a password field that did not agree with the confirm password.

consistency check

Input control that ensures that data entered into a field makes sense in relation to other data or in a situational context.

A **check digit** is an extra digit added to the end (or other part) of an account number to ensure that no transpositions (order change) or transcription (wrong number, omission, or addition) errors are made. For example, to create a check digit for a seven-digit vendor ID such as V890115, an entity would use a mathematical algorithm known as Modulus 11. This formula was invented for the purpose of creating a unique number that would be added (or appended) to the seven-digit ID, making it an eight-digit ID (including the check digit). Therefore, if we assume that Modulus 11 generates a check digit of 2 for vendor code V890115, the vendor code now becomes (if appending) V8901152. The check digit 2 is unique because the algorithm creates it so that if a user enters a vendor code with a check digit that does not contain the original digits in the proper order, an error message would be generated by the computer's input editing software. Here's a video that explains how the numbers on a product bar code are validated using the calculation to determine the check digit.

check digit

Input control that adds an extra digit to the end of an account number to ensure no transpositions or errors were made.

Bar Code Calculation to Determine the Check Digit

This is an example of using an algorithm to determine check digit of bar code.

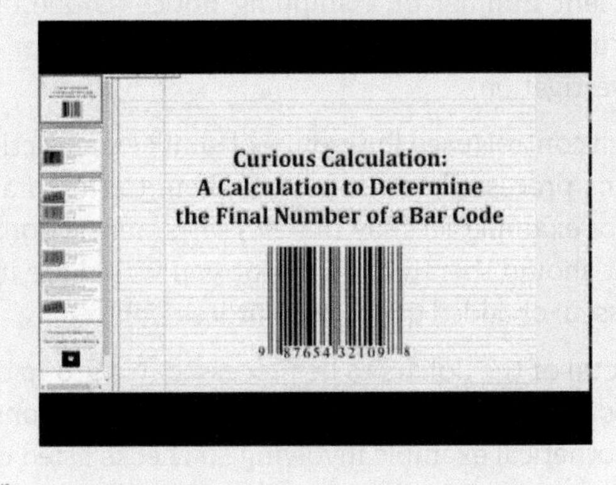

View in the online reader

A **limit check** is performed to be sure that pre-established limits are not exceeded. Common limits established in accounting might include the cost of an asset for testing total accumulated depreciation, total hours to be worked in a week, or the maximum amount of travel reimbursement allowed or the maximum number of products or shares of stock that can be traded without an additional special authorization code.

limit check

Input control that ensures pre-established limits are not exceeded.

To illustrate the speed and magnitude of damage that can be caused by poorly controlled software, take the "Flash Crash" of May 6, 2010, and the Knight Capital Trading Debacle of August 1, 2012. Due to trading imbalances caused by inadequate limit checks on supercomputer-initiated orders at 2:42 p.m. on May 6, the Dow Jones, which was already down more than 300 points for the day, began to fall rapidly, dropping an additional 600 points in 5 minutes for an almost 1,000-point loss for the day by 2:47 p.m.[3] This crash caused nearly $1 trillion of market value to evaporate. During this fluctuation, the prices of some stocks decreased to one cent per share, including Accenture, while others including Apple and Hewlett-Packard, increased to more than $100 thousand.[4] Twenty minutes later, by 3:07 p.m., the market had regained most of the 600-point drop. Due to undisclosed software problems (most likely caused by inadequate limit checks), Knight Capital, one of the largest members and electronic traders on the NYSE, entered erroneous trades of company stocks that caused major disruptions in the prices of 148 companies. Many of the trades had to be canceled or honored at large losses to Knight, which caused it to lose $480 million and 75 percent of its market value by the next day, and left the company teetering on the brink of bankruptcy.[5]

completeness check

Input control that ensures that all required fields are filled in.

A **completeness check** ensures that all required fields are filled in. For example, if an accounts payable clerk were to enter all of the data for paying a vendor, but failed to enter the due date, a completeness check would respond by stating that a required field had not been filled in and would delay processing the transaction.

field check

Input control that ensures the characters entered in a field are of the proper type.

A **field check** is a control that determines whether the characters entered in a field are of the proper type. For example, if a customer wishes to order ten (10) units of a product, but accidentally entered the number one (1) and the letter "o" (1o), then a field check would notify the customer that a number appears to have been input as an alphabetic character.

Processing Controls

processing controls

Application controls used to ensure that all legitimate transactions have been accurately processed.

prenumbered documents

Processing control relating to source documents used in transaction processing (e.g., purchase order) are sequentially prenumbered.

batch totals

Processing control that is a record count of a group of similar transactions.

control total

Batch total processing control where the total dollar amount of individual transactions processed equals the total on the report.

hash total

Batch total processing control where a nonfinancial attribute is added up to ensure all transactions are processed accurately.

Processing controls are controls used to ensure that all legitimate transactions have been processed accurately. These controls include **prenumbered documents** and **batch totals**.

Prenumbered documents such as receiving reports and shipping notices are used to keep track of transactions and to ensure that all authorized ones are processed once and only once. For example, by entering the document number of a shipping notice as one of the data elements in a transaction record, a computer program can check for any missing or duplicate shipments and report them for manual investigation.

A record count is a batch control (used for groups of similar transactions), which counts up the total number of transactions processed and compares them to the total number of transactions that should be processed. For example, let's say that 543 sales transactions occurred for the month. The processed record count should therefore be 543, or you would see if either a transaction had been lost (if 542 were processed) or added (if 544 were processed).

A **control total** is the total of the dollars to be processed in a group of like transactions that is arrived at by adding up the dollars in the financial field of the transactions. An example of a control total can be found in a hypothetical example involving 50 checks listed on a disbursements sheet. If the total on the sheet is $56,090, then the processed control total generated by the computer should be $56,090. Any other processed total would indicate that at least one of the checks was processed incorrectly.

A **hash total** is another type of batch control that is used to add up otherwise meaningless data—meaning that the accounting department would not normally add up these figures. For example, general ledger (G/L) account numbers would not normally be totaled but might be added up to make sure that all of the individual accounts were processed accurately. Such a control would be useful if a G/L account number was incorrectly processed due to a transposition or transcription error because a record count or control total would not reveal such an error. Hash totals should only be used on nonfinancial attributes such as G/L account numbers, customer account numbers, and inventory identification numbers.

Output Controls

output controls

Application control that ensures output is not lost, misdirected, or seen by unauthorized individuals.

Output controls include procedures designed to ensure that accounting system reports or other outputs are not lost, misdirected, or seen by unauthorized individuals. Output controls include a variety of distribution checks and reasonableness tests.

Distribution checks are a type of control intended to ensure that computer output is distributed to only authorized users. For example, some reports may need to be marked confidential or indicate to whom they may be distributed. Confidential data should also be sent to a printer that is not in a public area. After viewing confidential reports, they should either be locked away or put through a paper shredder.

distribution checks
Output control to ensure that output is distributed only to authorized users.

Reasonableness tests involve someone reviewing reports, transaction listings, and other output (such as expense checks) to make sure there are no obvious problems or errors. This can be a very important control procedure for payroll and expense reimbursements. For example, reviewing a printed trial balance may show an expense account with a zero-balance, indicating that an accrual may have been missed, or an expense report run with an unusually large amount, indicating that there may be an error or irregularity.

reasonableness tests
Output control that ensures output has no obvious errors and is reasonable.

10.3 General IT Controls

Learning Objectives

At the end of this section, students should be able to:

1. Identify and explain the overall objective for each category of general IT controls.
2. Explain and recognize access controls.
3. Explain and recognize change controls.
4. Explain and recognize operational controls.
5. Understand the need for and parts of a disaster recovery plan.
6. Recognize controls to protect privacy and confidentiality of information.
7. Explain what encryption is and how it is used in accounting systems.

General IT controls are designed to ensure that access to the entire computer system and data is authorized, that the IT infrastructure is physically protected, and that all computer systems and data are available when needed. These controls are referred to as general IT controls because they are not application specific. Security measures are a special type of general control and are intended to protect physical assets and data. In this section we discuss three categories of general IT controls: access security, change, and operational controls.

Access Security Controls

Access controls are concerned with the possible loss or unauthorized access to an organization's data. The likelihood of these threats posing a problem is often increased when a company's computers are networked. Data access and protection security measures include domains and access control lists, passwords, lockout procedures, callback procedures, firewalls, virtual private networks, encryption, virus and other malware protection, phishing protection, and intrusion detection. The overall goal is for the systems to keep doing what they are supposed to be doing and prevent access where not allowed. Access controls are virtual and physical.

access controls
General IT control that ensures only those authorized can access the data.

network domain

Collection of network resources of the organization.

access control lists (ACL)

A list of user accounts who have access to an organization's network domain resources.

To control access to a computer network's data and resources in an organization, a system administrator is normally placed in charge of creating a **network domain** and **access control lists (ACL)**. A domain is essentially a collection of network resources that certain users are allowed to access. To allow access to the domain, the system administrator creates a list of user accounts. These user accounts allow respective users to log into the network domain and access its resources. Since a company may have multiple servers and multiple domains, a network administrator may then have to create multiple access control lists. These lists define which network resources a user can access.

For example, in a company that has two domains—one for the accounting system and one for the rest of operations—an administrative employee with a user account will probably be granted access to the operations domain and its servers and, hence, be given such privileges on the operations domain access control list. That same employee will probably not be given access to the accounting system domain and its servers. That same employee will also not likely have access to servers maintained by the human resources department. Even employees in accounting who have access privileges for both the operations and accounting domains will probably be restricted by an ACL from accessing any of the payroll files. As you can imagine, it is essential that the administrators of a computer system understand how to manage the access privileges or there will be serious control problems.

contra-security behavior

Behavior that defeats the purpose of a good security practice (e.g., posting password on the computer monitor).

In addition to user accounts, computer network users need to have passwords. Passwords are needed to log into a network domain and to access particular servers, files, and printers. Employees should be instructed to select passwords that are not easily guessed. Common words such as love, sex, and god are examples of common passwords that can be easily guessed. A password like ilny1984 which stands for "I love New York" and someone's birth year would be much harder to guess. Passwords that use a combination of letters, numbers, and symbols are referred to as strong passwords. Passwords should also be changed on a regular basis. Never paste your password to your monitor with sticky notes for others to see. Such actions are referred to as **contra-security behavior**.

lockout procedure

Access control security measure that locks you out of the system after a certain number of failed attempts at a password.

A **lockout procedure** is a security measure that allows a certain number of tries at a password and then the system shuts off. For example, bank ATM machine normally allow you to try your password three times and then it "eats" (doesn't return) your card.

callback procedures

Access control security measure that allows you to log in, but then shuts off the connection and calls you back at the authorized location.

Callback procedures allow users to log in to a system, and then they shut off the connection and call the user back at their authorized location. This is used to minimize the effect of stolen passwords. Therefore, if someone has stolen a password and attempts to log into a system protected by callback, the system will disconnect and return the call to the authorized location where the hacker is assumed not to be (theoretically). Callback procedures are commonly used by companies for people who have authorization to electronically transfer (EFT) large sums of money by phone.

firewalls

Used to filter data packets from the internet and drop data packets coming from unauthorized network servers.

data packets

Small amount of data sent over the network that includes the data itself, source, and destination.

Firewalls are used to filter incoming data packets from the internet. They are often installed between an internet router and the organization's internal network to protect it from unauthorized network traffic. Firewalls can be configured to drop **data packets** from sources that are not authorized to access certain servers within a company's network. Network administrators, who are normally in charge of a company's firewall, may then configure the firewall to allow connections to certain servers, such as a website server, etc.

Many organizations have employees who travel or work from home, and the organization needs to give these employees access to files and the network in a secure manner. **Virtual private networks (VPN)** allow employees to have a secure connection over the internet to access the organization's network and files.

virtual private networks (VPN)

Access control that provides a secure connection over the internet to access the organization's files.

Encryption is a process of encoding information in such a way that unauthorized individuals who might gain access to it cannot read it. It uses an algorithm to scramble the data using an encryption key. Authorized individuals must then use the de-encryption key to see the original information. There are two types of encryption: symmetric and asymmetric. **Symmetric encryption** uses the same key to encrypt and decrypt the data. **Asymmetric encryption** uses two keys: one is public to encrypt the information, and the other key is private to decrypt the data.

encryption

Process of encoding information by using an algorithm to scramble the data so unauthorized individuals cannot read it.

symmetric encryption

Type of encryption that uses one encryption key to encrypt and decrypt the data.

asymmetric encryption

Type of encryption that uses one public key to encrypt the data and one private key to decrypt the data.

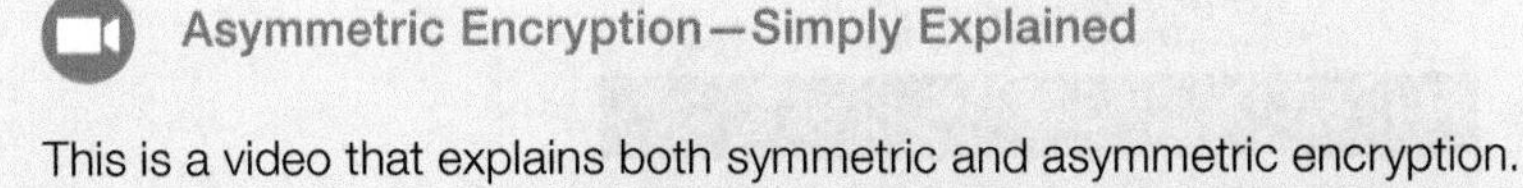

This is a video that explains both symmetric and asymmetric encryption.

View in the online reader

Encryption can be helpful in protecting confidential data from the eyes of hackers who find a way to circumvent a firewall or other security measures. Sensitive and confidential information (e.g., employee social security numbers) should always be encrypted.

Malware protection is software that prevents malicious code (sometimes called a virus) from infecting your computers. This will prevent hackers from stealing your data or taking control of your data. Anti-malware software can even prevent **phishing attacks** and can warn you before you click on a link that is deemed malicious. Phishing attacks can lead to a serious problem for businesses in the form of **ransomware**, which can lock out all employees from the system and become very expensive to gain access back to the data.

malware

Software that prevents malicious code from infecting your computer.

phishing attacks

Fraudulent act to obtain data through disguise (e.g., clicking on a link in an email that appears trustworthy, but it is not).

ransomware

Malware that locks you out of the system and requires you to pay a ransom in order for your data to be unlocked.

 Ransomware–Cybersecurity for Small Business

This is a video that explains ransomware and how businesses can protect themselves.

View in the online reader

intrusion detection software (IDS)

Software that monitors and analyzes the data on the network for suspicious activity.

biometric identification

Security measure that can identify your unique physical characteristic e.g., fingerprint.

In addition to anti-malware software, organizations can virtually monitor their networks by using **intrusion detection software (IDS)**. An IDS can monitor and analyze the data on the network and send alerts of suspicious activity to the information security professionals.

Access controls also include preventing physical damage to any computer facilities. Physical damage can occur as result of human actions or unfortunate events such as natural disasters and accidents. The controls to minimize physical damage include a secure area, biometric identification, smoke detectors and fire retardants, file libraries, disaster recovery plans, and alternate processing facilities. An organization can restrict who has access to its servers and other essential physical elements by setting up a secure area where critical servers are stored. This can be accomplished through something as simple as a locked door or as complicated as building a data center underground. Appropriate personnel can gain access to the secured area though the use of a key card or secure pin code. Should an organization require a greater degree of security for their critical hardware and have the necessary funds, it can acquire lock systems that require biometric identification to gain access. **Biometric identification** is a type of security measure that can identify unique physical characteristics such as fingerprints, voice patterns, and retina prints.

Facilities containing essential IT hardware should be equipped with smoke detectors and fire retardants. Smoke detectors should be checked regularly to ensure that they will function in the event of an actual emergency. These areas should also be equipped with one of a variety of fire retardants. Fire retardants include sprinklers and halon gas. Halon gas works by sucking the oxygen out of a room and is more expensive than installing a traditional sprinkler system. That being said, sprinkler systems that use water can damage servers or other sensitive electronics stored in a secured area, rendering the infrastructure they are intended to protect useless. Therefore, organizations should carefully examine the costs and benefits to both options before deciding which fire prevention measure to install.

Change Controls

The overall goal of management **change controls** is to avoid changes that could break the system or prevent changes with unintended consequences. All changes to program codes or data conversions must be tested and validated prior to placing in the production environment. Programmers should never be allowed to work on the computer code in the production environment. In general, the new code is developed, tested, and documented in a test environment. Direct changes of code in a stable environment create risks of deleting application controls already in place. Changes need to be authorized and documented. For example, if depreciation expense calculation is changed from straight line to an accelerated depreciation method, this change needs to be authorized, tested, and documented. In addition, when organizations upgrade their software or transition to new software (patch management), management change controls are needed to validate data conversion.

change controls

General IT control relating to management control focused on preventing breaks of a system from program codes or data conversions.

IT Auditing and Change Management, Part 4

This is a video that explains why change controls are important.

View in the online reader

Patch management is when most software vendors continue to update their applications and fix bugs by issuing a "patch" to fix the software. Not installing a patch to fix vulnerabilities in the software on a timely basis leaves an organization open to hackers. This was the case with the Equifax breach that happened in 2017.[6] In addition, patches need to be tested before rolled out into the production environment.

patch management

Update to fix software bugs.

Operational Controls

Operational controls are focused on keeping the systems operational and available to users with minimum downtime. Controls include system backups, physical data center controls, disaster recovery, and system monitoring and troubleshooting.

operational controls

General IT control that is focused on keeping information systems operational to users with minimum downtime.

Machine-readable file media should be backed up routinely, and the backup copies should be stored in a secure, off-site location in case of fire or theft. Backed-up files should also be recovered on a test basis periodically to ensure that the recovery process is sound and that the backups are functional. Checking to make sure your data files are properly backed up and can be recovered without any corrupt files will save time and money that would otherwise have to be spent recreating the lost data.

colocation

Third party data center provider who hosts your server.

disaster recovery plan

Comprehensive plan that outlines the procedures and actions needed to ensure continuity of operations after a disaster event.

Using a data center to host an organization's servers is called **colocation**. The benefit of server colocation is better security and faster speeds to process transactions over the internet. These data centers would have physical and virtual security to protect the servers and are often certified under ISO 27001, which is a global information security standard.

Every organization should have a written **disaster recovery plan** that is stored at a safe, off-site location. Disaster recovery plans are comprehensive outlines of the actions that should be taken before, during, and after a disaster, such as an earthquake, fire, or terrorist attack. Plans should contain clearly described, tested procedures to ensure the continuity of operations. Such a plan should be proactive and be clearly defined before a disaster takes place to ensure a smooth transition and to minimize the damage and confusion associated with such a disaster. A disaster recovery plan should include an alternate processing facility, a list of critical applications, backup and recovery procedures, a disaster recovery team, and tests to ensure that the plan will work when needed. A disaster recovery team should also be appointed with specific assignments.

Alternative processing facilities serve as a backup in the event of a catastrophic occurrence or service outage. The options available include a reciprocal arrangement, an empty shell, an internally provided backup, or a recovery operations center. The choice will often depend on an organization's estimate of how long they can operate without their information system versus the cost of the processing alternative. For some companies, such as those engaged in e-commerce, they would not be able to function without their information system.

reciprocal arrangement

Option of disaster recovery plan that allows two or entities to partner and share a facility to resume operations.

empty shell

Option of disaster recovery plan that allows a company to have a space to set up their hardware and software to resume operations.

recovery operations center

Option of disaster recovery plan that is a fully equipped space for an organization to resume operations.

access logs

Records the user activity on the system.

Reciprocal arrangement: A reciprocal arrangement is a partnership of two or more entities to share their facilities in case one or the other partner is in need. This option is generally considered to be the least costly but limited and having a potentially high risk. The success of this type of arrangement depends on the other organization having excess processing capacity when it is needed and will not work if both organizations are significantly affected at the same time.

Empty shell: An empty shell is a "cold" site that a company purchases and holds in reserve or leases in the event it is needed. The site would normally be internet-access ready but still have to be equipped with the necessary hardware and software for the company to resume operations. An organization can acquire the equipment and software themselves or contract with an outside vendor to do it within some agreed-upon time period. Backup data would then need to be restored.

Recovery operations center: A recovery operations center is a fully equipped, highly secure backup center that is shared by several companies. These service providers usually offer a range of services to clients who pay an annual fee for access rights. The services are normally available in a short period unless a widespread disaster affects several of the recovery operations center's customers at the same time.

Not only should organizational data be backed up on a regular basis, system monitoring should also occur on a regular basis. **Access logs** are a form of systems monitoring and are used on systems to keep a record of user activity by password, user account, and IP address accessing the account. Such logs can be used to investigate problems after the fact or be monitored in real-time to detect certain patterns that warrant investigation.

10.4 How Do IT Auditors Work with Financial Auditors?

Learning Objectives

At the end of this section, students should be able to:

1. Understand how IT auditors work with financial statement auditors.
2. Understand information provided by entity and the risks involved when clients use that information.
3. Explain the three types of information provided by entity report testing and validation.

Students graduating with an accounting degree have many career opportunities. Many students begin their careers as auditors, which can mean they work for a public accounting firm that does external financial audits, work for a company and become an internal auditor, or work for the government as an auditor. When a public accounting firm conducts an external audit of its client's financial statements, it would also have specialized IT auditors that will test the client's systems and controls that are underlying to the financial statements. Why is this important? Because the financial statement auditors need to rely on the fact that the systems and data used to generate the financial statements are reliable. In addition, all publicly held companies require auditors to have an opinion on internal controls. To do this, the audit team will have IT audit experts test reporting controls and IT security controls, whereas the financial statement auditors test the accounting controls.

Report Testing and Validation

A majority of an IT auditor's work, in conjunction with a financial statement audit, will be report testing and validation in three areas: report logic, report parameters, and source data. Auditors use the term "**IPE**" which stands for "information produced (or prepared) by the entity" (which is the audit client) and covers report logic, report parameters, and source data. IT auditors will test the IPE for accuracy and completeness because using IPE carries several risks:

IPE
Information produced by the entity.

- IPE report did not include all the data.
- IPE report has sorting or formula errors.
- IPE report has incorrect filters (parameters).

These risks require the IT auditor to directly test the data as well as the controls over the data used in the IPE.

Report logic is considered the formula or algorithm to extract the data from the AIS and may come from standardized reports from the accounting system or from customized report writers used to extract from the AIS. It can also include manually prepared reports using a spreadsheet, or a combination of the two, such as data download from the AIS exported to a spreadsheet. The IT auditor would want to know if the report is a standardized report coming from the system or if it is post-processed using a spreadsheet or a custom report writer. For example, if a spreadsheet is relied upon to produce the depreciation expense journal entry, the IT auditor will check the formulas in the spreadsheet.

report logic
The formula or algorithm used to extract the data from the AIS.

report parameters
Used to filter the data when extracting data from the AIS (e.g., date).

Report parameters work similar to a filter where the report user can filter out unwanted information and only keep the information that is important to them. A common filter often used is a date range filter. A standardized report from the AIS might have a date parameter. As we found in Chapter 3, data analytics requires prepping the data, which may also include joining two separate data sources together. To rely on a report that is generated using a data join, this would also need to be validated.

source data
Identifies where the data from a report is stored.

Source data basically answer, "Where do the data from the report reside?" If they are in an ERP system, the underlying infrastructure is a relational database. The important consideration for the source data for a report is that it is accurate and complete. For example, if we are testing the validity of a payroll report, the risk is that terminated employees are receiving paychecks. The IT auditor would look at the report logic of the terminated employee report from the human resources module in the ERP system. The report parameter would have a criterion of only employees determined after a certain date, and the source data would be tested for accuracy and completeness from the HR database.

Working Together Example—Purchasing

Both the financial statement auditor and the IT auditor will work together to understand risk. The financial statement auditor is concerned with any material risk in the purchasing function that involves purchasing inventory/supplies and payment to vendors. The financial statement auditors will rely on the segregation of duties' internal control as a key control so that the authorization, custody, and recording functions of purchasing are reliable.

The IT auditor will help the financial auditors in identifying the correct information systems to test relating to the purchasing function. The IT auditor would perform application controls and general IT controls, such as user security, data access, and maintenance security. The IT auditor will also help the financial auditors with testing how the system enforces segregation of duties for the purchasing function. If no significant issues are discovered, it allows the financial auditors to use the system and rely on the outputs generated by the system for their financial auditing procedures. If the financial auditors are able to rely on the IT controls, it reduces the amount of testing that they would need to do. Thus, the IT auditors are a support function of the financial auditor to help address risk.

Key Takeaways

In this chapter we learned why we need IT controls and IT control frameworks. As accountants, we also learned about the importance of application controls and general IT controls and how testing of these controls helps the financial statement auditors. While this is only one chapter to provide basic awareness to an accounting student, many accounting or management information systems departments at your school may have an entire course devoted to IT auditing. In addition, you can become certified in this specialty area. To learn more, go to www.isaca.org.

10.5 End-of-Chapter Exercises

Exercises

1. What is a computer security audit?
2. How might a computer security audit be performed?
3. What type of controls are tested in a computer security audit?
4. What is the main difference between application and general IT security controls?
5. What are the three types of application controls? Provide an example.
6. What is phishing, and why is it a threat?
7. What is a ransomware, and why is it harmful to businesses?
8. Why is encryption used in accounting?
9. Why is change control important for a business?
10. What is patch management?
11. What is a disaster recovery plan? Are they necessary? What should be included in the plan?
12. What are the three different types of options an organization can choose from in a disaster recovery plan?
13. Which of the following would reduce the likelihood of someone receiving an expense check for $65,000 more than he was entitled to?
    a. validity check
    b. consistency check
    c. check digit
    d. limit check
14. Which of the following batch processing controls would minimize the likelihood of someone transposing an expense account number in a cash disbursement run?
    a. record count
    b. hash total
    c. control total
    d. All of the above
15. One of the categories of general controls is project development. Which of the following is not an example of a project development process?
    a. long-range plans
    b. system performance measurements
    c. disaster recovery
    d. post-implementation review
16. Which type of batch total should only use nonfinancial information?
    a. hash total
    b. control total
    c. All of the above
    d. None of the above
17. All except which of the following are controls that can be used to prevent damage to computer facilities?
    a. secured area
    b. fire retardants

biometric identification

d. reciprocal arrangement

18. Which of the following best describes what would be classified as a computer virus?
    a. a program that inflicts some form of damage on a computer
    b. a hidden list of instructions on a computer that do not execute and cause damage to a computer until triggered
    c. a list of instructions to a computer that can replicate itself and attach to another program
    d. a computer program that can monitor users' actions on a computer and steal their personal data
19. Which of the following approaches to alternate processing facilities would generally present the least risk to a company?
    a. reciprocal arrangement
    b. empty shell
    c. internally provided backup
    d. recovery operations center
20. Physical access and protection is a subdivision of which of the following categories of control?
    a. application control
    b. processing control
    c. implementation control
    d. general control
21. Indicate one or more application or general controls that could effectively reduce the likelihood of each of the following errors or irregularities:
    a. The due date of an upcoming vendor payment was entered as 2001 instead of 2010.
    b. The due date of an upcoming vendor payment was inadvertently omitted from the payment input.
    c. The accounts payable clerk sent 52 check requisitions to the computer center for processing. For some reason, only 51 were processed.
    d. A high school student was able to log in to the school's computer remotely and change his grade from F to A in bookkeeping after discovering the password, which had been written on a note on the secretary's desk just outside the principal's office.
    e. An employee coded an expense on their travel reimbursement form to department 3262. There is no department 3262.
    f. A payroll employee inadvertently entered the letter O for zero deductions in a new employee's input form to set up the new employee's payroll tax withholding information.
22. Sony, Inc., better known for its outstanding "best-in-class" TV picture tube technology and its PlayStation gaming console, is also known for creating a now infamous copy protection scheme on 22 million CDs between 2005 and 2007 from its BMG music division, a scheme that turned into a public scandal. Sony, intent on protecting its copyrighted music CDs from being copied, decided to include a program on its music CDs that when read by a computer would install a program that would modify the operating system and allow it to run undetected. The malware computer program, now called a "rootkit," allowed Sony to monitor the music copying habits of its customers and to send this data to the company anonymously without the customers knowing about it. Thanks to Sony, and despite the class action suit against the company and its abandonment of copy protection, hackers have copied its "rootkit" scheme and now use them to hide key loggers and many other types of malware on unsuspecting computers.

    According to Bloomberg News, at 12:25 a.m. on December 2, 2014, using the high-speed network at the St. Regis Hotel in Bangkok, from either a guest room or lobby, hackers began leaking confidential Sony data to the internet. By the time it was over, private details of 47,000 Sony employees as well as Hollywood stars, including their salaries, addresses, phone numbers (including Brad Pitt's), emails (including some from producers that discussed why they canceled the planned movie about Steve Jobs and one saying that Angelina Jolie was a minimally talented spoiled brat), and social security numbers, were leaked to the world. Rather than trying to steal money or somehow profit from their action, the hack seemed to focus on making Sony employees' lives difficult. For example, in addition to leaking embarrassing private information, the hackers also sent threatening emails to Sony employees and their families. Although the company had not made an official announcement, some cybersecurity experts believe that the hack had something to do with (perhaps retaliation for) Sony's pending release of a movie called *The Interview*, a comedy starring Seth Rogen and James Franco (the stars of *Pineapple Express*). *The Interview*'s plot involves an attempted assassination of North Korean leader Kim Jong Un. According to The Verge (dot com), "North Korean officials had denounced the film as an act of war." Although the exact method of the attack is yet unknown, The Verge speculates that it had something to do with recent phishing attacks and a recent attack on the PlayStation network that contained enough passwords to give the hackers full access to the network servers. Once the hackers took over, the entire corporate system locked up,[7] showing a red skeleton that bluntly announced, "You've been hacked by #GOP." Hard drives were wiped, email accounts were frozen, and employees were cautioned not to connect to the office Wi-Fi.

Required

a. What do you think was the cause(s) of the Sony hack?

b. Is a rootkit a virus (as they are often reported by the press)? If not, what are they?

c. Is there a way to protect computers against rootkits?

d. How do you think the hack was traced back to Bangkok? (Use the internet to research it.)

e. Is it possible to fake your IP address? (Use the internet to research it.)

f. Is it possible to protect an accounting system that is connected to the internet from damage?

g. Do you think it was smart for Sony to make a movie about the assassination of a foreign leader?

h. Are there any solutions you would recommend to protect Sony and other companies from similar attacks?

23. Equifax is one of the three largest credit rating bureaus, along with Experian and Transunion, in the United States. These are the guys who collect our personal information from banks and credit card companies and then turn around and charge you, or anyone else who wants access, for the credit rating that they have created for you. Equifax has been a very profitable company over the last decade, and its stock has appreciated more than 500 percent until recently.

In March of 2017, Nike Zheng, a Chinese developer and noted hacker,[8] discovered a vulnerability in the Apache Struts software that works with Apache's widely used web server. Apache Struts is an open-source development tool for creating JAVA web applications. It is widely used by many Fortune 100 companies and the IRS.[9] It uses a plug-in software architecture that supports both REST, AJAX, and JSON. Zheng apparently posted to an international information database that a vulnerability in the REST plug-in existed after he discovered it. The Apache Software Foundation, the organization that acts as custodian for the Struts software, noted the posted vulnerability and released a security patch to fix it within one day. For some reason, Equifax did not apply the patch that Apache had created. In this day and age, one would think that either Apache would notify anyone using their software of the vulnerability and the need to update or that Equifax would continuously monitor sites that contain the latest databases or posts of such potential threats.

Hackers, on the other hand, apparently scan the internet regularly to discover the latest security threats (often referred to as zero-day vulnerabilities) and then use hacker tools to scan the internet to find websites that have not been properly patched. In this instance, hackers found that Equifax was vulnerable and exploited the unpatched weakness to enter the Equifax network and set up as many as thirty backdoors. The backdoors allowed the hackers to enter the system as though they were authorized users. The hackers then explored the Equifax hard drives and ultimately downloaded personal data, including names, birth dates, credit card accounts, credit ratings, and social security numbers for more than 143 million people.

Equifax supposedly did not detect the "suspicious" activity on their network until the end of July 2017 (3 months after the Apache Strut vulnerability was first disclosed). Equifax then began an internal investigation, which they say took all of August to complete before they announced the breach to the public and notified the FBI. The amount of time it took appears to be a matter of question since most well-run companies would have a network "blackbox" that would help them identify unauthorized traffic and even the internet addresses of those doing the hacking. In the meantime, several senior executives at Equifax sold millions of dollars of company common stock when it was at an historic high of roughly $150 per share. The stock subsequently declined by roughly 30 percent in the days following Equifax's disclosure of the breach.

Required

a. How did hackers penetrate Equifax's network?

b. What are the primary ethical issues in this case?

c. What are the internal control issues (other than ethics) that Equifax should address?

d. What steps should Equifax take now to fix the problems?

e. Should the government begin regulating the credit rating industry?

24. Using the internet, do a search on "hacked," "hacking," or "ransomware" for your local area. Has anything been in the news in the last 6 months or year? Summarize the problem, why it occurred (risk), and suggest how this problem could be prevented in the future.
25. What was the material in this chapter about and how does it relate to other chapters in this textbook?
26. How will understanding this subject material help you in the future?
27. Read the following excerpt and answer the questions below.

EXP Fundamentals Corp.

Alice Smith, assistant controller and the new chief technology officer at EXP FundamentalsCorp. met recently with Mark Ross of the Enterprise Risk Services division of Deloitte and Touche to discuss the potential impact of automating EXP Fundamentals' expenditure cycle. Alice explained that EXP Fundamentals was currently unable to track requisitions and open purchase orders, which often resulted in parts shortages and related employee complaints. Alice continued by telling Mark that she was also concerned about input integrity and the general threats that automating the company's manual system might create, including network security and the possibility of being hacked.

Mark replied, "You're right Alice. There is definitely a need to check the data for accuracy before it is processed because of the specific threats created by automating the system. We call these application controls because they are intended to ensure the accuracy of the specific applications input, processing, and output. In addition, when computers are utilized in processing, you will also need to have some general security measures to protect you from system-wide threats that could cause damage to the physical assets or make them unavailable as well as lead to the possibility of unauthorized access or loss of data."

Mark began by outlining a few application controls. Mark said, "To minimize any garbage in, you need to validate the vendor field to be sure that the vendor exists in your database before you input the data. This is called a validity check. You should also make sure that the data in each field are of the correct type. For example, if the field is numeric, you want to make sure that there are no letters or nonnumeric characters in the field. This is what we call a field check. It is also a good idea to test input to make sure amounts do not exceed predefined limits for such things as overtime hours and expense reimbursements. You should also make sure that all required fields have been filled in before you submit the input for processing."

Mark then continued, explaining general controls that would be needed to protect all of EXP Fundamentals' computer operations as well as the purchasing cycle. Mark said, "For starters, you will need to have password protection at all important access points. You should also maintain an access log so you know who has been accessing the system and when. In addition, the computers should be physically located in a safe place with appropriate fire protection, such as halon gas. It is also extremely important to have copies of important files backed up and stored off site. In this day and age, you also need to be aware of cybersecurity risks and how to mitigate them. Finally, you should develop a disaster recovery plan."

Alice thanked Mark for his suggestions and indicated that she felt much more confident now and wanted to continue her investigation of needed application and general controls as soon as possible.

Required

i. Why does the CTO of EXP in the case feel that the system needs to be changed? What appears to be the weakness(es)?

ii. a. What were the needs Alice identified?

b. What were the risks of meeting them?

c. What did Mark suggest EXP could do to address these risks?

iii. If she makes these changes, what new (a) specific threats and (b) general threats will the company face? Hint: Use the following headings to organize your answer:

Threat		
Category	Examples	How Controlled

Endnotes

1. ISACA, COBIT 2019 Framework: Introduction and Methodology (2019).
2. NIST Cybersecurity framework accessed via https://www.nist.gov/cyber-framework.
3. Tom Lauricella, "Market Plunge Baffles Wall Street—Trading Glitch Suspected in 'Mayhem' as Dow Falls Nearly 1,000, Then Bounces," *Wall Street Journal* (May 7, 2010): 1.
4. Stephen Grocer, "Six Mega Drops of the Flash Crash; Sam Adams Goes Flat," *Wall Street Journal* (May 6, 2010).
5. Caroline Vatekevitch and Charles Mikolajczak, "Error by Knight Capital Rips Through Stock Market," Reuters.com (August 1, 2012).
6. https://www.reuters.com/article/us-equifax-breach/equifax-failed-to-patch-security-vulnerability-in-march-former-ceo-idUSKCN1C71VY
7. http://www.theverge.com/2014/11/24/7277451/sony-pictures-paralyzed-by-massivesecurity-compromise
8. https://threatpost.com/attacks-heating-up-against-apache-struts-2-vulnerability/124183/ and https://www.theregister.co.uk/2017/03/09/apache_under_attack_patch_for_zero_day_availabl e/ and https://thehackernews.com/2017/09/apache-struts-flaws-cisco.html
9. https://thehackernews.com/2017/09/apache-struts-flaws-cisco.html

CHAPTER 11

Expenditure Cycle and Controls

The remaining five chapters of this book focus specifically on understanding risk as it relates to the transaction cycles and financial reporting. This chapter focuses on the expenditure cycle.

11.1 Overview of the Expenditure Cycle

Learning Objectives

At the end of this section, students should be able to:

1. Explain what an expenditure cycle is and identify its main functions.
2. Understand the objective of each expenditure cycle function.
3. Know the source documents generated and used for each expenditure cycle function.

The purpose of the expenditure cycle is to efficiently and effectively exchange cash with suppliers for needed goods and services. An organization's trading partners are called vendors or suppliers of these goods and services. The organization's goal is to minimize costs. As with most systems, the expenditure cycle is made up of parts that must work together to achieve the system objective. Overall control activities for the expenditure cycle are to minimize the risk of misappropriation of assets (e.g., cash, inventory) and financial statement fraud (e.g., understating expenses and liabilities).

Expenditure Cycle

This is a video that gives an overview of the expenditure cycle.

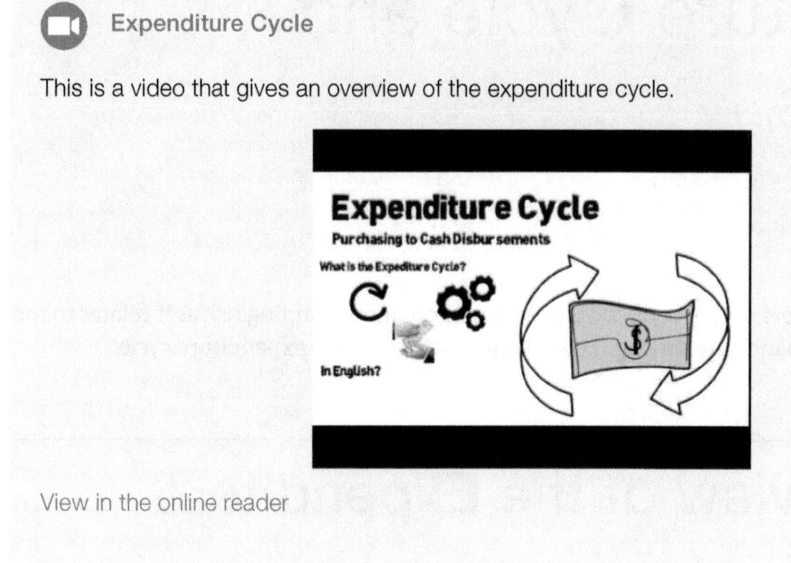

View in the online reader

Objective and Conceptualization

The following functions can be found in the expenditure cycle:

1. Requisitioning
2. Purchasing
3. Receiving
4. Accounts payable
5. Cash disbursements

requisitioning

Function within the expenditure cycle to ensure that needed goods are requested given available resources.

Requisitioning is an internal function that initiates the purchasing process. The objective of the requisitioning function within the expenditure cycle is to ensure that needed goods are requested, given available resources. It is usually preferable to have the person who needs the item to make the request formally to the appropriate manager for approval. This "request" for approval may be formal, requiring a signed document, or may be informal with an email to the manager. Most large organizations will formalize this function with a source document, whereas a smaller business may require the employee to ask the company owner for permission to make the purchase.

purchasing

Function within the expenditure cycle that authorizes the purchase of goods from a vendor by issuing a purchase order.

In **purchasing**, a company must ensure that needed goods are ordered and received in a timely basis. Purchasing is initiated within the organization with the trading partner (e.g., vendor) to purchase goods or services. A purchasing agent often handles this function when there is enough purchasing activity to justify the cost. A purchasing agent is responsible for keeping track of the purchasing activities and ensures that the company acquires the most appropriate quality of goods at the lowest price. At this stage in purchasing, the authorization to purchase goods and services is done.

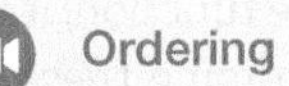

Ordering

This is a video explaining the function of ordering in the expenditure cycle.

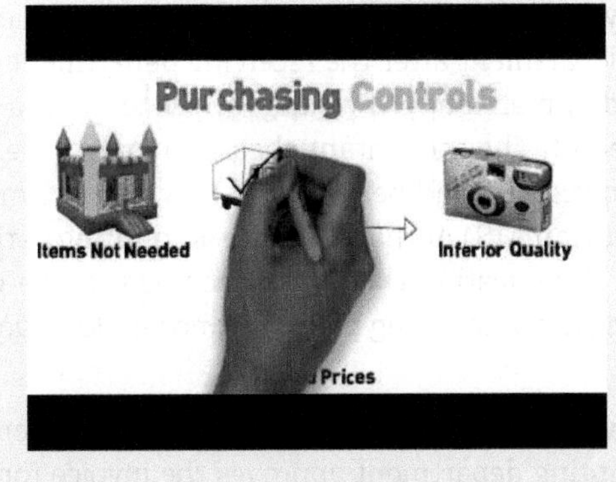

View in the online reader

Receiving is a subsystem within the expenditure cycle where goods should be properly identified and safeguarded. To accomplish this objective, competent and trustworthy people must receive the goods (i.e., take custody of the goods) in a reasonably secure area. The goal is to receive only what the organization ordered and ensure it is of good quality. Many errors can happen at this stage of the expenditure cycle, such as receiving the wrong item or receiving items of poor quality. Prior to receiving the goods from the vendors, the receiving clerks actually count and properly inspect the goods for possible damage or defects. Once the goods are received, the organization has an *obligation to pay* for those goods. (Hint: This is an event that now requires the organization to account for the event.) At this stage of the cycle, the custody of inventory and the inventory records should be updated.

receiving

Take custody of ordered goods.

Receiving

This is a video that explains the receiving function of the expenditure cycle.

View in the online reader

accounts payable

Administrative function that keeps track of who to pay, when to pay, and how much to pay them.

In **accounts payable (A/P)**, the objective is to keep track of who to pay, when to pay, and approving how much to pay your vendors. While this is purely an administrative function, it is one of the most important functions of the accounting department because performing these functions effectively is important in maintaining a company's cash flow and credit rating. It is important to note that this administrative function must make sure that the expenses from the vendor invoices are properly posted in the correct period. Most of the time, vendor invoices are received in the accounting department after the receiving department receives the goods. At this stage, the invoice is processed by matching the vendor invoice to either a copy of the purchase order or a copy of the receiving report. The accountant checks to make sure that the vendor invoice is also accurate and adds up correctly. (You'd be surprised how many companies create invoices in a Word document and do not use an AIS.) At the end of the accounting period, the accounting department needs to ensure that all obligation events are recorded in the general ledger, meaning if inventory was received during the accounting period but no vendor invoice was processed, then an accrual should be made.

cash disbursements

Function of the expenditure cycle that processes a check to pay a vendor.

For **cash disbursements**, the objective should be to pay the supplier the correct amount at the proper time. Once the accounting department approves the invoice for payment, payment to the vendor is processed (e.g., check written) and signed by the treasurer's office. If the organization is small and does not have a separate treasurer's office, then the business owner will sign the check. Delaying payments to a vendor can have a negative impact on an organization's credit. Here is a video that explains the function of approving the vendor invoice and cash disbursements of the expenditure cycle.

Supplier Invoice and Cash Disbursements

This is a video about the accounts payable and cash disbursement functions of the expenditure cycle.

View in the online reader

Source Documents of the Expenditure Cycle

source documents

Original records that substantiate the functions throughout the cycle.

Depending on the function of the expenditure cycle, source documents are original records that substantiate the functions throughout the cycle. **Source documents** can be generated within the organization or come from outside the organization and are used as evidence of key data for the expenditure transaction. Table 11.1 provides a list of source documents commonly used for each function of the expenditure cycle and designates the function as an internal or external activity.

The next series of figures show the source documents for a transaction that involves an employee requesting office furniture. In Figure 11.1, you will see the requisition of the office furniture and approval by the manager. The purchase requisition then goes to the purchasing department, and a purchase order is issued, which is shown in Figure 11.2. When the office furniture comes into receiving, Figure 11.3 shows you an example of the receiving report. The accounting department uses the A/P voucher (see Figure 11.4) to process the vendor invoice (see Figure 11.5) and input it into the AIS.

TABLE 11.1 Source Documents for Expenditure Cycle

Function	Source Document	Internal/External
Requisitioning	Purchase Requisition*	Internal
Purchasing	Purchase Order	Internal
Receiving	Receiving Report	Internal
Accounts Payable	Vendor Invoice	External
	A/P Voucher*	Internal
Cash Disbursements	Check	Internal
* Organizations may not require this source document		

Figure 11.1 is an example of the **purchase requisition**, which is generated internally by the employee who is asking permission from management to make a purchase. To keep track of these requests, the requisitions should be dated and prenumbered. Dating and prenumbering allow the purchase requisitions to be tracked and periodically accounted for so none go missing. In addition, the requisition must be approved prior to ordering the goods.

purchase requisition
A source document that needed goods are requested.

FIGURE 11.1 Example Purchase Requisition

Vandy-Dramen, Inc.
Purchase Requisition
No. 30931

Requested by Vicki Ross
Date Prepared 5/27/2020

Part No.	Quantity	Description
318	2	*Two-Drawer Lateral File Cabinet*
120	1	*Office Desk*

Approved by M. Dramen

The **purchase order** is generated from the approved purchase requisition in large organizations; smaller organizations may just begin the expenditure cycle with the purchase order. Figure 11.2 shows an example of a purchase order. This source document is internally and prenumbered to account for of all purchase orders. In addition, the purchase order is dated and the purchase authorized by management. The purchase order is considered a commitment to the vendor that if the goods are received as ordered, the organization will pay for them.

purchase order
A formal source document needed to formally request a purchase.

FIGURE 11.2 Example Purchase Order

Vandy-Dramen, Inc.
Purchase Order
No. 27159

To: Chad's Furniture
1234 Main Street
Las Vegas, NV 89194

Bill To: Vandy-Dramen, Inc.
1111 Central Street
San Diego, CA 92101

Ship To: Vandy-Dramen, Inc.
1111 Central Street
San Diego, CA 92101

Date Ordered 5/28/2020

Requisition No. 30931

Part No.	Qty	Description	Price	Ext Price
318	2	2-Draw Lateral File Cab	259.99	519.98
210	1	Office Desk	499.99	499.99
			Total	1019.97

Approved by H. Vandy

receiving report

A formal source document that records the goods received and their quality.

Figure 11.3 provides an example receiving report. The **receiving report** is an internal document that shows who received, counted, and checked the goods for quality. It's important to know that the receiving report should refer back to a purchase order that authorized the order. In addition, this source document is also prenumbered and dated. This source document would be accounted for at the end of an accounting period to determine what items received have vendor invoices processed and what items received need to be accrued because the vendor invoice has not arrived in the mail or been processed.

FIGURE 11.3 Example Receiving Report

Vandy-Dramen, Inc.
Purchase Order
No. 10061

Receiving Report

Vendor Chad's Furniture

PO No. 27159

Date Received 6/9/2020

Qty	Description
2	2-Draw Lat File
1	1 Office Desk

Counted by B. Taylor

Condition OK

The accounts payable function will process the **vendor invoices**, which are considered an external source document. Sometimes, if an organization has several transactions with the same vendor during the month, the accounting department may use a voucher, which is an internal source document. As you can imagine, keeping track of all this activity in a company can get very complicated. To enhance control over incoming invoices, some companies attach a payment voucher to incoming vendor invoices. A voucher is a prenumbered document that assigns numeric control to the vendor's invoice in accordance with your company's numbering system (as opposed to the vendor's). The voucher also has spaces for dates, accuracy checks, and approval-to-pay signature(s). While vouching invoices can provide a benefit, not all companies use them because they increase processing costs. Again, we see that the system decision boils down to a trade-off of costs and benefits. Figure 11.4 is an example of an accounts payable voucher used to process multiple invoices for the same vendor during an accounting period. Notice that the voucher shows the accounting period that the invoice will get posted to in the general ledger. Also note that the voucher has the debit side of the journal entry for the expense or asset general ledger accounts that will get posted with the total posting a credit to accounts payable. The **voucher** allows for flexibility in processing invoices because a vendor invoice may have more than one general ledger account that would be processed.

vendor invoices

Source document provided by the vendor for payment of goods and services rendered.

voucher

Source document used internally in the accounting department for processing vendor invoices.

FIGURE 11.4 Accounts Payable Voucher

Vandy-Dramen, Inc.

Voucher # 165 **Accounting Period: June 2020**

Vendor Name Chad's Furniture

Vendor # 2995

Invoice Date	Invoice #	G/L Amount	Amount
6/10/2020	572	2600	$1,019.97
6/25/2020	602	2600	$ 748.95
6/30/2020	613	2600	$ 579.99

Total A/P $2,348.91

Checked and Processed by L. Jones

FIGURE 11.5 Vendor Invoice

Chad's Furniture

Invoice # 572

Invoice Date 6/10/2020

Customer: Vandy-Dramen, Inc.
1111 Central Street
San Diego, CA 92101

Terms: net 30

Product #	Description	Qty	Price	Ext Price
318	2-Draw Lateral File Cab	2	259.99	519.98
120	Office Desk	1	499.99	499.99
			Total Due	1019.97

Notice that the invoice from Figure 11.5 would be matched up with the purchase order in Figure 11.2 and the receiving report in Figure 11.3 to ensure accuracy of what was ordered, what was actually received, and the amount invoiced.

Finally, for the cash disbursements function, the check is the source document generated by the organization to pay the vendor. Figure 11.6 shows the processes and documents that flow into the receiving department assuming the use of basic accounting technology and procedures, and Figure 11.7 provides a basic flowchart of the processes and documents involved in accounts payable and cash disbursements and how they might be separated.

FIGURE 11.6 Flowcharting Example of Purchasing and Receiving

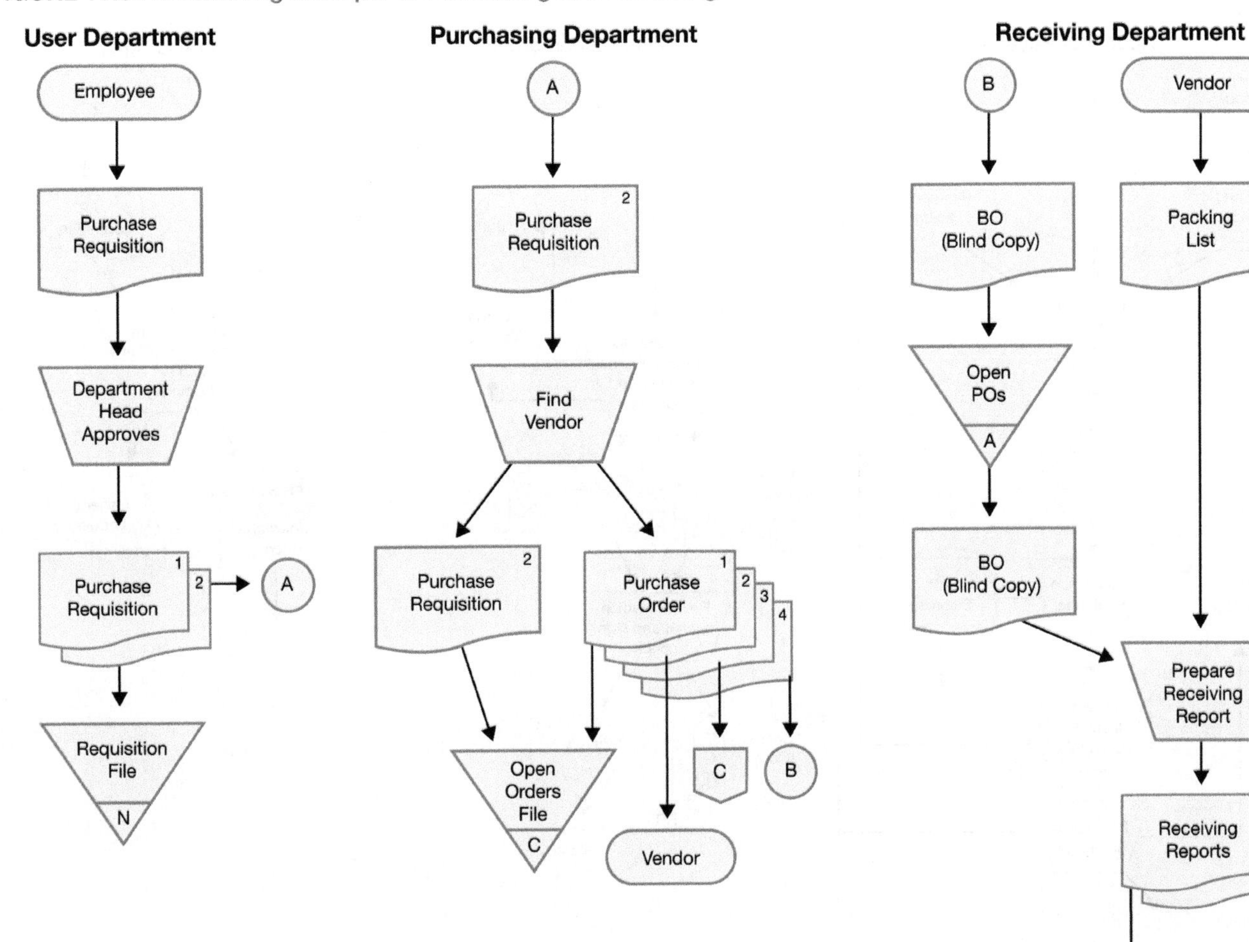

FIGURE 11.7 Flowchart Example of Accounts Payable and Cash Disbursements

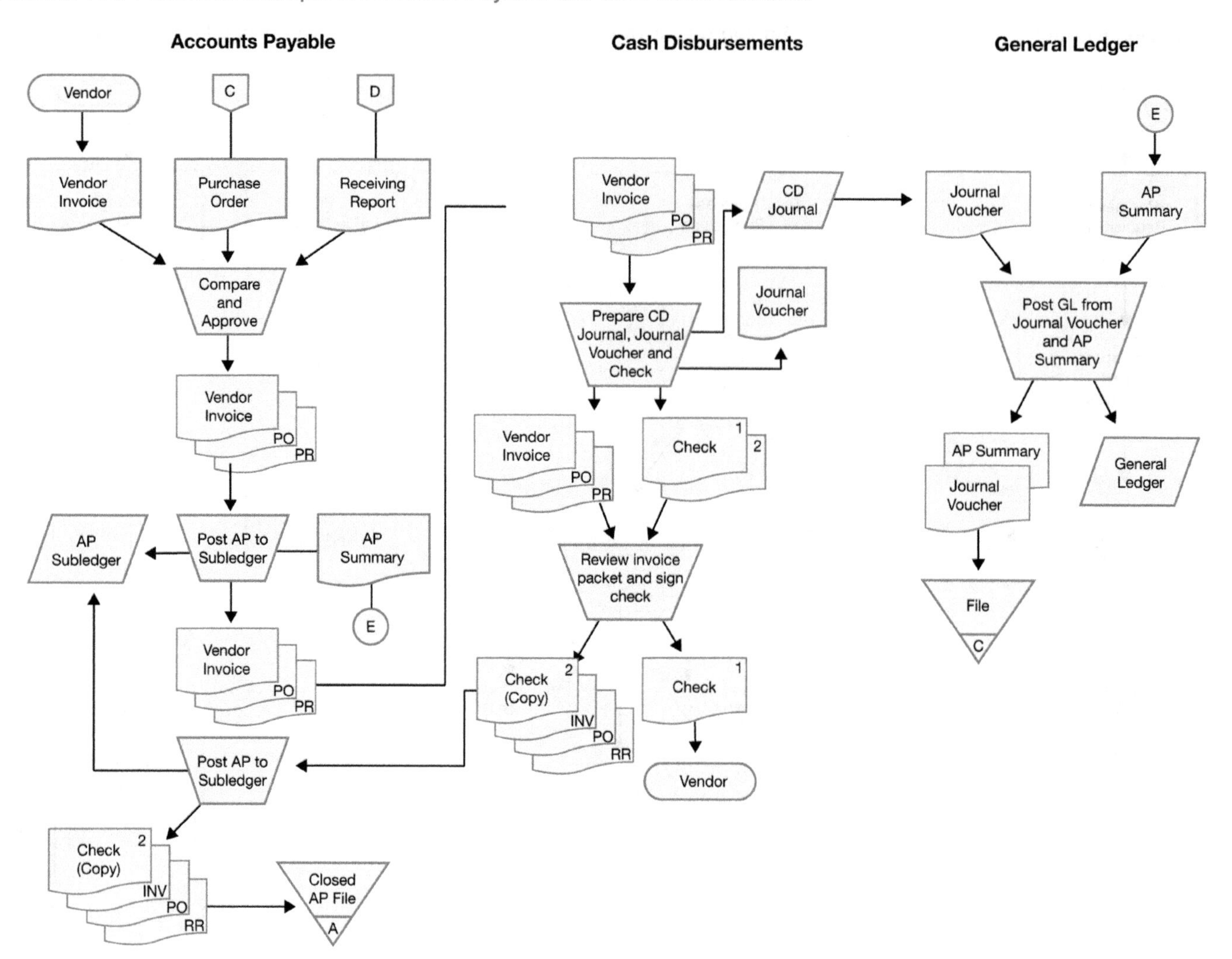

11.2 Risks and Controls

Learning Objectives

At the end of this section, students should be able to:

1. Identify the risks that may be present in each of the functions.
2. Describe the control activities associated with each function and how they ensure their operating effectiveness.
3. Evaluate how well an expenditure cycle is performing.

The next sections of this chapter specifically address the risks and control activities for each function of the expenditure cycle. Overall, possible risks to financial statements for the expenditure cycle include paying for goods not ordered, paying for goods not received, paying for damaged or poor-quality goods, overpaying for goods, not posting transactions in the proper accounting period, or misstating the transaction into the wrong general ledger account.

Requisitioning and Purchasing

As stated previously, the objective of requisitioning and purchasing is to ensure that needed goods are ordered and received on a timely basis and minimizing costs. To meet its purchasing objective, a company must have the right combination of people, technologies, and controls. For example, purchasing agents really need to know the markets they are dealing with and cannot be distracted by conflicts of interest. Effective and efficient purchasing requires a lot of research.

Risks associated with the requisitioning and purchasing function include the following:

- Purchasing items that are not needed
- Purchasing items that have high prices
- Purchasing items of poor quality
- Purchasing from unauthorized suppliers
- Kickbacks

Purchasing agents use the purchase order to keep track of goods ordered; purchase orders must have the appropriate authorization. By having the authorization from a manager who will be held accountable, the risk of purchasing unneeded items is reduced. For example, if anyone could go and order office supplies whenever they wanted without management authorization, you would probably see some employees with every color of pen and unnecessary office supply gadget possible. Having proper authorization for a purchase order prevents the risk of purchasing unneeded items. Outstanding purchase orders should be tracked and vendors contacted to expedite any orders that are not received on a timely basis.

To prevent purchasing items at inflated prices or items of poor quality, vendors should be approved, and purchasing agents should use only vendors on the approved vendor list. An approved vendor list has suppliers and service providers who have met certain criteria for attributes such as quality, delivery, ethics, and price. For example, in this day and age, companies must protect themselves from accepting a low bid only to find out that the vendor's products are of poor quality or made in unsafe or forced working conditions. In addition, using an approved vendor list prevents purchasing items from unauthorized suppliers or suppliers who have not been vetted by the organization.

A company can also improve the efficiency of its purchasing by requesting competitive bids or request price quotes (**RFQ**s) directly from multiple vendors. This can help reduce the cost of items purchased, but it can raise the cost of processing the transaction. In attempting to obtain the lowest prices, however, companies risk purchasing inferior-quality goods. From experience and research, buyers can learn which vendors provide the best-quality goods for the lowest prices. This kind of information should be considered when an enterprise establishes its approved vendor list.

RFQ
Request for quotation.

Electronic Data Interchange (EDI) arrangements can also lower purchasing costs and help ensure that goods are received on time. Under such arrangements, purchasing agents may be replaced by software that tracks quantities on hand and inventory reorder points and sends electronic purchase orders to suppliers via some type of network. The decisions about whether or not to establish such partnerships and choosing the most appropriate technology option in the circumstances can be very complicated. Hence, effective system thinking must be utilized to achieve the best trade-off.

In addition, purchasing agents should not be tempted by sales people offering gifts or other matters of personal interest, such as doing business with friends or relatives. Such behavior may be permissible when you own your own business, but it is generally not acceptable when you work for someone else. To control these types of distractions, a company should have a code of ethics that provides guidelines on how to handle these matters properly. In certain cases, requiring employees to disclose potential conflicts (preferably on a form) may be sufficient and prevent the risk of kickbacks. These reports would then be reviewed by an ethics officer or committee and either be allowed, limited, or prohibited.

Receiving

The importance of the receiving function cannot be stressed enough; risks associated with this function include the following:

- Receiving unordered items
- Receiving items of poor quality
- Mistakes in inventory
- Theft of inventory

To prevent receiving unordered items, the receiving clerk should have an approved purchase order prior to receiving the items. The receiving clerks actually count and properly inspect the goods for possible damage or defects to prevent mistakes in counting or receiving poor quality items. In addition, companies blank out the quantity field of a purchase order that may be sent to receiving to ensure that receiving clerks do not just copy the quantity during busy times when incoming receipts are backed up. Many organizations have updated the inventory process by using bar-codes to scan the items coming into the warehouse, which reduces mistakes in counting and provides for more accurate inventory.

To reduce the risk of inventory theft, organizations should restrict physical access to the warehouse (and receiving of inventory to the warehouse). This includes having a lock on the warehouse door and allowing only authorized personnel to access areas of the warehouse. All transfers of inventory should be documented. Organizations periodically take inventory counts and reconcile that information to the inventory records in the AIS.

It is also important for the receiving clerks to keep track of their work. To track their work effectively, receiving clerks should prepare some type of prenumbered receiving report. A receiving report may be a source document or an entry on a computer as a result of scanning a bar code. The report should be dated and signed by the responsible employee with accounting getting a copy of the receiving report. The prenumbering is important because it is used to establish the month-end accounts payable cutoff to properly accrue for the liability (obligation).

Accounts Payable

Risks during this stage of the cycle include the following:

- Vendor invoice errors
- Accounts payable posting errors

Even for companies that do not use vouchers, a number of verification procedures must be performed before an obligation should be recognized. One of the first of such verifications is to make sure that the goods were actually ordered and authorized. Comparing the vendor invoice to the company's purchase order can accomplish this.

If the goods were in fact ordered and authorized, you must make sure that everything billed was actually received. This can be done by comparing the quantities as per the vendor invoice to the quantities received as per your receiving report (assuming you prepared an accurate receiving report, of course). Therefore, the vendor invoice is matched to the purchase order and the receiving report. Next, the mathematical calculations on the invoice should be checked (based on some reasonableness policy). Many AIS systems actually check automatically. Finally, the person who will ultimately use the goods should approve the invoice for payment. If that person is not satisfied with the received goods, the accounts payable clerk should be contacted, who will contact the purchasing agent and ultimately the vendor to resolve the problem.

To minimize the risk of posting errors, the accountant processing the vendor invoice needs to look at the date the items were received and not the date of the invoice itself, since invoices generally arrive after items are received into the warehouse. For example, if goods are received into the warehouse on June 29, 2020, and the vendor invoice is dated July 3, 2020, what accounting period (month) will inventory and accounts payable be posted in the general ledger, June or July?

The answer is the inventory and the accounts payable amounts are posted to the June 2020 accounting period to properly account for inventory received and the obligation to pay. At the end of each accounting period, a reconciliation of amounts between the accounts payable subledger and the accounts payable balance in the general ledger should occur.

Cash Disbursements

Risks during this stage include the following:

- Paying for items not received
- Paying the same invoice twice
- Theft of cash
- Cash flow problems

Before signing a check, the authorized check signer should review the supporting documentation (purchase order, receiving report, and vendor invoice) to make sure that the invoice has been approved for payment. This prevents the risk of paying a "fake invoice" for items not received. The supporting documentation would include the purchase order, receiving report, and vendor invoice matched and checked by accounting and proper vendor invoice approval. The check should then be mailed under the control of the check signer and not be physically delivered to anyone in the accounting department. After the check is signed, the invoice and all supporting documentation should be canceled as "paid" to prevent paying the same invoice twice. Organizations should only process original invoices and not copies because this helps prevent duplicate payments on the same invoice.

The question of who handles the responsibility of cash disbursements can be a significant control issue in many companies. Because this stage involves custody of cash, the person who signs the checks should not be able to authorize or perform any accounting functions concerning these transactions. This separation of incompatible duties can be significant in reducing the incidence of unintentional errors or embezzlements. The general rule on segregation of duties states that "no one person should be able to authorize, account for, and handle the assets relating to a single transaction." When one person can handle two or more of these transaction responsibilities, the possibility of error or fraud increases. In small companies, this can be a significant problem because there are simply not enough people to separate the incompatible duties. While this may appear to create a control nightmare, the risks involved with concentrating duties can be minimized by direct supervision from the business owner.

Check signers should normally come from the Treasurer's Department. The treasurer's function deals with the physical custody of a company's liquid assets, such as cash and marketable securities. The Accounting Department should handle the accounting records and not the liquid assets of the company. Cash flow budgets can help organizations in managing their cash flow. Many vendor invoices have discounts (e.g., 2/10, net 20) for paying earlier than the normal 30-day terms. In this case, companies can risk losing these discounts if they do not have invoices processed and organized by due dates.

Finally, cash accounts should be reconciled on a timely basis by someone who cannot authorize transactions or have the physical access to cash or incoming customer receipts. Table 11.2 summarizes the functions, objectives, and controls of the expenditure cycle.

TABLE 11.2

A system whose purpose is to efficiently and effectively exchange cash with suppliers for needed goods and services.					
Functions:	Requisitioning	Purchasing	Receiving	Obligation Recognition	Cash Disbursements
Objectives:	Ensure needed goods are requested given available resources.	Ensure needed goods are ordered.	Identify received goods and safeguard them.	Keep track of who to pay, how much, and when.	Pay suppliers correct amount at roper time.
Parts:					
People	Department head or reorder point via EOQ	Purchasing Agent	Receiving Clerks	Accounts Payable Clerk(s)	Check Signer
Technologies					
Documents:	Purchase Requisition	Purchase Order	Receiving Reports	A/P Voucher	Checks
					Vendor Invoices
Records:	Request File	Open PO File	Inventory Master File	Open-to-Pay File	CD Transaction File
		Vendor File		AP Subledger	
Controls	Prenumber Authorization (relative to budget)	Prenumber Code of Ethics	Prenumber	Prenumber	Prenumber
		Approved Vendor List	Inspect for Damage	Match PO & RR	Authorized Signer
		Competitive Bids	Blind Counts	Extensions and footings checked	Review supporting documents
		RFQs	Physical Security	Approve Payment	Cancel Invoice
					Control Mailing

Key Takeaways

In this chapter, we discussed the objective of the expenditure cycle and the relevant functions it includes. We examined each individual function of the expenditure cycle, noting that a bill can be paid in many ways and many things can go wrong in the process. Our examination focused, in large part, on the objectives associated with each function (requisitioning, purchasing, receiving, obligation recognition, and cash disbursements) as well as how each objective is achieved. We learned about the risks associated with the achievement of these objectives and the controls that are needed to ensure that the objectives are met.

11.3 End-of-Chapter Exercises

Exercises

1. Who does the company transact externally with during the expenditure cycle?
2. What are the functions in the expenditure cycle?
3. What are the objectives of each function?
4. How are the objectives achieved?
5. What are the risks involved in requesting goods and services and how can they be mitigated?
6. Who should be in charge of purchasing? Do they need any special training? Could they be influenced by conflicts of interest? How can purchasing risks be mitigated?
7. How can a company effectively determine who to pay, what to pay, and when to pay it?
8. What are risks involved in cash disbursements and how can they be mitigated?
9. What is the best way for a company to pay its bills?
10. Preventive controls
    a. are needed because corrective controls often do not work.
    b. are more costly than detective controls.
    c. are generally not effective.
    d. are, usually, more cost beneficial than detective controls.
11. Employers bond employees who handle cash receipts because fidelity bonds reduce the possibility of employing dishonest individuals and
    a. protect employees who make unintentional errors from possible monetary damages resulting from their errors.
    b. deter dishonesty by making employees aware that insurance companies may investigate and prosecute dishonest acts.
    c. facilitate an independent monitoring of the receiving and depositing cash receipts.
    d. force employees in positions of trust to take periodic vacations and rotate their assigned duties.
12. Which of the following is not a function of the expenditure cycle?
    a. determining who to pay, when to pay, and how much to pay your customers
    b. selecting appropriate vendors from an approved vendor list
    c. ensuring that received goods are appropriately identified and safeguarded
    d. paying suppliers the correct amount at the proper time
13. What is the difference between a purchase requisition and a purchase order?
    a. Purchase requisitions need to be authorized, whereas purchase orders do not.
    b. Purchase requisitions are used to ask for goods internally, whereas purchase orders are used to request goods from an external supplier.
    c. Purchase requisitions are required, whereas purchase orders are not.
    d. Purchase requisitions are created on paper, whereas purchase orders are done electronically.
14. In order to meet the purchasing objective, purchasing agents should avoid temptations such as gifts and distractions. A company should, therefore, implement which of the following in order to control these behaviors?
    a. peer reviews
    b. management meetings
    c. an approved purchase requisition
    d. a code of ethics

15. Which of the following control procedures will best reduce the risk of paying an invoice twice?
    a. Attach a payment voucher to incoming vendor invoices.
    b. Paid invoices should be marked as "paid."
    c. Compare the vendor invoice to the company's purchase order.
    d. Compare quantities on the vendor invoice to the quantities received on the receiving report.
16. To minimize errors in the accounts payable function, which of the following procedures should be performed?
    a. approving the purchase requisition
    b. following up on open purchase orders
    c. double checking the math on the bank reconciliation
    d. matching the supplier's invoice to the receiving report
17. In the cash disbursements process of the expenditure cycle, the most appropriate person to sign the checks would be?
    a. a staff accountant
    b. the AP clerk
    c. someone in the Treasurer's Department
    d. the controller
18. After sending a purchase order, ordered goods are normally shipped into a warehouse. Which of the following procedures would normally ensure that receiving clerks actually count the goods received?
    a. Blank out the quantity field on the purchase order that was sent to the receiving area.
    b. A supervisor takes the packing slip from the incoming goods and watches the receiving clerks perform their duties.
    c. Prenumber the receiving report.
    d. Both a and b
19. A transaction was recorded that debited inventory for $1,000 and credited accounts payable for $1,000. Which of the following would most likely be used as the internal source document for this transaction?
    a. purchase order
    b. vendor invoice
    c. purchase requisition
    d. receiving report
20. Which of the following would be an advantage to using prenumbering?
    a. It prevents items from being added to a sequence of events.
    b. It allows you to keep track of documents or forms and to detect if something is lost.
    c. Prenumbering enables you to determine where certain events end and possibly others start up again.
    d. Both b and c
21. Using the Internal Control Questionnaire at the end of this section as a resource, please read the narrative below for the expenditure cycle. You will need to evaluate the company's internal controls for the expenditure cycle and make the recommendation that best mitigates this problem.

    Amy is a consultant hired by the CEO of Jensen's Sports Equipment Company. This company orders and sells sports equipment to individual, government, and corporate customers. After talking to the accounting department, Amy has documented the following processes that currently occur at Jensen's:

    Jensen's has a separate Purchasing Department that issues purchase orders (POs) for items needed to maintain an adequate level of stock in inventory for sale. The purchasing employees issue a PO based off department purchase requisitions. Most of the time, the purchase agents use a vendor list to purchase stock. There are a few times, though, when the suppliers do not have the stock and the purchasing agents will use Google to find a supplier who can deliver the items within the "need by" date. If they are happy with the quality of goods from this new supplier, they will add the supplier to their list for next time. The purchasing department sends a copy of the PO to the warehouse and to accounting. When the goods are received in the warehouse, the receiving employees receive the shipment and inspect the goods. They securely store the goods in the warehouse and add it to the receiving report that goes to accounting at the end of the week. Once the vendor invoice is received, the accountant will check the receiving report to confirm it was received and then pay the vendor invoice by check. The general ledger posting for both the vendor invoice and check posts on the check date. The checks are only signed by the owner of the company. The bank reconciliation is done by the senior accountant, who is not involved in custody, recording, or authorization duties of the expenditure cycle.

After further discussions with the accounting staff, they have mentioned that the warehouse seems to have high levels of items that the company doesn't seem to use. Amy also noticed that the accounting department has a file drawer full of POs, and the accounting staff wasn't sure what to do with them. In addition, a few times they noticed that the vendors returned their payments because the invoice was already paid.

Required:

Identify the five internal control problems that are specific to this scenario and make the recommendations that best mitigates each problem.

22. Using the Internal Control Questionnaire at the end of this section as a resource, please read the narrative below for the expenditure cycle. You will need to evaluate the company's internal controls for the expenditure cycle and make the recommendation that best mitigates this problem.

Beth is a consultant hired by the CEO of Blair Fishing & Camping Supply. This company orders and sells fishing and camping equipment to individuals. After talking to the accounting department, Beth has documented the following processes that currently occur at Blair:

Blair has a separate Purchasing Department that issues POs for items. The purchasing department decides what to order based on sales projections. In addition, purchasing agents also order items at least every quarter to make sure they don't run out of stock. The purchasing employees only issue POs to vendors who are on the approved vendor list. The purchasing department sends a copy of the PO to the warehouse and to accounting. When the goods arrive in the warehouse, the receiving employees only receive the shipment if there is a PO for the goods. The receipt is logged onto a daily receiving report with a copy delivered to the accounting department. They then move the inventory to an area in the warehouse to get it out of their way. It is eventually moved to the warehouse shelves if someone in the company has extra time. Since Blair is a small company, any employee is able to go and check the inventory levels or talk to warehouse personnel if they have questions about inventory or reports. Once the vendor invoice is received, the accountant will match the PO to the daily receiving report and process the invoice in the accounting system. Vendor invoices are paid each Friday, and the inventory and A/P is posted on that date in the system. Checks are signed by the owner of the company. The vendor invoice is then stamped "paid" and filed in the vendor file. The bank reconciliation is done by anyone in the accounting department who has time.

After further discussions with the accounting staff, they have mentioned that in the past the warehouse seems to have high levels of discontinued items. Upon further review, it appears that the purchasing department was not looking at the new products and discontinued products report from management. Beth also noticed that the accounting department has had to credit customers for poor quality products shipped to customers.

Required:

Identify the five internal control problems that are specific to this scenario and make the recommendations that best mitigates each problem.

Internal Control Questionnaire for the Expenditure Cycle—Requisitioning

Control Objective: *Accurately identifies needs given budget constraints and addresses them in a timely manner*

Risks: *Unnecessary goods requested, requests exceed available resources, and requisitions lost or not filled on a timely basis*

1. *Are needed goods identified by someone who actually needs or uses them?*
2. *Does the company use reorder points monitored by computer?*
3. *Do they have a purchase requisition form of some type (written or computer)?*
4. *Does a department head review and approve requests for goods in relation to a budget or other form of management control?*
5. *If they have requisitions, are they prenumbered and tracked?*

Purchasing

Control Objective: *Ensures that needed quality goods are ordered and received on a timely basis at the best price*

Risks: *Inadequate vendor screening or vendor favoritism, kickbacks, poor quality, excessive prices, order not filled or filled on a timely basis*

1. *Do they use a purchase order form?*
2. *Is the purchase order prenumbered?*
3. *Are open purchase orders tracked and reviewed for timely follow-up?*
4. *Are purchase orders authorized by approved purchase requisitions?*
5. *Do they have a purchasing agent with the appropriate amount of authority?*
6. *Is there a code of ethics for purchasing that addresses conflicts of interest?*
7. *Is there an approved vendor list?*
8. *Do they get competitive bids through RFQs?*
9. *Do they evaluate vendor performance?*

Receiving

Control Objective: *Properly identifies received goods and safeguards them*

Risks: *Lost receiving reports, shortages or damaged goods not detected, receiving reports inaccurate, or inadequate physical security over goods received*

1. *Do they use a separate receiving report to track received goods?*
2. *Is the receiving report prenumbered?*
3. *Do the receiving clerks inspect incoming goods for damage?*
4. *Do the receiving clerks actually count the goods?*
5. *Are the receiving clerks prevented from copying the quantity from the purchase order?*
6. *Do they maintain good physical security over goods?*

Accounts Payable

Control Objective: *Keeps track of who to pay, how much, and when*

Risks: *Wrong vendor paid, vendor not paid, amount paid incorrect, not paid on time, or goods paid for that were not ordered or received*

1. *Do they use a prenumbered voucher to establish control over incoming invoices?*
2. *Do they match invoice quantities to a copy of a receiving report to ensure they do not pay for more goods than were actually received?*

3. *Do they match invoice descriptions to a copy of the purchase order to ensure that they do not pay for goods they did not order?*
4. *Do they perform a math check on the invoice's extensions and footings?*
5. *Do they ensure proper distribution of invoices by reference to a chart of accounts with clear descriptions?*
6. *Are the invoices approved for payment by the person or department that requested them in order to ensure that the items are of acceptable quality?*
7. *Are adequate computer edit checks performed on input to ensure that erroneous data are not entered into the computer?*

Cash Disbursements

Control Objective: *Pays suppliers the correct amount at the proper time*

Risks: *Inaccurate, untimely, or unavailable vendor information or due dates, fictitious documentation, documentation reused or not reviewed, or invoices paid late*

1. *Do they use prenumbered checks?*
2. *Are the people who handle checks separated from accounting record keeping responsibilities?*
3. *Are the check signers segregated from other accounting responsibilities?*
4. *Do they have second signatures on large checks to reduce the likelihood of embezzlements?*
5. *Does the check signer properly review the supporting documentation before signing the checks?*
6. *Is the supporting documentation canceled as paid to ensure that it is not used again?*
7. *Do the check signers ensure that the checks are mailed to ensure that persons inside the company do not improperly receive company funds?*
8. *Do they maintain adequate security over any signature plates?*
9. *Do they reconcile the bank accounts on a regular basis?*

CHAPTER 12

The Revenue Cycle

12.1 Overview of the Revenue Cycle

Learning Objectives

At the end of this section, students should be able to:

1. Describe the revenue cycle and its major functions.
2. Understand the objective of each function.
3. Know the source documents generated and used for each revenue cycle function.

Most businesses today sell to other businesses on credit and receive payment in the form of cash, check, credit cards, or electronic funds transfer. To grasp the material in this chapter, it is important for you to understand that revenues can be collected from customers in many ways and that many things can go wrong in the process. The overall goal of the revenue cycle is to provide the right products for the right price at the time and the place the customer wants. To lay the foundation for what we refer to as the revenue cycle, we need to cover the fundamental processes involved. The revenue cycle is a system whose purpose is to efficiently and effectively receive cash from customers for requested goods and services.

Revenue Cycle Overview

This is a video that is an overview of the revenue cycle functions.

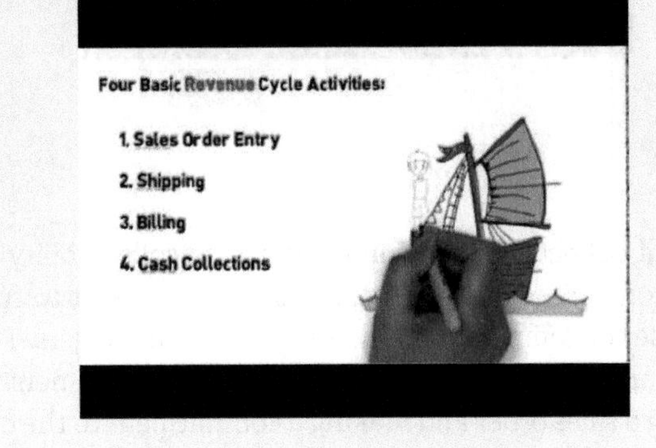

View in the online reader

Objective and Conceptualization

The following functions can be found in the revenue cycle for credit sales:

1. Order entry
2. Credit and collection
3. Shipping
4. Billing and accounts receivable
5. Cash receipts
6. Sales returns

order entry

Function of the revenue cycle where the objective is to accurately enter approved orders on a timely basis.

sales order

Source document that is the formal authorization to ship goods to a customer.

The objective of **order entry** is to accurately enter approved orders on a timely basis. The process begins with the receipt of an order from a customer that authorizes the transaction. The order may be received in writing or by phone, web form, or standard electronic transmission (i.e., EDI). The system then needs to place the data into some type of sales order. A **sales order** is a formal authorization (subject to credit approval) to ship goods to a customer. In other words, the company is committing to ship the goods to the customer when a sales order is accepted and credit is approved. A sales order is generally prepared by the order department or created automatically by the system. Sales orders should be prenumbered for accountability purposes. If shipment is delayed, the customer should be notified.

Sales Order Entry Video

This is a video on the sales order function of the revenue cycle.

View in the online reader

credit and collection function

Function of the revenue cycle that ensures the collectability of customer accounts and maintains the quality of the account receivable assets.

An effective **credit and collection function** ensures the collectability of customer accounts and maintains the quality of the account receivable assets. For credit to function properly, there must be an adequate number of competent credit analysts and managers. These people will establish and monitor credit for the company's current and potential customers. Customer credit must be checked *before* accepting a sales order and making a commitment to the customer to ship goods.

The credit process normally begins with the completion of a credit application and the provision of required credit information. The credit information may include a credit history and audited financial statements. Depending on the size of the customer, a review service or compiled financial statements may be accepted. In addition, the credit manager may obtain a credit report from an independent credit agency such as Dun & Bradstreet. The credit information is then analyzed and rated according to a company policy and rating system. The credit analysis should then be properly documented so it can be reviewed and updated where necessary.

After customers are granted credit, their payment histories should be periodically reviewed to determine if credit limits should be increased, decreased, or suspended. Delinquent accounts are contacted, and if necessary, the credit manager or an outside collection agency takes action to collect the account. Once an account gets to this stage, some portion of it most likely needs to be written off.

In shipping, a company must ensure that requested goods are properly identified and shipped. The process starts in the warehouse where the goods are identified based on a picking list, which is generated by order entry based on the approved sales order. The picked goods are moved to a physically secure shipping area, where the quantities are doubled checked by the shipping clerks before the goods are shipped. The warehouse must be properly secured and only authorized individuals should be allowed entrance. Upon shipment, the shipping clerks prepare a prenumbered shipping report. A **packing slip** is also generally included with the goods to describe the contents of the order, as well as a **bill of lading**, which describes who is responsible for the items in transit when an outside shipping company is handling the shipment. A copy of the shipping report is sent to the billing clerk, and the shipping department should retain one copy for tracking purposes. A **shipping report** is a document or form that provides evidence of the quantity and date that the goods were shipped. The prenumbered shipping report facilitates the establishment of a clean month-end sales cutoff. This information is important for determining the last sale of the fiscal period. Shipping reports should be entered by the shipping clerks into a shipping log.

packing list

Source document that lists the goods packed in an order.

bill of lading

Shipping source document used by an outside shipping company that describes who is responsible for the items in transit.

shipping report

Report or source document that provides evidence of the quantity and date that the goods were shipped.

Shipping Process

This is a video on the shipping function of the revenue cycle.

View in the online reader

Billing and accounts receivable determine who owes the company money for goods shipped, how much is owed, and when the amounts are due. To accomplish these objectives, a billing clerk needs to prepare a **sales invoice** based on the shipping report and the sales order. It is important to make sure that the sales revenue is posting to the proper accounting period. Any discounts for early payment are also included on the sales invoice. The sales invoices must be prenumbered so they can be tracked and accounted for. The sales invoices should also be mathematically checked, and the terms of sale should be properly disclosed.

sales invoice

Source document that is prepared in the accounting department to bill the customer for items ordered and shipped.

remittances

Payments from the customer.

remittance advice

Source document that customer returns with the payment.

lockbox

An arrangement made with the bank to receive all customer payments at a P.O. box that the bank will process and deposit providing the organization with a detail of all checks received and deposited in the bank account.

A copy of the invoices is provided to the accounts receivable clerk who maintains the accounts receivable subsidiary records. When **remittances** (payments) are received from customers, the accounts receivable clerk obtains a copy of the **remittance advice** and post the credits to the customer accounts based on the remittance advice document (recording function) and should not handle the actual checks (custody function). A remittance document is generally a part of the customer invoice that the customer tears off from the invoice and returns with the payment so their account is properly posted. Companies that have a high volume of customer receipts may want to set up a **lockbox** with their bank, which allows cash to be deposited immediately, and the bank provides a report of all cash remittances so the accountant can properly credit the customer's account without handling cash.

In cash receipts, the objective is to accurately and safely determine what funds are received from customers. One thing to keep in mind is that the person who opens the mail and handles the incoming checks should not be able to initiate any accounting entries or handle any other accounting records. Inadequate separation of incompatible duties increases the risk of irregularities. Again, authorization, recordkeeping, and custody of assets must be separated. Some companies address the segregation of duties issue by having customers remit their checks directly to a bank lockbox. This is called a lockbox arrangement, which has many advantages: (1) it keeps the receipts out of the hands of employees, and (2) it speeds up the cash flow. Banks charge a fee for the service where the customer payment goes directly to the bank and the bank provides a list of the payments to the accounting department to post the cash receipts and post the deposit to the general ledger. If organizations have a large number of transactions of cash receipts each month, the benefit would outweigh the cost, providing a more secure and efficient means of processing cash receipts.

Lockbox Services

This is a video on lockbox arrangements.

View in the online reader

For companies that receive remittances directly, it is recommended that the checks be listed immediately by the person opening the mail and restrictively endorsed "For Deposit Only." The listing can be compared later to the entry in the cash receipts journal, and the endorsements make it less likely that someone might try to cash the checks. Again, after the incoming receipts have been listed, the cashier can prepare a deposit slip and forward the remittance advices to the accounts receivable clerk for posting.

Billing and Cash Collections

This is a video on the billing and cash collection functions of the revenue cycle.

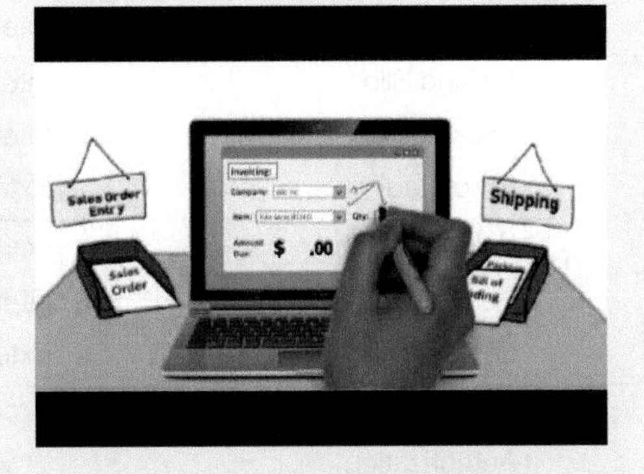

View in the online reader

Sales returns are handled ideally by a customer service department to ensure that they are properly authorized and tracked. Before goods are returned, authorization should be obtained and a code provided to the customer. When the goods arrive at the receiving dock, they are accepted when accompanied by a proper **return merchandise authorization (RMA)** code. The goods are then inspected and a receiving report for returned goods is prepared. The goods should be returned to the warehouse, and the receiving report should be sent to the customer service area. If the goods are in acceptable condition, the customer service department can then issue a credit memo to the customer, a copy of which should then be sent to the accounts receivable clerk for posting to the customer's AR record.

return merchandise authorization (RMA)

Authorization number authorized by customer service to track returned goods.

Source Documents of the Revenue Cycle

As we found with the expenditure cycle, source documents are generated internally and externally to the organization. Table 12.1 provides details of source documents used at each stage of the revenue cycle. Customers initiate their orders via phone, web, or by sending a purchase order that begins the sales order process for the organization. The sales order is an internally generated document that must have the customer's written authorization for the order. If the order is called in by the customer, then the organization will want to send the customer the sales order for a written signature. If the customer sent a purchase order, this will be used to generate the sales order. Figure 12.1 provides an example of the sales order. The sales order is prenumbered so the organization can periodically account for all orders. In addition, sales orders include basic information, such as what customers are ordering, how much they need, when they need it, and where they would like it to be shipped. It's important to make sure that accurate and relevant information are on the sales order to ensure that customers get what they ordered when they need it.

TABLE 12.1 Source Documents for Revenue Cycle

Function	Source Document	Internal/External
Order Entry	Sales Order	Internal
Credit and Collection	Credit Application	Internal
Shipping	Picking Slip Packing Slip Bill of Lading	Internal Internal External
Billing	Sales Invoice	Internal
Cash Receipts	Remittance Lockbox Report	Internal External
Sales Returns	Return Merchandise Authorization	Internal

FIGURE 12.1 Example of Sales Order

Sales Order

No. 7212019

DeLuca Security Equiment, Inc.
2564 Third Street
San Francisco, CA 94107

Order Date: 7/15/2020
Customer PO#: 3215

Bill To: Ross, Inc.
195 First Street
San Diego, CA 12129

Ship To: Ross, Inc.
195 First Street
San Diego, CA 12129

Part No.	Qty	Description	Cost	Subtotal
30110	1	Digital Video Recorder-2TB	599.99	599.99
35190	8	HD 4MP Coax Camera-Wide Angle	169.99	1,359.92
35800	4	Coax Connections	1.50	6.00
60112	16	60' Coax Video/Power Combo Cable	19.99	319.84
			Total	2,285.75

Approved by H. Vandy

The shipping stage of the revenue cycle includes two internally generated source documents. The picking ticket is used to pick the goods for the sales order from the warehouse, and the packing slip is included in the box of items shipped to the customer. The packing slip includes the inventory item descriptions, the quantity packed in the box, as well as who is billed and where the items are shipped. Sometimes the items are shipped to a different warehouse from where the customer's accounting department pays their bills. Figure 12.2 provides an example of a packing slip.

FIGURE 12.2 Example Packing Slip

DeLuca Security Equipment
Packing Slip

No. 629305

Customer: Ross, Incorporated
Ship to address: 195 First Street
San Diego, CA 12129

Part No.	Qty	Description
30110	1	Digital Video Recorder-2TB
35190	8	HD 4MP Coax Camera-Wide Angle
35800	4	Coax Connections
60112	16	60' Coax Video/Power Combo Cable

Checked by K. Donahue Date Shipped 7/27/2020

When an outside shipping company is used to transport the goods to the customer, a bill of lading is generated by the transport company. The bill of lading is therefore an externally generated source document that describes who is responsible for the items after being loaded (e.g., truck, rail, ship) and in transit.

What Is a Bill of Lading?

This is a video that explains the basics of a bill of lading.

View in the online reader

Once the goods are shipped to the customer, the accounting function will prepare the invoice to send to the customer. This is an administrative function and requires someone in the accounting department to match the sales order and shipping documents. An example of a sales invoice is shown in Figure 12.3.

FIGURE 12.3 Example Sales Invoice

Invoice

DeLuca Security Equipment, Inc
2564 Third Street
San Francisco, CA 94107

No. 651350
Date: 7/28/20
Terms: Net 30

Bill To:
Ross, Incorporated
195 First Street
San Diego, CA 12129

Ship To:
Ross, Incorporated
195 First Street
San Diego, CA 12129

Part No.	Qty	Description	Cost	Subtotal
30110	1	Digital Video Recorder-2TB	599.99	599.99
35190	8	HD 4MP Coax Camera-Wide Angle	169.99	1,359.92
35800	4	Coax Connections	1.50	6.00
60112	16	60' Coax Video/Power Combo Cable	19.99	319.84
		Shipping		20.00
			Sub-Total	2,305.75
			Tax	194.29
			Total	2,500.04

Make all checks payable to DeLuca Security Equipment, Inc.
If you have any questions about this invoice, please contact Greta Keton at 888-555-1212.
Thank You for Your Business!

aged trial balance
Report that is generated by the company that shows all the accounts receivable invoices outstanding and aged based on their invoice date. Generally, the columns of the report sort the invoices by customer name and then sort each customer invoice by the number of days outstanding: <30 days, 30–60 days, 60–90 days, and >90 days.

A copy of the invoices should be provided to the accounts receivable clerk who maintains the accounts receivable subsidiary records. When payments are received from customers, the accounts receivable clerk obtains a copy of the remittance advice and posts the credits to the customer account based on the remittance document and should not handle the actual checks. At the end of each month, someone other than the AR clerk reconciles an **aged trial balance** of the accounts receivable (see Table 12.2), to the general ledger to ensure independent verification.

TABLE 12.2 Example Aged Trial Balance

DeLuca Security Equipment, Inc. Aged Trial Balance					
Customer	**Balance**	**Current**	**30–60**	**60–90**	**Over 90**
5Commerce	76,000	38,000		38,000	
AccessBank	165,008		165,008		
Agular, Inc.	70,990	47,000	15,800	8,190	
Alpha Industries	67,000	23,000	41,000		3,000
ATM	29,650	13,250	16,400		
Balance Diodes	45,973	30,997			14,976
Burton Consulting	60,000	20,000		40,000	20,000
Ross, Inc.	2,500	2,500			2,500
Virtual Worlds	345,000			270,000	75,000
WilTel	57,650	57,650			
Yamaha Industries	(20,000)		(20,000)		
Zefer Electric	44,567		22,555		22,012
Zylon Electric	10,000	10,000	–	–	–
Totals	954,338	242,397	240,763	356,190	242,397

Figure 12.4 provides a basic flowchart of the processes and documents involved in order entry, credit, and shipping, and Figure 12.5 is a basic flowchart of the accounts receivable and cash receipts.

FIGURE 12.4 Flowchart Example

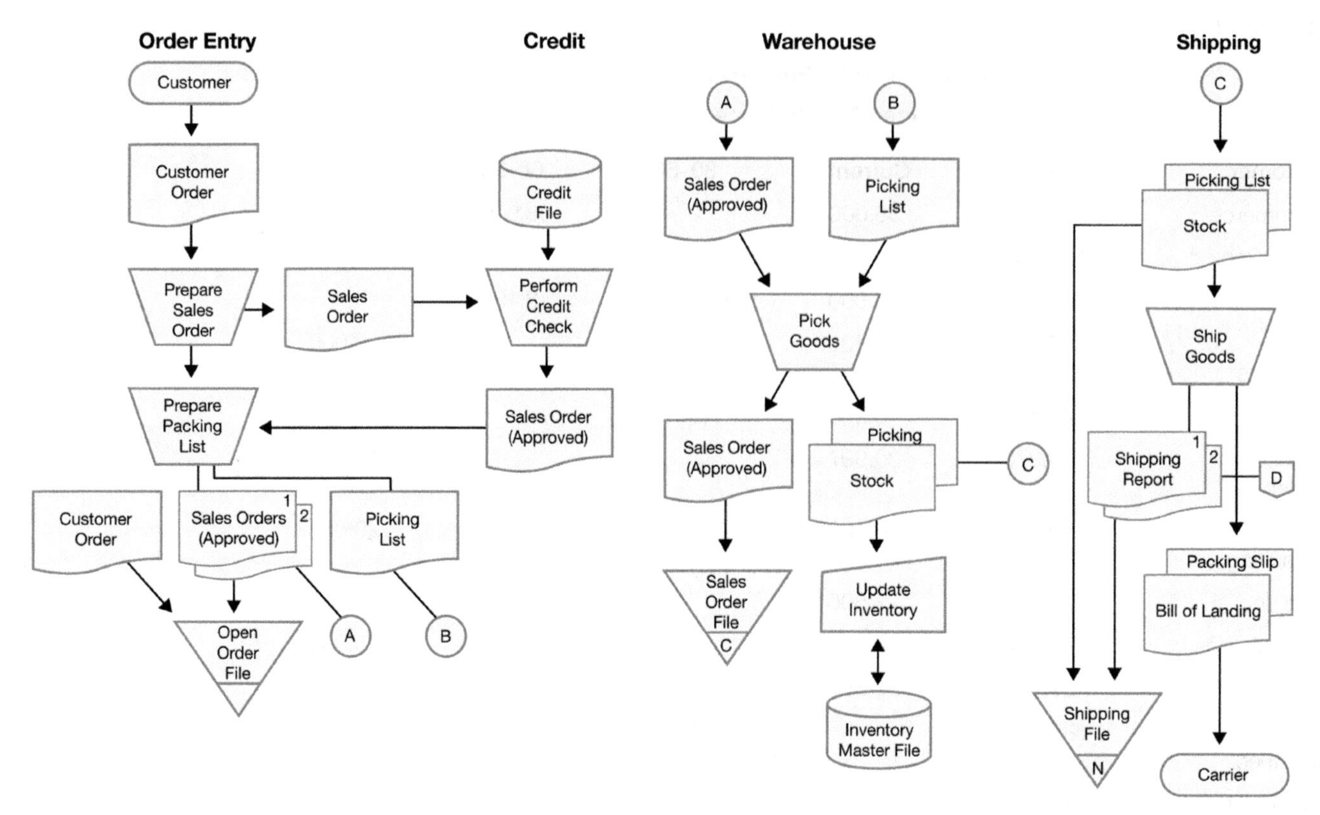

FIGURE 12.5 Flowchart Example of Cash Receipts and Accounts Receivable

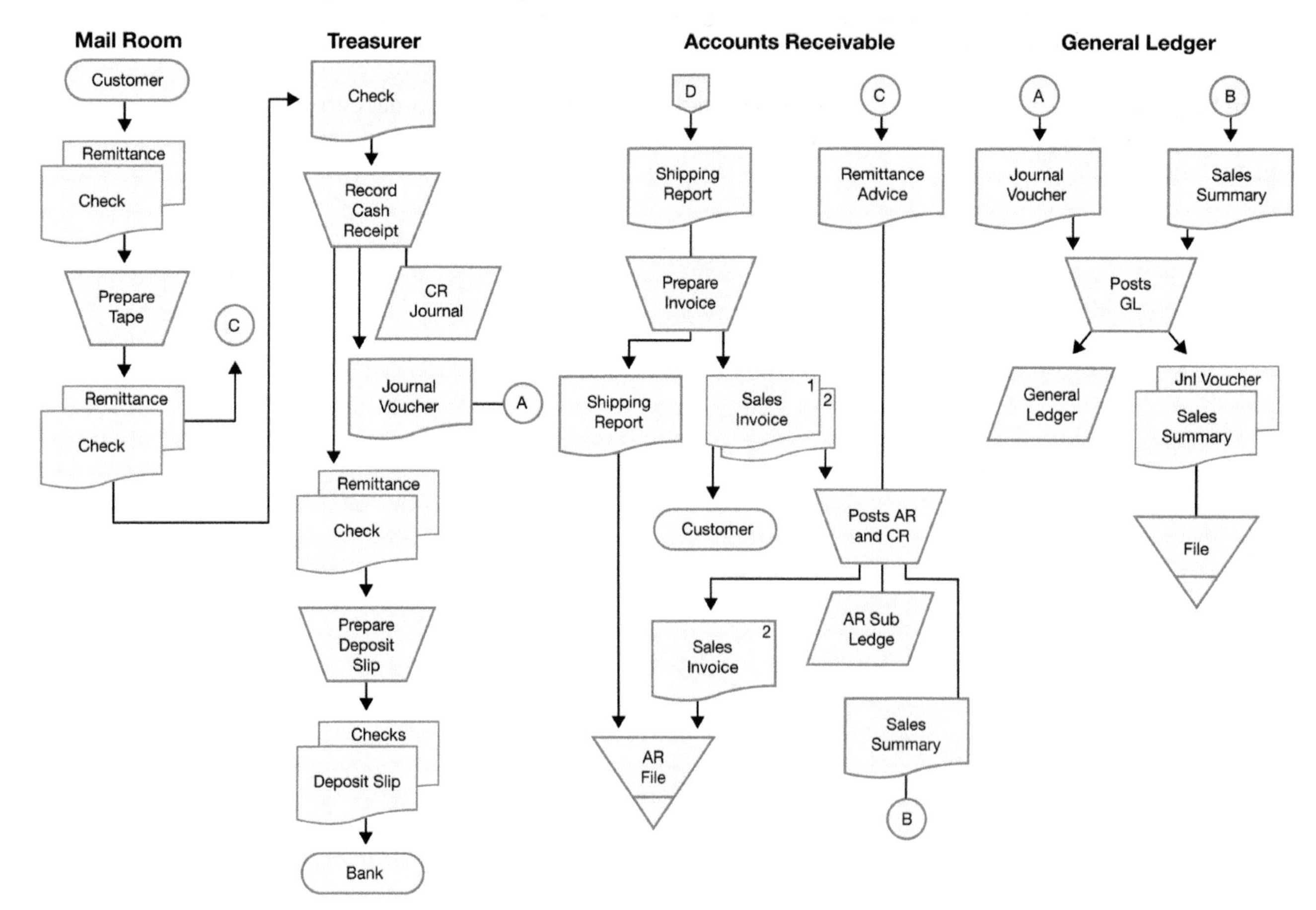

12.2 Risks and Controls

Learning Objectives

At the end of this section, students should be able to:

1. Identify the risks that may be present in each of the functions.
2. Describe the controls that can help ensure the operating effectiveness.
3. Apply the above and evaluate how effectively a revenue cycle is functioning.

The next sections of this chapter specifically address the risks and control activities for each function of the revenue cycle. Overall, possible risks to financial statements for the revenue cycle include theft of cash, running out of inventory stock, and inaccuracies leading to poor service. In addition, inaccuracies in posting transactions to the wrong accounting period, misstating a transaction into the wrong general ledger account, or simply not billing a customer are problematic.

Sales Order

Several substeps occur during the sales order function of the revenue cycle. First, the organization takes a customer's order. Then credit is checked, and providing that the customer has enough credit, the organization will check to make sure the items ordered are available in the warehouse. Lastly, customers are notified when their orders are accepted and when they can expect to receive their orders.

Risks associated with the sales order function includes the following:

- Inaccurate/incomplete sales orders
- Invalid/fake orders
- Uncollectible customer orders
- Inventory stockouts

Inaccurate and incomplete sales orders include sales orders that do not have a shipping address for the customer or items on the sales order that the organization does not carry. To prevent these risks, data entry controls are used. For example, incomplete orders can force the entry of all data fields prior to processing. Have you ever purchased something online and forgot to fill out part of the form, such as the zip code? When you try to complete your purchase, an error pops up on the screen letting you know that you didn't complete a field in the online form— this is a data entry control. We learned about the various types of data entry controls in Chapter 10.

To prevent invalid sales orders, which can lead to inflating sales revenues on the income statement as well as salespeople creating fake orders to inappropriately receive sales commissions (the order can be cancelled after receiving the commission), the organization must require all sales orders to be properly authorized by the customer. Most often, the authorization will come in the form of the customer's purchase order. If the order is made online or by phone, the organization must secure a proper written authorization of the customer order.

To prevent the possibility of uncollectible customer accounts, the organization must approve credit for new customers and check credit limits for existing customers prior to processing sales orders. It is imperative that this step occur prior to processing the customers' order and shipping it out.

stockout

A sale item not available in inventory.

RFID tags

Radio frequency ID tag used to keep track of inventory electronically.

Since inventory is an asset, many organizations like to manage their supply chain to keep just enough inventory in their warehouse, but not too much so they can maintain good cash flow. However, an unfortunate risk is having a customer order but being unable to deliver on the commitment because the inventory is not in stock, which is known as a **stockout**. To prevent stockouts, organizations maintain good inventory practices by having a perpetual inventory system and taking physical counts as well as reconciling those counts to the inventory system to maintain accuracy in inventory. Barcoding inventory or using **RFID tags** are useful ways to manage the perpetual inventory system.

Shipping

Two substeps are related to the shipping function: picking and packing the goods for the sales order and shipping the goods to the customer.

Risks associated with the shipping function include the following:

- Picking the wrong item
- Picking the wrong quantity of an item ordered
- Theft of inventory
- Not shipping the ordered items to the customer
- Shipping the items ordered to the wrong shipping address

To prevent the risks associated with picking errors (wrong item and wrong quantity), barcode or RFID systems are needed. To prevent the theft of inventory, the organization should restrict access to only those authorized to enter the warehouse. In addition, all inventory transfers should be documented and any movement of inventory in the warehouse can be tracked using barcode or RFID systems.

To prevent errors in shipping, the organization should reconcile the sales order with the picking ticket, packing slip, and the shipping documents to make sure the order was shipped to the customer and shipped to the correct address.

To prevent errors in shipping, the organization should reconcile the sales order with the picking ticket, packing slip, and the shipping documents to make sure the order was shipped to the customer and shipped to the correct address.

Billing

The billing function is administrative and occurs in the accounting department. Once the customer's order is shipped, the accounting department receives the information, matching the sales order to the picking ticket and shipping documents to prepare and send the customer invoice.

The billing function also has associated risks:

- Not billing the customer (not sending the invoice to the customer)
- Errors on the invoice
- Not posting the transaction to the proper accounting period
- Posting to the wrong customer account

To prevent the risk of not billing the customer, the accounting department must reconcile that all items from the warehouse are matched to a customer order and then invoiced. Generating an invoice in the accounting system just means that accounting needs to mail the invoice to the customer. What happens if the customer doesn't receive the invoice? They certainly won't pay you unless they get an invoice. Reviewing the AR aging report regularly may provide insights into potential billing issues as well. For example, if you notice that a customer who regularly pays their invoices within 30 days has invoices aged past 45 days, that means that there might be a problem. Did the customer receive the invoice? Or is the invoice incorrect? Was there a problem with the quality of the items shipped? Call the customer and find out the problem. To prevent the risk of errors on an invoice, such as the wrong amount on an invoice, data entry controls are used. Oftentimes, organizations will send out monthly statements to their customers to detect any issues with billing.

To prevent posting errors, data entry controls (see Chapter 10) are useful as well. In addition, it is important for the accountant to ensure that the sales invoice posts to the proper accounting period, such as the same month as the shipping date. Reconciling the accounts receivable total in the subsidiary ledger to the accounts receivable account total in the general ledger is needed monthly.

Cash Collections

Cash collections includes two tasks: First, the customer payment is deposited at the bank, and second, the customer's account is properly credited for the cash payment (think debit cash, credit customer).

Risks are associated with the cash collection function:

- Theft of cash
- Cash flow problems

To prevent the theft of cash, organizations should have proper segregation of duties in handling the cash and recording the customer payment. In addition, an organization can use a bank lockbox to reduce the theft of cash as well as improving cashflow. Figure 12-7 summarizes the functions, objectives, and controls of the revenue cycle.

TABLE 12.3 Revenue Cycle

A system whose purpose is to effectively and efficiently receive cash from its customers for requested goods and services.

Credit Sales						
Functions	**Order Entry**	**Credit**	**Shipping**	**Billings and Receivables**	**Cash Receipts**	**Returns**
Objectives	Accurately enter approved orders on a timely basis.	Ensure the collectability of customer accounts.	Ensure requested goods are identified and shipped.	Keep track of who owes how much and when.	Accurately determine what has been received from customers.	Authorize and track any product returns.
Parts						
People	Order Entry Clerk	Credit Analysts	Shipping Clerks	Billing Clerk	Cashier	Customer Service
		Credit Manager	Supervisor	AP Clerk		Clerks and Manager
Technologies Documents	Sales Order	Credit Application	Packing List	Sales	Remittance Advice	Authorization
		Credit Analysis	Shipping Reports	Invoice	Deposit Slip	Credit Memo
Records	Open Order File	Credit Files	Inventory Master File	Trial balance	CR Transaction File	Sales Return File
						Aged Trial Balance
Controls	Pre-number Approve	Approval	Double Check Pre-number	Review Aging	Restrictively Endorse	Authorize Code
		Credit Limits		Pre-number GL to AR	List Checks	Receiving Report
		Credit Review			Segregate Duties	

Key Takeaways

This chapter began by describing the revenue cycle and enumerating the functions contained within this business process. We described the objectives of each function and saw how these objectives are achieved. We learned which source documents are associated with each revenue cycle function. We addressed the risks associated with the revenue cycle and observed how activity controls can be placed at the critical control points throughout the process to mitigate these risks.

In the next chapter, we will focus on the conversion cycle. The purpose of the conversion cycle is to transform resources into products or services and to keep track of the associated costs. We will cover the functions of the conversion cycle for both manufactured and purchased inventory. For businesses that sell products, inventory is often a significant account. Regardless of how an entity's inventory is acquired, accounting information is needed to help an organization plan, operate, make decisions, and prepare necessary reports. In discussing the objectives of each function, we will describe the potential risks associated with each process and the purpose of identifying ways in which we can control the risks and maximize the system's effectiveness.

12.3 End-of-Chapter Exercises

Exercises

1. What is the revenue cycle?
2. What are the functions in the revenue cycle?
3. What are the objectives of each function?
4. How are the objectives achieved?
5. What is the purpose of a sales order? How is it different from a purchase order?
6. What is the purpose of the credit and collection function?
7. How does the credit and collection function work?
8. What is the best way to control the sales cutoff? Explain.
9. What is an aged trial balance? How is one prepared? What is the benefit of using one?
10. What are the risks in handling cash receipts, and how can those risks be mitigated?
11. Compare and contrast the revenue cycle to the expenditure cycle. What is similar, and what is different?
12. Which of the following is a formal authorization to ship goods to an approved customer?
    a. a customer order
    b. a sales order
    c. a shipping report
    d. a sales invoice
13. When an arrangement has been established with a bank to receive and deposit customer checks directly from the customer with remittances sent to the company, such an arrangement would be referred to as a
    a. funds transfer.
    b. lockbox.
    c. bill of lading.
    d. direct deposit.
14. Which of the following would be a possible threat to the ordering function?
    a. a bad customer credit score
    b. theft of inventory
    c. accepting incomplete customer information
    d. misplaced inventory
15. Which of the following would most likely help the credit manager adjust a customer's credit rating or limit?
    a. a back order list
    b. an aged trial balance
    c. a remittance advice
    d. a prenumbered shipping report
16. Which of the following would best facilitate an accurate sales cutoff?
    a. a sales order
    b. a shipping report
    c. an invoice
    d. a remittance advice
17. Which of the following duties within the revenue cycle should be separated?

a. removing cash receipts from the incoming mail and separating the remittance advices
b. account posting responsibilities and signing checks
c. billing customers and preparing the aged trial balance
d. handling cash receipts and approving bad debt write-offs

18. Which of the following would normally be the basis of a sales invoice?
a. a sales order
b. a shipping report
c. a bill of lading
d. a remittance advice

19. Which of the following would not be an effective control in the revenue cycle?
a. segregating credit approval from sales activity
b. adjusting the list of approved customers to reflect delinquent accounts
c. requiring the shipping clerks to double-check quantities and descriptions coming from the warehouse before shipment
d. allowing the AR clerk to reconcile the aged trial balance to the general ledger at the end of the month

20. **INTERNAL CONTROL EVALUATION:** RevCo, Inc.
Using the following table as a guide, describe each of the listed functions from the RevCo, Inc. case at the end of the chapter (following the exercises):
a. What can go wrong? (That is, what event or action can cause the organization to fail to meet its objectives?)
b. What control is being used to mitigate the risk?
c. For risks that appear to be inadequately controlled, indicate whether you believe the deficiency is inconsequential or significant.

Function	What can go wrong?	Controls
Order entry		
Credit		
Shipping		
Accounts Receivable		
Cash receipts		

21. **BAGEL CAFÉ Revenue Procedures**
Bagel Café is a small local café that sells bagels, pastries, coffees, and sandwiches. Katie is a new employee for the summer months. Her job responsibilities include taking customer orders, delivering food to the customers, and cleaning the tables. She works alongside two other high school students, two cooks, one dishwasher, and the owner of the café.

The owner, Sue, has instructed Katie and the other two high school students to handwrite all of the customer's orders and to pass them on to the cooks. Once the food orders have been prepared, the cooks place the handwritten order slips on top of the food. Katie is then instructed to tear up and throw away the slips before delivering the food to the customers.

Sue has placed herself in charge of the cash register and enters very few of these orders into the register. A chalkboard menu behind the counter describes the items as well as their costs. However, Sue recognizes the "locals" who come into the café, and she usually charges them a few dollars (an amount that she finds reasonable). She does not enter these transactions into the cash register. The money that she does not place into the cash register is placed into an envelope that is kept underneath the countertop. In addition to the money envelope, Sue also keeps money in a small safe in her office behind the kitchen.

Katie has also noticed a daily pattern: Sue takes money out of the white envelope or the safe and leaves for approximately one hour to buy groceries. During this time period, Sue has given all of the employees the option to eat and drink whatever they would like during their work shifts. While Sue is gone, Katie proceeds to record and place every transaction into the cash register; she also saves the food orders that she records.

When Sue returns to café, she does not record the grocery expenses. Katie does not know how Sue maintains other expenditure records, such as rent, utilities, etc. Sue is also very upset when she finds out that Katie has been recording every transaction in the cash register and instructs her to not do that again while she is out.

After two weeks of employment, Katie receives her first paycheck, which is a handwritten personalized check from Sue. The check amount was determined by the number of hours that Katie had worked multiplied by her hourly wage rate of $8.00/ hour. Since it is a personalized check, no taxes were deducted from the paycheck. As for tips, a jar sits in front of the cash register, labeled "tips," which the girls who work the front of the café empty out at the end each day and divide up among themselves. Sue never checks to see how much money is in the jar. Katie is becoming more and more wary about the café's business practices.

Required:

a. Identify problems in the operations and revenue practices at the Bagel Café.
b. How would the owner create, given the procedures used, the required fundamental information required for taxes and earnings reports?
c. If you were Katie, what would you recommend to the owner of the Bagel Café?
d. Would you continue to work at the Bagel Café? Why or why not?

22. **RevCo, Inc.**

RevCo, Inc. is a manufacturer and seller of high-tech solar panels. It is a relatively new business and so its sales have just crossed the $50,000,000 mark. Although its manufacturing is outsourced to China, the primary staff is located predominantly in California. The following provides a description of the company's revenue cycle:

Order Entry: The company's sales staff is made up of four sales representatives and the vice president of marketing. Sales staff members take orders from customers on their iPads and then email the orders to the main office. At the main office, Peggy, the receptionist, creates a sales back-order file on her laptop. In this file, she enters the customer account number, salesperson number, product numbers and quantities, and the requested delivery date. The customer number is used to access the customer's record, which includes the customer name and address, and is used to complete the sales order. The product number is used to retrieve the item description and price. A sales order is generated and sent to the credit department from the back-order file.

Credit: Sales orders are then received in the credit department where the sales amount is compared to the customer's available credit. Orders that fail the credit check are rejected. Customers that do not have a credit limit established must fill out a credit application, which includes their billing address and the requested credit limit. To obtain credit, the customer must follow the RevCo credit policy. Customers are normally given a standard 30 days to pay their bills. In some cases, credit limits are raised by the credit manager or the sales manager for customers who exceed their available credit as a courtesy to the customer. For customers who pass the credit check, their sales orders are sent to the shipping department.

Shipping: Warehouse employees use the sales order to determine which products to pick from inventory. They then mark the sales order for the items picked and enter the reductions into the inventory file. Completed sales orders are then moved to the shipping dock. Shipping employees prepare a prenumbered shipping report after the items are shipped. One copy is then sent on to accounts receivable.

Accounts receivable: Upon receipt of the shipping report, Jerry, the accounts receivable clerk, looks up the original sales order and adds the freight. A two-part sales invoice is prepared from the sales order and shipping report. Pricing is based on the standard price list or quotes from the sales manager. Invoices over $10,000 are double checked for math accuracy. The first copy is mailed to the customer, and the second part is placed in the customer's file after it is posted to the accounts receivable subsidiary ledger. The accounts receivable clerk also prepares a sales journal from the prenumbered sales invoices. The AR clerk later sends monthly statements to delinquent customers. From the accounts receivable subsidiary ledger, the AR clerk creates an aged trial balance and reconciles it to the general ledger at the end of the month. The controller estimates bad debts on a monthly basis, using the percentage of credit sales method and writes off accounts when they become uncollectible.

Cash receipts: The receptionist opens the mail and separates any customer checks and related remittance advices. The customer checks and advices are then forwarded to the accounts receivable department. In processing the cash receipts, the AR clerk prepares a two-part deposit slip. The deposit slips and checks are then taken to the bank. The remittance advices are used by the AR clerk to update the accounts receivable subsidiary records. The clerk also uses the advices to create a cash receipts journal.

Required:

Using the supplied Internal Control Questionnaire (below), evaluate the internal control strengths and weaknesses relating to the revenue cycle of RevCo, Inc. for each of the following functions or subsystems:

a. Order entry
b. Credit
c. Shipping
d. Accounts receivable
e. Cash receipts

Internal Control Questionnaire for the Revenue Cycle—Credit Sales

Order processing

Control objective: *Accurately enter approved orders on a timely basis*

Risks: *Orders may be lost, not processed accurately, or entered on time.*

1. *Do they use a sales order document or satisfactory equivalent?*
2. *Is the sales order record prenumbered?*
3. *Do they maintain a file of open orders and review them periodically for shipment delays?*
4. *Do they use a list of approved customers or its equivalent?*

Credit and collection

Control objective*:* *Ensure the collectability of customer accounts*

Risks: *Information may be incomplete, inaccurate, or out-of-date and result in bad debts.*

1. *Do they have a clear credit policy?*
2. *Do they perform credit checks on new customers who do not appear on the approved list?*
3. *Do they adequately document credit approvals including the process?*
4. *Do they adjust their list of approved customers and credit limits to reflect delinquent accounts?*
5. *Do they segregate credit approval from sales activity?*
6. *Do they keep customer correspondence files related to overdue accounts current?*
7. *Are write-offs approved by someone independent of the sales and cash receipts functions?*
8. *Do they use prenumbered documents to evidence write-offs?*

Shipping

Control objective: *Ensure that requested goods are properly identified and shipped*

Risks: *Improper products or quantities may be shipped, packing materials may be inadequate, or shipment may be late or not properly authorized.*

1. *Do they use a shipping report or satisfactory equivalent?*
2. *Is the shipping report prenumbered?*
3. *Are shipments made subject to approval from the credit department?*
4. *Are orders picked based on a picking list?*
5. *Are quantities and descriptions double-checked before shipment?*
6. *Is access to inventory adequately restricted?*

Billing and receivables

Control objective: *Keep track of who owes you money, how much, and when*

Risks: *Customers might not be billed, billed the wrong amount, or billed for something not ordered or shipped.*

1. *Do they use a prenumbered sales invoice for billing?*
2. *Do they have standard terms of sales?*
3. *Do they match quantities billed to the shipping records?*
4. *Is an up-to-date master price list used?*
5. *Do they verify the extensions and totals on the invoice?*
6. *Do they*
   a. *prepare an aged trial balance of receivables on a regular basis?*
   b. *reconcile the general ledger to the aging or subledger?*
7. *Do they properly send monthly statements to customers?*

Cash receipts

Control objective: *To accurately and safely determine what has been received from customers*

Risks: *Funds could be lost, stolen, or inaccurately recorded.*

1. *Is the handling of receipts separate from other accounting functions and sales-related activities?*
2. *Do they properly use remittance advices as evidence of amounts received?*
3. *Do they restrictively endorse all checks received or use a lockbox service?*
4. *Do they prepare a list of all receipts immediately and reconcile it to the monthly journal entry?*

CHAPTER 13

The Conversion Cycle

Inventory is often a significant dollar amount on the balance sheet for businesses that sell products. Most businesses today acquire their goods from a variety of vendors to resell. Many others manufacture their own products. Still others outsource all or part of their manufacturing process to third parties. Regardless of how an organization's inventory is acquired, accounting information is needed to help an organization plan, operate, make decisions, and prepare necessary reports as its inventory is sold and converted to cash. The process for turning raw materials and labor into finished goods is what we refer to as the **conversion cycle**. Sometimes you may also hear it referred to as the **production cycle**. In this chapter, we cover the functions in the conversion cycle for both manufactured and purchased inventory. We also discuss what can go wrong in the process and how an organization can best mitigate these risks.

conversion cycle

The process for turning cash or raw materials and labor into finished goods.

production cycle

Another name for the conversion cycle.

13.1 Overview of the Conversion Cycle

Learning Objective

At the end of this section, students should be able to:

1. Understand the purpose of the conversion cycle and the major functions that comprise its operation.

The conversion cycle is a system whose purpose is to transform resources effectively and efficiently into products or services and to keep track of their costs. In manufacturing, the process involves planning and then turning raw materials, labor, and overhead into finished goods. In distribution, the process is concerned with planning, acquiring inventory, and tracking costs.

Objective and Conceptualization

The subsystems of the conversion cycle depend on whether finished goods are manufactured or purchased. The following functions are found in the conversion cycle for a manufacturing organization:

1. Product design
2. Production schedule development

3. Inventory control
    a. Work order, materials requisition, and move ticket creation
    b. Raw material issuance to production
    c. Convert raw material to finished goods
4. Cost accounting
    a. Product cost accumulation for the work in process
    b. Transfer finished product to finished goods inventory

For entities that distribute already-manufactured products (merchandisers), the cycle involves two parts:

1. Inventory control
2. Inventory costing

The overall objective is for organizations to efficiently and effectively fulfill their inventory needs and to preserve their gross profit margins. You may recall from your financial accounting that a company with a good gross profit margin means that it knows that it is selling a profitable product.

Production Cycle

This is a video that shows the activities of the conversion (production) cycle.

View in the online reader

Simple Example—Jim's Chocolate Chip Cookie Company

Let's look at a simple example of how the steps would flow in the conversion cycle for Jim's Chocolate Chip Cookie Company.

Jim is the owner of a cookie company that specializes in chocolate chip cookies. He has perfected his recipe after much experimentation involving lots of tasting! He has opened a small shop downtown to sell his cookies. He uses his recipe to mix and bake these cookies. To begin making his cookies, he needs to plan out how many cookies he thinks he will sell each day. He realizes that more people are downtown on the weekends, so he adjusts his production schedule to meet the demand for each day of the week, meaning more cookies are made on the weekend to meet the higher demand. He also checks to make sure he has enough ingredients in stock to mix the cookie dough for the week, and if he runs low, he places an order with his suppliers. He has hired a full-time baker and some part-time staff to make the cookies and run the shop. At the end of the month, he calculates his gross profit margin and hopes he can cover his operating expenses (cookie ingredients, full-time baker's salary) and his sales and administrative expenses (e.g., rent, part-time staff, utilities).

Although this is a simple example, we can see how the different steps occur in the conversion cycle: first Jim perfected his recipe (product design); next, he matched his production schedule for baking cookies to meet the daily demand (this will continue to be refined as more sales information throughout the weeks and months are accumulated). The raw materials of the ingredients (cost of flour, sugar, chips, etc.) as well as payroll expenses of the baker's salary convert to the finished product cost of the chocolate chip cookies!

Provided that Jim continues to grow his business, because those chocolate chip cookies really are good, he could expand to a large factory. A large factory would include costs of increasing the production and the use of raw materials as well as an increase in the labor costs. However, if a large factory is making the cookies, can Jim keep his costs down? Perhaps. If the factory can produce more cookies and the process is more efficient, that means the cost per cookie should be less. While the process may have more steps and become complex, the objective is still the same—to fulfill the inventory needs efficiently and effectively. In addition, we will discuss some of the risks as well as the controls to mitigate those risks. Now that we've made you hungry, let's discuss each major function in detail!

13.2 Manufacturer Risks and Controls

Learning Objectives

At the end of this section, students should be able to:

1. Understand the objective of each function.
2. Recognize the risks of what might go wrong with the conversion cycle.
3. Be familiar with the controls that help ensure the operating effectiveness.
4. Be able to apply the above and evaluate how well an organization's conversion cycle is working.

Manufacturers are organizations that produce their own inventory. The goods flow throughout the production, converting raw materials and labor into finished goods. Throughout each subsystem of the conversion cycle, specific risks and controls help mitigate those risks. Overall risk, of course, is wasted time, resources leading to poor performance, and dissatisfied customers.

Product Design

"Good design is good business" was first said in 1973 by Thomas J. Watson Jr., president of IBM. Good product design is essential for manufacturing companies. A good design can help make the manufacturing process less expensive by streamlining processes as well as examining alternative materials that are as effective but cost less. In addition to having good design for the product, the company also needs to consider that the product has good packaging design. For example, why have a product that is good for the environment in a package that is bad for the environment?

What Separates Good Product Design from the Bad?

This is a video on good product design.

View in the online reader

Poor design is a product design risk. Poor design may mean that the cost to manufacture the product is too high, too complex, or results in poor quality of the manufactured item. The result of poor design is wasted time and money as well as dissatisfied customers. There is no such thing as 100 percent design perfection. However, an organization that understands the factors of product design understands that 80 percent to 90 percent of design translates to the manufacturing processes and then collaborates with the manufacturer on the remaining 10 percent to 20 percent, which can reduce time and money in the long run.

Mitigating the risk of poor product design includes communicating with the manufacturing and quality assurance personnel to ensure an effective and efficient production process that fits with the manufacturing capabilities. Any changes to the design process should be well documented in case quality and warranty issues arise.

Production Schedule Development

production schedule

Source document that determines the number of units that will be needed to meet customer demand and inventory needs and when units should be made.

The objective of the **production schedule** is to accurately determine the number of units that will be needed to meet customer demand and inventory needs. The production schedule will also specify when the units should be made. Customer demand for an organization's products is normally estimated by the marketing department and expressed in the form of a sales forecast. The desired inventory levels are often determined by the inventory control department. This objective can be met by having the right combination of people, technologies, and controls.

A production schedule, as illustrated in Figure 13.1, is the formal plan and authorization to begin production. A production schedule is generally prepared by production planners.

FIGURE 13.1 Example Production Schedule

Production Schedule

Dec 2020

Product Number	Quantity	Start Date	Finish Date
C42911832	320	12/1/2020	12/6/2020
A32931654	740	12/4/2020	12/7/2020
B72921835	410	12/4/2020	12/8/2020
C42912943	1180	12/7/2020	12/12/2020
A12911731	950	12/11/2020	12/14/2020

One of the biggest risks involved in production scheduling is over- or underproduction. Overproduction can result in excess inventory that may end up having to be written off as obsolete or significantly marked down as new models are introduced. Excess inventory also increases carrying costs and reduces cash flow. Underproduction, on the other hand, can result in lost sales and customer dissatisfaction because of insufficient quantities to meet customer demand. These risks are more likely to be significant for companies who manufacture goods affected by seasonality, such as clothing vendors, than for companies who make food products, such as the vendors for Joe's Ristorante' in Chapter 1.

Manufacturing has two major approaches: **materials requirement planning (MRP)** and **just-in-time manufacturing**. MRP is based on sales forecasting and demand.

materials requirement planning (MRP)

Approach to manufacturing goods and is based off of sales forecasting and demand.

just-in-time

Approach to manufacturing that does not need future planning and makes sure you have everything you need just in time to manufacture based on the order.

Materials Requirement Planning

This is a video providing a simple example of MRP.

View in the online reader

Just-in-time, however, focuses on making sure you have everything you need "just in time" to manufacture, based on the order. No future planning is involved. Sometimes this is called "**lean manufacturing**" and is used in auto manufacturing.

lean manufacturing

Just-in-time manufacturing.

What Is "Just-in-Time"?

This is a video that explains just-in-time manufacturing.

View in the online reader

A good way to mitigate the risks of over- and underproduction is to ensure that production schedules are properly prepared and approved. Proper preparation is more likely to occur when a sound risk assessment process is in place that ensures adequate research is conducted and a commitment to personnel is made that ensures competent people are performing the function. The preparation of the production schedule should also be reviewed and approved by an independent person, such as the operations manager.

Inventory Control

Inventory control consists of work orders, materials requisitions, and move tickets. These are source documents to authorize the issuance of raw materials to production. Once the goods are manufactured, the goods move from a status of "work-in-process" to "finished goods" inventory. It is important to note that many times at the end of an accounting period, all three types of inventory will be on the balance sheet: raw materials inventory, work-in-process inventory, and finished goods inventory. The difference among all three of these is how much labor is applied to the inventory goods value as they move from one category to the next for accurate financial reporting.

work order

Source document used to initiate the manufacturing process in the production department and to control the bill of materials and move tickets for each production run.

bill of materials

Source document that identifies all materials needed to produce a product.

A **work order**, as shown in Figure 13.2, is used to initiate the manufacturing process in the production department and to control the bill of materials and move tickets for each production run. Upon issuance, an entry is made in the open work order file. The **bill of materials**, as illustrated in Figure 13.3, specifies the types and quantities of raw materials used to produce a single unit of product. The route sheet specifies the sequence of operations and the estimated time for each production task. Figure 13.2 illustrates an example work order for 320 units of product number C42911832 (the first product shown in Figure 13.1).

FIGURE 13.2 Example Work Order

Work Order

Order	Product No.	Product Name: Production
No. 1201	C42911832	Panel Assembly Quantity: 320

Work Area	Operation Number	Operation Description	Start Date	Estimated Hours	Actual Hours
A101	1a	Assemble	12/1/2020	2.8	2.8
A105	2c	Finish	12/4/2020	1.3	1.4
C201	3a	Paint	12/4/2020	0.7	0.8
B150	4	Inspect/Test	12/5/2020	0.6	0.5

Approved by MAC

route sheet
Source document based off the work order that identifies the steps for manufacturing a product.

Although production is partially controlled with the production schedule, initiation of the production process via the work order should be approved by an independent person to ensure that it is accurate and that the production areas are ready. Review of the work order should include a review of the bill of materials and **route sheet** for accuracy. Work orders also need to be prenumbered so they can be tracked and reviewed to ensure that none are lost or unnecessarily delayed. Production planning and control should also be organizationally segregated from the work areas since some of the documentation they create will be used to evaluate performance in the work areas.

Both the bill of materials and route sheet originate in the product engineering department, where the materials and procedures necessary to manufacture a product are designed and documented for the production planners. The bill of materials is illustrated in Figure 13.3. An example route sheet is shown in Figure 13.4.

FIGURE 13.3 Example Bill of Materials

Bill Of Materials

Product No:	Product Name:
C42911832	Panel Assembly

Part No.	Quantity	Description
201	1	Base Unit
202	1	Front Panel
203	1	Back Panel
210	1	Flux Capacitor
220	4	Edge Guards
225	8	Screws
230	2	Rotator Cuffs
250	1	Display Unit

FIGURE 13.4 Example Route Sheet

Route Sheet

Product No:	Product Name:
C42911832	Panel Assembly

Work Area	Operation Number	Operation Description	Estimated Hours
A101	1a	Assemble	2.8
A105	2c	Finish	1.3
C201	3a	Paint	0.7
B150	4	Inspect/Test	0.6

materials requisition
Source document identifying the materials needed from a work order.

When issuing raw materials to production, the objective is to ensure that material issuances are properly authorized and accurately tracked on a timely basis. Before raw materials can be issued from the factory storeroom to production, they must be requested with a materials requisition. A materials requisition is prepared based on the bill of materials. Figure 13.5 illustrates a materials requisition. The **materials requisition** includes the work order number, the issue date, and a list of the needed parts. Subsequent transfers are documented on move tickets. Upon issuance of the raw materials from the storeroom, a copy is sent to inventory control where an entry is made to transfer the raw materials costs to work-in-process inventory.

FIGURE 13.5 Example Materials Requisition

Materials Requisition

Requisition Number: 3183	Work Order Number: 1201	Issue Date: 11/30/20	Issue To: A101

Part No.	Description	Quantity Issued	Unit Cost	Total
201	Base Unit	320	15.75	15.75
202	Front Panel	320	12.25	12.25
225	Screws	2560	0.12	0.96
203	Back Panel	320	9.96	9.95
				$38.91

Issued by: WLG
Received by: EAS
Costed by: BHO

Raw materials are subject to theft and waste. To reduce this risk, they should be physically segregated and made the responsibility of storeroom personnel. Only authorized personnel should be in the warehouse. All movements should also be documented. They should be periodically counted by an employee who does not have custodial responsibility for the raw materials. Materials requisition is a source document that authorizes the release of raw materials to production. This document should be signed by the employee who maintains custody of the raw materials inventory and the employee receiving the raw material for production to acknowledge release of the raw materials to production. In the material requisition (no. 3183) above in Figure 13.5, the issuance and receipt are signed by WLG and EAS, respectively. Any requests for additional materials more than the amount specified in the bill of materials should be documented and approved by a production supervisor. Unused raw material should also be documented and returned to the storeroom with a materials return form.

When converting raw materials to finished goods, the objective is to do so efficiently and effectively and to keep track of the costs. In other words, the objective is to make the product according to specifications and to do it in a reasonable amount of time and with a minimal amount of waste. When a task is complete, an authorized person signs the **move ticket**. This in turn authorizes the work in process to move to the next work area and adds the related cost to the work-in-process inventory in cost accounting. When a stage of production is completed, a copy of a move ticket, as illustrated in Figure 13.6, is sent to production planning and control department to update the open work order file.

move ticket

Source document used to document the completion of each step on the route sheet.

FIGURE 13.6 Example Move Ticket

Move Ticket

No. 8354

Work Order No: 1201

Units: 320

Move to:	A105
Operation	2 Finish
Start Date:	12/1/2020
Finish Date:	12/4/2020

Received by: BT

work-in-process inventory

Inventory identified as "in process" meaning that it is not raw materials nor is it yet finished goods, but has some labor hours associated with the raw materials.

Since move tickets are used to authorize work in process to move to the next work area and add the related cost to the **work-in-process inventory** in cost accounting, all move tickets need to be prenumbered and accounted for. This will minimize the chance that one is lost and that work orders and product costs are not properly updated. They should also be signed to establish accountability in case of any problems.

Cost Accounting

From a system perspective, the objective in product costing is to accurately accumulate product costs for inventory and cost of goods sold in accordance with generally accepted accounting principles (GAAP). Product costing is normally handled by the cost accounting department. The process begins when production planning sends the cost accounting department a copy of a work order. The work order then initiates the creation of a work-in-process record in the work-in-process file or subsidiary ledger.

As the production process moves forward, materials requisitions and completed move tickets are sent to the cost accounting department. This information is then used to update the work-in-process accounts with costs for raw materials and direct labor. Indirect costs relating to factory overhead are then estimated and applied by the cost accounting department. Indirect manufacturing costs are those that are difficult to trace directly to a production run. Examples include factory supplies, electricity, salaries for production supervisors, and rent for the factory.

The production (conversion) process is generally considered to be complete when the last move ticket for a production run is received. Cost accounting should then close the work-in-process account for the respective work order. Journal vouchers are posted to the general ledger to increase the finished goods inventory control account and reduce work-in-process inventory.

One of the biggest risks in this process is inaccurate cost data. These inaccuracies can result in poor decisions related to manufacturing performance evaluation and product pricing. They can also lead to misleading financial statements that affect user decisions.

To minimize the likelihood of inaccurate cost data, control procedures should be used to either verify data input or automate the input process with barcode scanners. Cost accounting can also create standards for each manufacturing process, which enables them to compare the standard to the actual manufacturing cost and identify possible errors as well as performance problems.

Properly accounting for the movement of goods from work-in-process to the finished goods inventory requires the preparation of the final move ticket. The final move ticket is then sent to not only production planning, but to cost accounting, where the work-in-process account for the respective work order is closed. Entries are then prepared for the general ledger to increase the finished goods inventory account and reduce work in process.

13.3 Merchandiser Risk and Controls

Learning Objective

At the end of this section, students should be able to:

1. Understand risks and controls as it relates to merchandising inventory organizations.

Merchandisers are organizations that purchase goods to sell to customers; they do not manufacture their own products. For merchandisers, the objective of the inventory control is to maintain an optimal level of inventory. This generally involves minimizing the total inventory cost while ensuring that adequate inventory is on hand to meet expected demand. Inventory requirements are normally determined based on a sales forecast and desired ending inventory levels. Maintaining an optimal level generally involves determining how much inventory should be purchased and when the inventory should be purchased.

Inventory Control

One way to determine an optimal order quantity is to use the **economic order quantity (EOQ)** model. The model requires certain assumptions that make it useful when demand for a product is relatively constant. For example, businesses such as McDonald's and Walmart use EOQ. The EOQ model uses estimated carrying costs and ordering costs to reduce total inventory costs. The following equation is used to calculate the EOQ:

economic order quantity (EOQ)

Formula used to determine the optimum number of an inventory item.

$$EOQ = \frac{\sqrt{2DF}}{CC}$$

Where:

D = annual demand

F = fixed ordering cost

CC = carrying cost per unit

For example, if an organization has a product with an annual demand of 5,000 units, a fixed cost of $20 per order, and a carrying cost of 50 cents per unit, the economic order quantity would be equal to 632 as follows:

$$EOQ = 632 = \frac{\sqrt{2(5,000)(20)}}{0.50}$$

reorder point (ROP)

Formula used to calculate when an inventory item should be reordered.

In addition to determining how much to purchase, entities also need to know when to purchase. The main factors that determine when to purchase inventory include daily demand and lead time. Accordingly, the **reorder point (ROP)** can be expressed as follows:

$$ROP = D \times L$$

Where:

D = daily demand (total demand / number of work days)

L = lead time

For example, if total demand is 2,600 units, there are 260 workdays, and a lead time of 7 days is needed, the reorder point, or when an order should be placed with vendors, is when the quantity on hand equals 70 units, calculated as follows:

$$ROP = 70 = \left[\left(\frac{2600}{260}\right) \times 7\right]$$

Therefore, the reorder point for the above data indicates that an order should be placed with vendors when the quantity on hand equals 70 units.

When the parameters of the reorder point formula are stable, the inventory on hand should decline to zero just as the organization receives the ordered quantity of inventory. Since this can be risky if either of the parameters are estimated incorrectly, many organizations will add some additional inventory to the reorder point as a cushion against possible stockouts.

One of the main risks in inventory control is over- or understocking of goods. Understocking goods leads to stockouts and the risk of customers going elsewhere. Overstocking risks having cash tied up into inventory on the balance sheet and, depending on the type of product, the possibility of obsolescence. This risk is not unlike that experienced in a production planning and control operation. Therefore, inventory control for a merchandising company also needs a sound risk assessment process in place that ensures adequate research is conducted and a commitment to personnel is made that ensures competent people are performing the function. The preparation of order quantities and reorder points should also be reviewed and approved by an independent person.

Cost Accounting

perpetual inventory

Inventory is updated automatically in the AIS as inventory is purchased and sold.

barcode scanner

Hardware and software that scans a barcode and updates the inventory in the AIS.

Inventory costing in a merchandising company must also be performed to accurately assign costs to inventory and cost of goods sold in accordance with GAAP. Therefore, to minimize the likelihood of inaccurate inventory costing, control procedures should be put in place to ensure that the individuals doing inventory costing are qualified and that any incentives for doing anything less than a competent job are minimized. The work of inventory costing should also be reviewed and approved by an independent person. **Perpetual inventory systems**, the use of **barcode scanners**, and periodic inventory accounts during critical cut-off periods, such as year-end and reconciliation to the general ledger, reduce the risk of inaccurate reporting of inventory on the balance sheet.

What Is a Barcode Scanner?

This is a video that discusses what a barcode scanner does in keeping track of inventory.

View in the online reader

Key Takeaways

In this chapter, we learned about the conversion cycle and the major functions that comprise its operation for both manufactured and purchased inventory. We examined the objectives of each individual function and how these objectives are achieved. Within each function, the most important procedures and tracking mechanisms were identified and discussed. We also looked at the various risks inherent to each part of the business process as well as the controls that can be utilized to mitigate the likelihood of their occurrence.

13.4 End-of-Chapter Exercises

Exercises

1. What is the conversion cycle?
2. What are the functions in the conversion cycle?
3. What are the objectives of each function of the conversion cycle?
4. What are the main risks in production planning, and how can they be controlled?
5. What are the similarities and differences between a production schedule and a work order?
6. Compare and contrast a bill of materials with a materials requisition.
7. What are the similarities and differences between a route sheet and a move ticket?
8. What does cost accounting use to accumulate work-in-process costs?
9. How are the functions for merchandise inventory similar and different from manufactured products?
10. What information does the economic order quantity and reorder point models provide?
11. What are the key limitations to using the economic order quantity and reorder point models?
12. Who accumulates factory overhead costs, and how do they get applied to work-in-process inventory?

13. Which of the following functions or subsystems would not be contained in the conversion cycle?
    a. production schedule development
    b. converting raw material to finished goods
    c. paying vendor invoices
    d. production cost accumulation
14. Which of the following is generally not pertinent to the production schedule?
    a. a bill of materials
    b. a move ticket
    c. a route sheet
    d. a materials requisition
15. Which of the following records contains a list of part needed to manufacture a specific product?
    a. a route sheet
    b. a work order
    c. a bill of materials
    d. a production schedule
16. Which of the following records captures necessary information relating to the direct labor used in manufacturing?
    a. a bill of materials
    b. a move ticket
    c. a route sheet
    d. a materials requisition
17. Which of the following would not be a risk involved with production scheduling when overproduction occurs?
    a. inventory price mark downs
    b. increased carrying costs
    c. lost sales
    d. reduced cash flow
18. Which of the following initiates the creation of a work-in-process record in a work-in-process file or subsidiary ledger in cost accounting?
    a. a production schedule
    b. a work order
    c. a move ticket
    d. a materials requisition
19. To minimize the likelihood of inaccurate cost data in the cost accounting department, which of the following control procedures would not likely be useful?
    a. using barcode scanners
    b. comparing production standards to actual costs
    c. verifying data input
    d. comparing actual costs to product prices
20. Which of the following records is most likely used to indicate that a work order should be closed?
    a. a bill of materials
    b. a move ticket
    c. a route sheet
    d. a materials requisition

21. Which of the following is not a control procedure related to the development of the production schedule?
    a. requiring the production schedule to be prenumbered
    b. requiring the production schedule to be reviewed and approved by someone outside of production planning
    c. requiring the use of a sales forecast to assist in planning
    d. requiring proper estimations of factory overhead rates based on past experience and projections
22. Which of the following does the EOQ model not include?
    a. considers inventory carrying costs
    b. minimizes total inventory cost
    c. considers inventory ordering costs
    d. determines when inventory should be ordered
23. A merchandising company sells a particular product that is estimated to have approximately 1,500 sales this year. The purchasing department estimates that it will cost approximately $200 to place an order for this product: $180 fixed and $20 variable. The total annual carrying cost for this product is $1,500. What is the product's EOQ?
    a. 775
    b. 19
    c. 735
    d. 20
24. **Robotic Medical Systems**

    Robotic Medical Systems is a manufacturer and seller of quality medical equipment and devices located in Lexington, Massachusetts. The company has been serving hospitals and clinics nationwide since 1995. In recent years, its profits have declined due to increasing inventory and overhead expenses. This has caused the company's board of directors to reexamine the organization's accounting system in order to discover the reason for the rising costs. The following provides a description of the company's conversion cycle:

    Production schedule development: The firm's production planners generate a schedule based on a sales forecast created by the firm's marketing department. Once the production schedule is established, it must be approved by the production manager. The production planning department further reviews the production schedule for shipment delays on a monthly basis.

    Work order: Independently verified, prenumbered work orders are then used to initiate the manufacturing process. The work areas and production planning department are located on the same floor of the facility, and the floor boss and the head of the planning department have been friends since high school.

    Raw materials issuance: The inventory control clerk must approve material requisitions based upon the bill of materials by checking the quantities and descriptions of items listed. Upon issuance of the raw materials from the storeroom, a copy is sent to inventory control where an entry is made to transfer the raw materials costs to work-in-process inventory. A production supervisor is responsible for approving and documenting any request for additional materials, and any unused material is documented and returned to the storeroom.

    Raw material conversion to products: Company employees use prenumbered move tickets approved by management to authorize the work in process to move to the next area. Such documents are based on bills of material and route sheets and are used to add the related cost to the work-in-process inventory to cost accounting. A copy of each move ticket is sent back to production planning and control to update the open work order file.

    Product costing: The production planning department sends the cost accounting department a copy of a prenumbered work order, which initiates the creation of a work-in-process record. Materials requisitions and move tickets are also sent to the cost accounting department to update the cost of raw materials and direct labor in the work-in-process files. The cost accounting department is also responsible for estimating factory overhead rates. These rates are based on projections and historical figures. The last move ticket is used to close the work-in-process record. Journal vouchers are sent to the general ledger to increase the finished goods inventory control account and simultaneously reduce work-in-process inventory. The firm uses the first-in-first-out (FIFO) method of inventory costing.

Transfer to finished goods: The final move tickets are sent to production planning and cost accounting to indicate the completion of a production run. Journal vouchers are also used to send information to the general ledger to increase the finished goods inventory control account after a work-in-process record is closed.

Required:

a. Production schedule development
b. Work order
c. Raw materials issuance
d. Raw materials conversion to products
e. Product costing
f. Transfer to finished goods

Internal Control Questionnaire for the Conversion Cycle—Manufacturing

Production schedule: *Accurately determine the number of units that will be needed to meet customer demand and inventory needs.*

1. *Do they use a production schedule?*
2. *Is the production schedule prenumbered?*
3. *Is the production schedule reviewed and approved by someone outside of production planning?*
4. *Do they review the production schedule regularly for shipment delays?*
5. *Do they use a sales forecast to assist in planning?*

Work order: *Initiate the manufacturing process in the production department and control the bill of materials and route sheet for each production run.*

1. *Do they use work orders to initiate the production process?*
2. *Are work orders prenumbered and accounted for?*
3. *Are work orders approved by an independent person?*
4. *Is production planning organizationally segregated from the work areas?*

Raw material issuance: *Ensure that material issuances are accurately tracked on a timely basis.*

1. *Do they use a materials requisition?*
2. *Is the materials requisition prenumbered?*
3. *Are requests subject to approval before issuance from the storeroom?*
4. *Are materials requisitions prepared based on the bill of materials?*
5. *Are quantities and descriptions double-checked before issuance?*
6. *Is access to raw material inventory adequately restricted?*

Raw material conversion to products: *Make the product according to specifications, and do it in a reasonable amount of time and with a minimum of waste.*

1. *Is manufacturing partly controlled by a bill of materials?*
2. *Are route sheets used to partly control production?*
3. *Are prenumbered move tickets used to authorize work in progress to move to the next work area?*
4. *Is a copy of the move ticket sent back to production planning to update work order status?*
5. *Are move tickets properly signed to establish accountability?*
6. *Is waste or lost material properly reported to cost accounting?*

Product costing: *Accurately accumulate product costs in accordance with GAAP.*

1. *Do they use a prenumbered work order to initiate the creation of a work-in-process record?*
2. *Do they use approved materials requisitions to update raw material costs in work in process?*
3. *Do they use move tickets to update direct labor costs in work in process?*
4. *Do they use a record or system to track actual indirect manufacturing costs?*
5. *Do they properly estimate a factory overhead rate based on past experience and projections?*
6. *Do they compare actual overhead costs to those applied and report any variance on a timely basis?*
7. *Do they use the last move ticket in a production run to close the work-in-process record?*
8. *Are journal vouchers used to send information to the general ledger to increase work-in-process inventory for direct material, direct labor, and overhead costs?*
9. *Are entries to the general ledger reviewed and approved by an independent person?*
10. *Is the inventory costing method in accordance with GAAP (FIFO, LIFO, or average cost)?*

Transfer to finished goods: *Properly account for the movement of goods from work-in-process to the finished goods inventory.*

1. *Are final move tickets sent to production planning and cost accounting to indicate that a production run is complete?*
2. *Are journal vouchers used to send information to the general ledger to increase the finished goods inventory control account and reduce work-in-process inventory after a work-in-process record is closed?*

CHAPTER 14

Fixed Assets, Financing, and Payroll Cycle

In this chapter we will cover three additional areas that occur in all organizations: fixed assets, financing, and payroll. Fixed asset tracking as well as investments, stock, and debt tracking are considered the **investment cycle**. Organizations must invest in equipment if they manufacture products or invest in real estate (e.g., office building) to meet their growth needs. Many times, organizations need money from investors in the form of equity or debt to fund their growth strategies. Organizations also need to invest in people, which requires paying their employee wages and salaries along with benefits and required taxes. This chapter covers the objectives of each of these areas and the risks and controls to mitigate those risks.

investment cycle
Accounting cycle that includes organization activities of investing in fixed assets as well as issuing stock or debt.

14.1 Fixed Asset Cycle

Learning Objectives

At the end of this section, students should be able to:

1. Understand the objectives of the fixed assets cycle.
2. Evaluate risks and controls associated with fixed assets.

Some industries, such as manufacturers, have an intensive amount of fixed assets on the balance sheet, while others do not. Even organizations that have a minimal amount of assets on their balance sheet (i.e., service providers) need to have good asset tracking. Organizations should understand what physical assets they have and where they are. Maintaining an accurate list of fixed assets is needed for financial accounting purposes, tax reporting, and insurance.

Objective and Conceptualization

The main objective of the fixed asset cycle is to safeguard the company's assets. This is done by tracking the physical asset once it is acquired to when it is disposed. In addition, depending on the asset, it is informative to the organization for planning purposes to have maintenance and repair information on each asset. Thus, the fixed asset cycle has four major functions:

1. Acquisition
2. Depreciation
3. Repairs and maintenance
4. Asset disposition

FIGURE 14.1
Asset ID Tag Example

Property of Cotait Co.

1111

It may seem silly to think about why a company would need to keep track of all its assets. Well, assets do add up. And it's easy to lose assets if you don't know where they are and replacing lost assets can be costly. Check around your college some time and look for labels on the computers in the lab. Do you see a tag with your college's name and a number on it or a scannable barcode? Figure 14.1 shows an example of what an **asset ID tag** might look like. Once you look around, you will notice them almost everywhere in an organization. They may be different colors to distinguish the year the asset was placed into service or to represent assets from different departments. In addition, these asset tags may be difficult to remove to prevent theft.

asset ID tag

A tag that is affixed to a fixed asset used for fixed asset control purposes.

What Is an Asset Tag?

This is a video that explains the purpose of an asset tag.

View in the online reader

In addition, the organization should have a policy that sets a threshold amount and capitalizes assets that are above that certain value in each asset category. Organizational policy should also be in place for asset acquisition approvals. Many organizations use budgeting to gain a better understanding of their asset acquisitions for each year. For example, if I have a delivery company and I use only one van, would it make sense to budget an increase in sales without also understanding that I may need more delivery vans to meet my budgeted sales demand?

Organizations also need a policy on depreciation for each category of their assets. Keep in mind that depreciation expense on the same asset may be different for the financial statements than for the depreciation calculated for tax purposes. Many AISs maintain separate depreciation methods for the same asset to generate the reports for financial as well as for tax purposes. Some organizations that do not have many assets may use a spreadsheet to keep track of their fixed assets. However, for organizations that are asset intensive, they may choose to integrate a separate fixed asset system into their AIS to handle their needs. Of course, organizations will need to do a cost-benefit analysis to determine if it is worthwhile to invest in a specialized system.

Fixed Asset Accounting Software

This is an example of what fixed asset accounting software does.

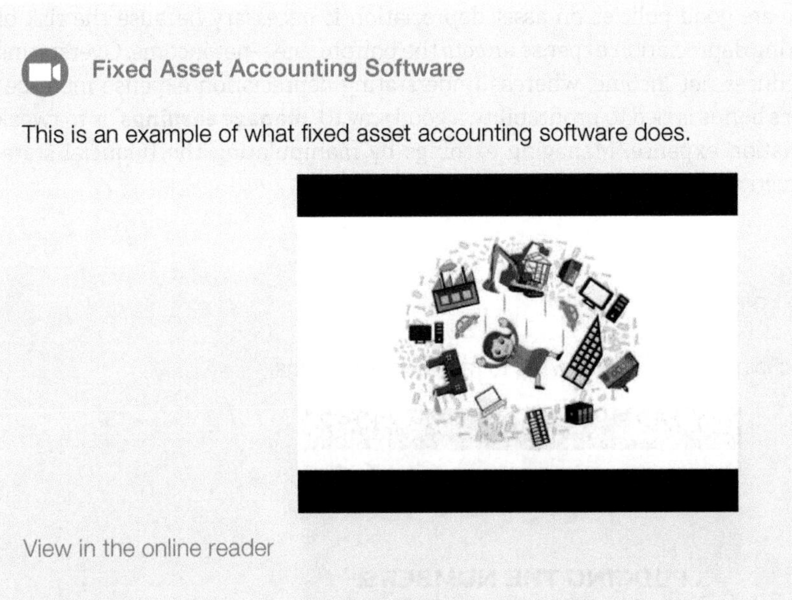

View in the online reader

Remember from your financial accounting courses how to account for repairs and maintenance? In certain cases, it is just a current expense; however, under certain circumstances the repair (if it extends the asset's life) may be capitalized. When processing an invoice for equipment repairs and maintenance, the accountant might not initially know that the repair extended the asset's life, so the cost of the repair could be improperly accounted for on the financial statements.

Depreciation is a means to show on the financial statements that an asset is used over time; however, **asset disposal** truly means the organization is ready to let the asset go. Organizations should have a policy regarding asset disposal and should also require authorization for disposal of assets.

An organization can have many transactions throughout the year that add new assets and dispose of old assets; it is important for organizations to track their assets and to reconcile assets to their ledger to ensure that all assets are accountable and usable. The importance of planning for asset purchases as well as asset dispositions cannot be stressed enough.

depreciation

A noncash transaction on the financial statements that estimates an asset's use over time.

asset disposal

Organization is no longer using the asset and sells it or disposes of the asset, which removes it from the financial statements.

Risks and Controls

Because the overall objective is to safeguard assets, risks are related to the fixed asset cycle:

1. Asset theft
2. Improperly accounting for the asset acquisition price
3. Improperly expensing or capitalizing repairs
4. Improperly calculating depreciation expense
5. Lack of authorization for asset acquisition or disposal
6. Inadequate insurance levels on assets

Controls needed to reduce the risk of asset loss include proper authorization to acquire the assets, tagging the physical assets, and reconciling physical assets to the amount on the general ledger annually to determine if any assets have been lost or are unusable. The risk of not properly accounting for asset capitalization requires good policies and knowledgeable personnel who understand how to account for assets according to generally accepted accounting principles (GAAP).

manage earnings

An unethical practice to manipulate the financial statements.

Ensuring that there are good policies on asset depreciation is necessary because the risk of understating or overstating depreciation expense affects the bottom line—net income. Overstating depreciation expense reduces net income, whereas understating depreciation expense increases net income. If a manager's bonus is tied to profitability, a good way to "**manage earnings**" is to tweak (understate) the depreciation expense. Managing earnings by manipulating the financial statements is an *unethical* practice.

 Techniques in Earnings Management

This video provides techniques of unethical ways to manipulate earnings.

View in the online reader

Proper authorization is required for asset disposal to reduce the risk of theft. The organization must ensure that good segregation of duties exist in the asset cycle. A common fraud scheme involves an employee who has authorization and custody of assets. The employee could steal the asset, give it to a friend or sell it for money, and write the asset off the organization's books. Lastly, it is often a good policy for organizations that have a significant amount of assets on their balance sheet to review their insurance policies to ensure adequate coverage of their assets. This review on liability coverage can be done each year prior to renewing the insurance policy.

14.2 Financing Cycle

Learning Objectives

At the end of this section, students should be able to:

1. Understand the objectives of the financing cycle.
2. Evaluate risks and controls associated with equity and debt.

Most organizations at some point in their history need additional money to grow or sustain their business. Funds that come into the organization are in the form of equity (e.g., issuing stock) or debt (e.g., bank loan).

Objective and Conceptualization

The main objective of the financing cycle is to properly account for the equity or acquiring of capital for an organization and includes some or all the following functions:

1. Acquiring capital—issuing stock
2. Dividends
3. Stock options
4. Reacquiring stock (treasury shares)

Funds received by the organization through financing debt include some or all the following functions:

1. New debt (short-term/long-term obligation)
2. Interest expense
3. Debt retirement

Risks and Controls

Risks of acquiring financing through equity include improperly accounting for the equity, making errors when classifying equity, and improperly accounting for dividends. Good corporate governance and corporate boards provide a line of defense to reduce risks related to equity and debt. Properly accounting for dividends and treasury stock are verified through the board minutes.

Risk associated with stock options requires proper authorization of stock option issuance to employees and properly accounting for the value of stock options on the financial statements. Proper segregation of duties is needed between stock option authorization and recording functions.

Risks associated with debt include improperly accounting for the debt, improperly classifying short- and long-term debt obligations, and errors in calculating interest. All debt should be properly authorized and accounted for according to the loan documents and amortization tables provided by the bank or leasing company.

14.3 Payroll Cycle

Learning Objectives

At the end of this section, students should be able to:

1. Understand the objectives of the payroll cycle.
2. Evaluate risks and controls associated with the payroll cycle.

All employees need to get paid, and all organizations must comply with federal and state payroll tax laws. Depending on the state, payroll taxes also include unemployment, disability, or city payroll taxes. The organization needs to make sure that employees are paid the correct amount and comply with the payroll tax laws.

Objective and Conceptualization

The primary objective of the payroll cycle is to pay employees for the labor (services) and comply with labor and tax laws. Employees are paid either through an annual salary or by an hourly wage. Hourly employees generally must use a timecard machine to record their hours worked. The payroll cycle has four major functions:

1. Onboarding employees
2. Processing payroll
3. Filing payroll related tax returns
4. Offboarding employees leaving the company

Depending on the size of the organization, these functions may be in-house or contracted to a third party (e.g., processing payroll checks and payroll tax returns). However, many functions must be managed throughout the cycle, such as when an employee begins working, his or her tenure at the company, as well as when the employee leaves the company.

Onboarding and offboarding employees usually begin in the human resources department and timely reporting of employee hires and exits is required to the accounting department. Employee and payroll information must be confidential, and limiting the access is required. In addition, when an employee leaves the company, laws require timely payment of all monies due, including wages and paid time off. Sometimes it is at the time of dismissal, while other states give up to 72 hours to make the payment. Hence, accounting and human resources must be in communication with each other.

Whether your organization does payroll in-house or uses a third-party processor, certain tasks or reviews occur within the organization:

1. Verify employees start and exit date for new employees or employees that have left
2. Verify time worked (timecards should be approved by the manager)
3. Authorization of salary increases or bonus payments
4. Review payroll report before and after processing
5. Timely submission of payroll tax reports
6. Conduct variance analysis

As with any systems-related decision, you would want to estimate the costs and benefits before deciding to outsource to a third party or bringing the payroll in-house. Most small businesses outsource their payroll and post a journal entry for the payroll each time it is run. Small businesses choose to outsource to a third-party payroll processor to reduce errors relating to tax compliance.

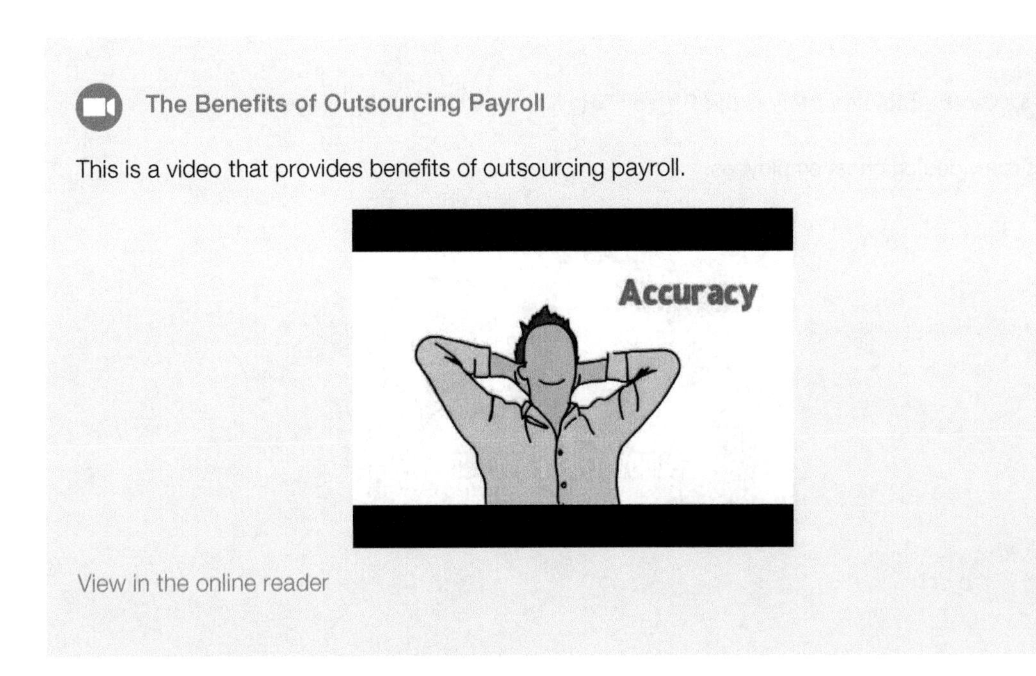

The Benefits of Outsourcing Payroll

This is a video that provides benefits of outsourcing payroll.

View in the online reader

Risks and Controls

Many risks are associated with payroll. The most obvious is theft of cash, which can occur when authorization and custody duties are not segregated. For example, someone who has access to the payroll records could increase her salary without proper authorization. In addition, a manager could set up paperwork for a fake or (ghost) employee and then take the fake employee's check and cash it for himself.

Risks associated with the payroll cycle include the following:

1. Theft of cash (payroll checks)
2. Unauthorized changes to the payroll system
3. Inaccurate wage or tax calculations
4. Incorrect posting to the wrong accounting period
5. Noncompliance with laws

Controls to help mitigate these risks include limiting access to payroll records and the payroll system. Only authorized employees should have access to the payroll records, and proper access controls should be limited to only certain areas of the system.

A payroll change report should be run and reviewed to verify all changes are matched with supporting documentation (i.e., wage increase). All changes to employees' pay must be authorized to prevent fraudulent payment or creating "**ghost employees**." Ghost employees are when someone is not an employee of the company but is getting a paycheck! Besides making sure that you have hired honest and reputable employees and have done preventive controls of verification and authorization of employee pay, the business owner can hand out paychecks to employees.

ghost employees

Someone who gets a paycheck but is not an employee of the company.

 Old Employees Still on the Payroll? How to Spot Ghost Employees

This is a video on ghost employees.

View in the online reader

imprest account

Separate bank account used to handle specific payments of a fixed amount such as payroll.

Many organizations, large and small, create a separate checking account only for payroll to limit their exposure to fraud (called a payroll clearing or **imprest account**). When payroll is run for each pay period, sufficient funds are provided to cover the employees' pay and the taxes. This amount can be moved over to the payroll checking account. A separate checking account for payroll can limit employees from trying to increase the amount on their paychecks or someone fraudulently writing a check off the account itself. By limiting the amount of money in the payroll checking account, fraudulent activity would be more pronounced, particularly if the bank notifies management of insufficient funds in the account. If payroll checks cleared from the organization's main operating bank account, it would be much harder to catch this type of problem.

To prevent errors in calculating pay and taxes, verifying hours worked from the timecard after the manager has reviewed them can detect any potential errors. Reviewing the payroll report before submitting to the payroll processing company can prevent errors input into the payroll system. Automating payroll as much as possible can prevent human error. Conducting variance analysis often related to payroll as well as using budgeted information can identify potential areas of fraud. For example, a manufacturing organization may increase production to a second shift. This increase in hours would be accounted for after conducting variance analysis with production information. For organizations that are service based, again variance analysis would show that any increases to salary expense should have an explanation (e.g., bonuses given in December).

Key Takeaways

In this chapter we have learned about three functions that impact organizations: fixed assets, financing, and payroll. In addition, we have learned about risks involved with each of these areas as well as controls that mitigate these risks. In the next and final chapter, we will discuss financial and management reporting risks and controls.

14.4 End-of-Chapter Exercises

Exercises

1. What is the fixed asset cycle?
2. Why is it important to keep track of fixed assets?
3. Why is separation of duties important when disposing of fixed assets?
4. How can earnings management occur with fixed assets?
5. What is the financing cycle, and what functions are associated with it?
6. What is treasury stock?
7. What is the primary objective of the payroll cycle?
8. What is a ghost employee?
9. What is an imprest account?
10. What is the benefit of using an imprest account for payroll?
11. What function is not part of the fixed asset cycle?
    a. disposition
    b. acquisition
    c. repairs and maintenance
    d. lease payments
12. ID asset tags can be designed with ________.
    a. color coding
    b. barcoding
    c. numbers
    d. All of the above
13. Which of the following statements is false?
    a. A company can have different depreciation expense for an asset-book depreciation and tax depreciation expense.
    b. Depreciation expenses can be different for each asset category.
    c. Lost assets should still be depreciated on the books.
    d. Depreciation expense is an administrative task to show on the financial statements how assets are used over time.
14. Which one of the controls below prevents improper disposal of an asset?
    a. authorization
    b. asset ID tag
    c. reconciliation of physical assets to the general ledger
    d. verifying depreciation expense
15. The financing cycle includes which of the following functions?
    a. issuing stock
    b. issuing stock options
    c. reacquiring stock
    d. All of the above
16. Which risk is not associated with issuing debt in the financing cycle?
    a. properly classifying short- and long-term debt obligations
    b. lack of authorization

c. errors in calculating amount of dividends
d. errors in calculating interest expense

17. Which of the following functions are not part of the payroll cycle?
    a. filing sales tax report
    b. onboarding new employees
    c. updating promoted employee salary
    d. offboarding employee who left the company
18. A ghost employee is
    a. someone who works at the company during the night shift.
    b. someone who telecommutes and works from home.
    c. a fake employee set up in the payroll system.
    d. an employee who is out sick.
19. What control helps detect potential fraud associated with payroll?
    a. imprest account
    b. authorization of wages
    c. timeclocks
    d. reviewing insurance levels
20. What control helps prevent errors associated with calculating pay?
    a. review of timecards by manager
    b. review of payroll report before submitting payroll to third-party payroll processor
    c. automating payroll
    d. All of the above

CHAPTER 15

Financial Reporting

Throughout this book you have learned about the different transaction cycles; in this chapter, we put it all together to see that the detail transactions are aggregated to create financial statements and other management reports. These various reports are used by management to make decisions in operating the business. As accountants, you may find yourself involved with more than just the financial statements and responsible for preparing management reports that use key performance indicators. **Key performance indicators (KPIs)** can be financial or nonfinancial as well as quantitative or qualitative. Going back to Chapter 1, we learned about the different types of data that may be used for KPIs.

key performance indicators (KPIs)

Key measure identified by management and may be either quantitative or qualitative.

15.1 Preparing Financial Statements

Learning Objectives

At the end of this section, students should be able to:

1. Identify the processes involved in generating an organization's financial reports.
2. Understand how the general ledger is updated, how adjusting entries get posted to the general ledger, and the role of reversing entries.
3. Understand and evaluate risks and controls related to financial reporting.
4. Understand what XBRL is and why it's useful.

After an organization's revenue and expenditure transactions are captured and processed as described in the preceding chapters, the data must be transferred to a centralized general ledger where they are stored and organized in a way that enables reports to be prepared to meet the information management needs. We learned in Chapter 2 how transactions are organized into a chart of accounts.

Objective and Conceptualization

The processes for accomplishing the task of financial reporting are as follows:

- Post/update the general ledger
- Prepare a preliminary trial balance
- Prepare and post adjusting entries
- Prepare financial statements
- Create other managerial reports

In a manual system, the bookkeeper would normally post the totals from each of the transaction journals to the general ledger. In a computerized system, each of the computerized subsystems would create a summary journal entry that represents the results of all transactions that occurred during a given period (usually a month). For example, the revenue cycle subsystem would generate a summary journal entry debiting cash and accounts receivable and crediting sales for all transactions in the subsystem made during the accounting period.

The main risks to the system at this point are inaccurate or unauthorized journal entries. The controls to minimize these problems would include edit checks to ensure the accuracy and completeness of the data and approvals to ensure that only authorized entries are being made.

After the journals have been summarized and posted to the general ledger, each account is then balanced; that is, a net figure is derived by balancing all of the debits and credits. This is called a trial balance. The bookkeeper or computer would then make a list of each account in the chart of accounts with its accompanying debit or credit balance. All of the debit balances would then be added up and a total created. All of the credit balances would be similarly added up and a total produced. The totals of all the debits should equal the totals of all the credits.

Role of Adjusting Entries

adjusting journal entries

Journal entries.

Adjusting journal entries are normally prepared by high-level accountants after they have performed various account analyses to ensure that previous accounting is accurate. Four types of adjusting entries occur at the end of an accounting period:

1. Correcting
2. Accruals
3. Deferrals
4. Estimates

correcting journal entries

Journal entry used to correct an error.

Misposted or erroneous amounts are normally fixed with **correcting journal entries**. In addition, accruals are made for expenses that were incurred in the accounting period and not yet paid. Deferrals are for revenues that have not been earned in the accounting period but monies have been received. Estimates are also necessary for such items as bad debts, depreciation, and warranty expense.

accrual journal entry

Adjusting journal entry made at the end of an accounting period for expenses incurred but not yet paid.

Adjusting journal entries should be authorized and accounted for and generally use a standard journal voucher form to make the journal entry (post to the general ledger). The journal voucher should be reviewed and approved by an independent person in accounting. Figure 15.1 is an example of a journal voucher authorizing an expense **accrual journal entry** where the vendor invoice is for expenses incurred during the accounting period (December), but the vendor invoice was not processed in the accounts payable system until January 4. When processing the vendor invoice, the system automatically posts the expense to January, leaving a dilemma—the expense was for December, but it posts to January. Because the accrued expense was done in December, to properly have the expense in the correct month, the expense from processing accounts payable is posting to January; reversing the accrual will offset the January accounts payable posting. Therefore, the expense is not double counted.

reversing journal entry

Journal entry that automatically reverses the accrual on the first day of the following month.

Because this happens all the time at the end of an accounting period, it is important to note that many accounting systems will have a feature where the accrual adjusting entry will "reverse" automatically in the subsequent period. This is called a **reversing journal entry** so the accounting department doesn't have to remember to manually reverse the accrual when the expense is processed in the next month. This is generally an option that you would need to select when you are posting the journal entry.

FIGURE 15.1 Journal Voucher Example

Journal Voucher

Number 1152
Date 12/31/2020

Account	Account Name	Amount Dr.	Amount Cr.
7250	Equipment Repair Expense	$ 8,990	
2450	Accrued Expenses		$ 8,990

Description: To accrue vendor invoice #2348 for equipment repairs in December but processed/paid in January.

Approved by H. Fisher

As a reminder from your introductory financial accounting course, the debits and credits from the accrual in Figure 15.1 for December and January in the general journal as well as what was processed from accounts payable on January 4 ensure that the expense is recorded in the appropriate accounting period. Figure 15.2 shows the sequence of these journal entries related to this one transaction.

FIGURE 15.2 Sequence of Entries

	Account #	Account Name	Dr.	Cr.
Accrual	December 31			
	7250	Equipment Repair Expense	8,990	
	2450	Accrued Expenses		8,990
Reversing	January 1			
	2450	Accrued Expenses	8,990	
	7250	Equipment Repair Expense		8,990
A/P	January 4			
	7250	Equipment Repair Expense	8,990	
	2300	Accounts Payable		8,990

Deferral journal entries include when cash is received before the revenue is earned, which is known as deferred revenue.

deferral journal entries

Adjusting journal entry made at the end of an accounting period for revenues not earned but monies collected.

 Adjusting Journal Entries

This is a video that explains adjusting journal entries for unearned revenues.

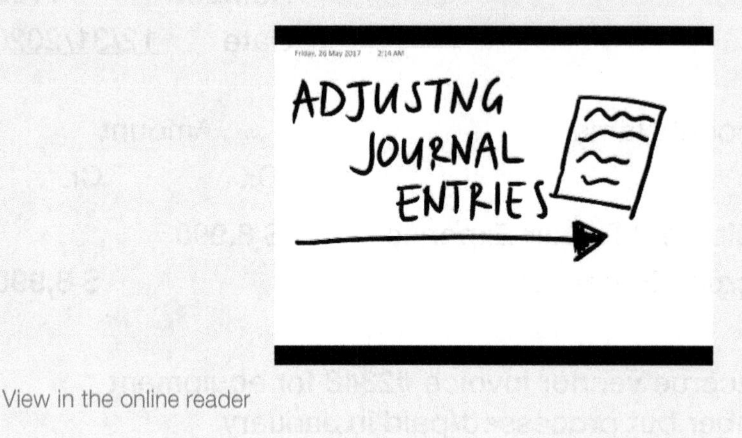

View in the online reader

estimate journal entry

Adjusting journal entry for depreciation or bad debt expense for the accounting period.

At the end of each month, adjusting **estimate journal entry** is to book depreciation expense for each month. You might recall doing this journal entry in your entry level accounting course. After adjusting entries are posted, financial statements are generated and reviewed for completeness and accuracy.

Risks and Controls

internal controls over financial reporting (ICFR)

Controls over financial reporting that provide confidence in an organization's financial statements and are good for the capital markets.

More attention is on organizations having good **internal controls over financial reporting (ICFR)**. Good internal controls over financial reporting provide confidence in an organization's financial statements and are good for the capital markets. This allows investors to have trust in the capital markets. The process includes the following functions:

- Risk assessment
- Design and testing of controls
- Documentation

Internal Controls Over Financial Reporting Overview

This is a video that discusses the importance of ICFR.

View in the online reader

The overall objective of risk relating to financial statements is the risk of material misstatement. Organizations need to have a high-level review to understand what areas of the financial statements and the general ledger accounts are at risk. Data analytics is helpful in assessing this kind of risk because an organization can focus its assessment on accounts that may be at a higher risk than other accounts. For example, assessing accounts at risk may be based on activity level, complexity of transactions, and type of transaction (e.g., manual versus automatic).

Controls to mitigate misstatements include automating routine transactions to reduce errors (e.g., robotic process automation). Accountants rely heavily on spreadsheets to do analysis of calculations to post journal entries; however, spreadsheets can have errors, which create financial statement risk. Centralizing accounting systems and using software that is in-scope of the financial statements controls for this type of risk. Spreadsheets are considered "out of scope" of the AIS. An example of this is to look at a depreciation schedule that calculates the depreciation expense journal entry. If the formula on the spreadsheet is incorrect, depreciation expense could be under- or over expensed and affect the income statement. The recommendation is to use the fixed asset module in the AIS where the depreciation calculation does not rely on a human to code the formula. Some systems (e.g., Blackline.com) automate the accounting process, such as reconciliations, and standardize the process to reduce the risk of spreadsheet errors; these systems work within the scope of the AIS.

 Blackline Account Reconciliations Overview

This is a video that demonstrates the reconciliation process using Blackline software.

View in the online reader

What Is XBRL?

As a result of the internet, organizations are also able to produce their financial statements in digital form using a language called XBRL (Extensible Business ReportingLanguage). XML was developed in the late 1990s to describe the content of the data being presented on a web page. Digitized financial statements are easier for investors and analysts to use and allow them to spend more time on analysis than on gathering data for analysis. Among their many efficiencies, digital statements mean that users do not have to retype the financial information and the information is more easily transmitted and shared. Furthermore, public companies in the United States are being required to file their financial statements with the Securities and Exchange Commission (SEC) in this format.

inline XBRL

Format for filing financial statement with the SEC using HTML documents.

According to the SEC, **Inline XBRL** is a format that allows filers to embed XBRL code directly into their HTML formatted filings. This would alleviate the need for a separate file and the possibility of discrepancies between the official filing and the separate XBRL file. It also makes the filings human-readable as well as machine-readable. The SEC says that Inline XBRL has the potential to reduce preparation costs and to increase its use by investors and information intermediaries. It can also, combined with the features and capabilities of an Inline XBRL viewing tool, provide visual and other analytical information about the SEC filing. Moreover, an open source Inline XBRL Viewer has been made freely available to the public. In 2018, the SEC voted to begin requiring its filing in Inline XBRL format over the next three years, beginning in late 2019 through 2021, depending on the size of the filing organization.

This is a video that demonstrates how the Inline XBRL viewer works.

View in the online reader

In order to achieve the benefits of XBRL, the method for transporting the data must be cost effective. This will generally be accomplished by use of the internet. With XBRL built into the enterprise's financial reporting system and related internet connectivity, financial reporting will become continuous. In some cases, financial information will be available in real time. The advantage of this is that more current financial information will be available for decision-making. With more up-to-date information, decisions should become more accurate, and financial markets should become more efficient. XBRL in turn creates a standard digital language for business. By using this standard format, business and government can eliminate the time and expenses incurred each year to key and rekey all the financial information in the world. By using a standard format, the information can be directly transmitted to regulatory institutions, taxing authorities, financial analysts, and auditors without any conversion. The cost savings that will be created by these new standards will be significant.

15.2 Preparing Management Reports

Learning Objectives

At the end of this section, students should be able to:

1. Understand the role of management reporting.
2. Understand the purpose and benefits of balanced scorecards.
3. Understand the risks associated with management reporting.

The final activity in the financial reporting cycle involves the creation of various types of management reports. These reports range from responsibility accounting performance reports and flexible budgets to balanced scorecards or other specific reports using the KPIs that management needs. Responsibility reports break down an organization's performance by the specific subunits that directly control the activities.

Objective and Conceptualization

With the advances in relational database technology and enterprise resource planning systems, organizations can now produce performance reports containing financial and nonfinancial metrics on both financial and operational performance. This level of integration allows the accounting system to produce information of more strategic value. Simply focusing on balancing the budget or cutting costs may not be the smartest strategy. Improving quality and an organization's reputation may be as important or more in the long run.

balanced scorecard

Multidimensional report used to measure an organization's performance.

One such management report is the **balanced scorecard**,[1] which provides a multidimensional perspective of an organization's performance by containing goals and measures in four areas: learning and innovation, internal business processes, customer relations, and traditional finance. Instead of focusing on traditional financial measures alone and expecting that they will produce results on their own, the balanced scorecard method assumes that knowledge leads to improved business processes, which in turn lead to improved customer relations and that this ultimately shows up in improved financial results. Learning and innovation can take the form of human resource development as well as new products, product features, and approaches to making a product.

The Balanced Scorecard

This is a video that explains the Balanced Scorecard.

View in the online reader

For example, let's say that a company wants to improve its financial results and decides to provide specialized training to its employees. The assumption here is that the specialized training will result in better service to its customers, which in turn will improve customer satisfaction. Ultimately, the goal is to turn happy customers into increased sales. To implement this system, the company would not only develop learning, internal process, and customer goals, but also create measures (leading indicators) for each of the goals to monitor and targets to work toward. This holistic approach is designed to better enable the enterprise to add value. Figure 15.3 provides an example of a balanced scorecard.

FIGURE 15.3 Balanced Scorecard Example

	Goals	Measures	Targets
Financial Perspective	Increase Sales	Increase Number of Sales	10% Revenue Increase
Customer Relations	Enhance Customer Satisfaction	Survey Results	15% Improvement
Internal Business Processes	Improve Customer Service	Complaint Reports	Decrease 10%
Learning and Innovation	Provide More Specialized Training	New Targeted Courses	1–2 per Quarter

Adapted from the *Balanced Scorecard* by Robert S. Kaplan and Dave P. Norton. Harvard Business School Press, 1996.

Risks and Controls

Perhaps the greatest risk for organizations is using financial and nonfinancial indicators that measure the wrong thing! You may think this is obvious; however, you may have also heard this saying: "What gets measured, gets managed."

What happens then if you end up measuring the wrong performance indicator? It means you are focusing your time and energy on the wrong area, which has an overall impact on the organization.

For the most part, financial measures are easy for us to understand since there are **GAAP** and we all understand what cash and inventory are; however, issues can arise when an organization is determining its nonfinancial performance measures. According to Ittner and Larcker (2003), organizations need to tie their nonfinancial performance measures to strategy. Merely adopting a "boilerplate" balance scorecard may not be enough if it doesn't map back to your organization's specific strategy. In Ittner and Larcker's (2003) study, they found that out of 157 organizations surveyed, only 23 percent had verified the cause-effect model of the nonfinancial performance measure to the strategy driver outcome. The lesson from this study is that picking the right nonfinancial performance measure matters.

GAAP

Generally accepted accounting principles.

Key Takeaways

In this chapter, we examined the various processes involved in generating an organization's financial reports. We gained an understanding of how the general ledger is updated and how adjusting entries are posted and needed to produce month-end financial statements. We also learned that these adjusting entries can be reversed to prevent the transaction from being booked twice. We learned about the risks and controls related to preparing financial statements and how XBRL provides an efficient means of reporting financial information to the SEC. We learned about the balanced scorecard as a management report. We saw the threats that occur at every stage of the process and the controls that can be used to mitigate them.

References

- Ittner, Christopher D., and David F. Larcker. "Coming Up Short on Nonfinancial Performance Measurement." *Harvard Business Review* 81, no. 11 (2003): 88–95.
- Kaplan, Robert S., and David P. Norton. "The Balanced Scorecard—Measures That Drive Performance." *Harvard Business Review* (January–February 1992): 71–79.

15.3 End-of-Chapter Exercises

Exercises

1. How does the process of generating an organization's financial reports work?
2. Explain how the general ledger is updated, how adjusting entries get posted to the general ledger, and how financial statements are prepared.
3. Provide an example of each of the four types of adjusting journal entries.
4. During what step in the process of creating an organization's financial statements is the risk of fraud the greatest? Why?
5. What is ICFR, and why is it so important?
6. Discuss the various types of managerial reports that can be produced by an accounting system.
7. What are the purpose and benefits of balanced scorecards?
8. What is XBRL?
9. Why would a company want to publish it financial statements in XBRL?
10. Can you think of a reason why an investor would want to use the Inline XBRL viewer?
11. In a computerized accounting system, the source for updating the general ledger from the transaction cycles is usually
    a. a summary journal entry.
    b. an adjusting entry.
    c. a preliminary trial balance.
    d. a journal voucher.
12. If an accountant uses a preliminary trial balance and notes that an expense has been recorded for an insurance expenditure that will be incurred in a later accounting period when the coverage begins, the accountant should make which of the following entries?
    a. an accrual
    b. a deferral
    c. a summary journal entry
    d. an estimate
13. To minimize the risk that a depreciation entry might be overlooked in closing the books, which of the following would most likely reduce this risk?
    a. a summary journal entry
    b. an accrual
    c. a deferral
    d. a standard journal entry
14. A journal voucher is likely to be most effective in preventing fraud when it is

a. prepared by a competent high-level accountant.
b. accurately described in the description field.
c. used as a standard journal entry.
d. approved by an independent person.

15. Which of the following is primarily designed to improve the efficiency of the financial reporting cycle?
   a. a relational database
   b. XML
   c. XBRL
   d. a balanced scorecard
16. The number of goods counted per receiving department worker per day is a metric that would most likely appear in which performance category on a balanced scorecard?
   a. financial
   b. customer relations
   c. internal business processes
   d. learning and growth
17. Which of the following linkages show the implied causal relationships among the categories of the balanced scorecard?
   a. Financial -> Customer relations -> Internal processes -> Learning and innovation
   b. Customer relations -> Financial -> Internal processes -> Learning and innovation
   c. Internal processes -> Customer relations -> Learning and innovation -> Financial
   d. Learning and innovation -> Internal processes -> Customer relations -> Financial
18. Balanced scorecards in their current form are more likely applicable to which of the following type(s) of organizations?
   a. not-for-profit organizations
   b. governmental units
   c. for-profit enterprises
   d. They are equally applicable in their current form to all of the above types of organizations.
19. What is the biggest risk of managerial reporting?
   a. using qualitative measures
   b. not tying your measures to strategy
   c. not using a balanced scorecard
   d. not using responsibility accounting
20. Which of the following is not an advantage of using XBRL?
   a. continuous financial reporting and readily available financial information
   b. continuous auditing that can be performed by intelligent agents
   c. enterprises adopting XBRL benefiting from increased coverage and analysis by financial analysis and stakeholders
   d. the high cost of converting to XBRL being passed on to consumers
21. Which of the following is not a risk associated with updating the general ledger and an appropriate control procedure that could be used to minimize the risk?
   a. inaccurate journal entries: edit checks
   b. unauthorized journal entries: approvals
   c. neglecting to make a recurring adjusting entry: journal vouchers
   d. All of the above are adequate controls given the presented risk.
22. **CREATING A BALANCED SCORECARD Facebook:** Expanding Its View on Performance

   Facebook is an internet-based social networking service that has grown rapidly since it was launched in 2004. Unlike many internet startups that came before it and struggled to make a profit, Facebook was profitable when it had its initial public offering in 2012 and has grown its net income from $3.7 billion on $17.9 billion in sales in 2015 to $15.9 billion on $40.3 billion in sales in 2017. In order to continue its income and sales growth, Facebook must either increase its customer base (roughly 2.2 billion active users by January 2018), derive more profit from existing customers, or decrease its costs. Key to Facebook's success is the capabilities of its networking service and its ability to maintain positive customer relations. Although Facebook has enjoyed a warm reception in the financial markets, it has been criticized for its heavy reliance on coal for electricity to power its data centers. Facebook has also been criticized for some of its privacy policies, violating its own minimum age policy, and difficulties users have in controlling what appears on their home page and what gets emailed to them.

Required:

Assume that you have been asked by the Facebook's chief financial officer to help the company improve its financial results. Identify a financial goal that you believe it should be working on and establish goals, measures, and targets for each of the four perspectives of performance you think the company could emphasize to meet this financial goal using the format for a balanced scorecard as depicted in Figure 15.3. Create the table manually or with word-processing or spreadsheet software.

23. **Creating a Balanced Scorecard:** Link a strategy through measures on the balanced scorecard.

Select a publicly held company that you admire, such as Chipotle, Apple, Tesla, etc.

Required:

1. Create a balanced scorecard to communicate one strategy (some organizations will list out multiple strategies, but you just need to completely cover one); the format can be in a table so that it would look like this:

	Goals	Measures	Targets

Strategy: (this is where you put the strategy you are linking goals and measures to)

2. Write six short paragraphs explaining your balanced scorecard:
   a. First paragraph: the vision/mission of the organization and the strategy
      i. Why did you focus on this particular strategy? (Is it the main one or in your opinion the most important? Why?)
   b. Second paragraph through fifth paragraph, discuss the specific balanced scorecard component objectives and measures chosen and elaborate on how they connect back to the strategy.
      i. Examine the measures you have selected, keeping in mind that a good balanced scorecard should have a mix of measures (input/process/outcome). Make sure that in your paragraphs you identify your measures as input/process/outcome.
   c. Read the organization's discussion on risk and write a brief paragraph about your thoughts as to this discussion. Is the organization focused mainly on external risks or internal risks? In your opinion, what risk that is discussed is deemed to have the biggest effect on the strategy you chose for your balanced scorecard?

Endnote

1. Based on Robert S. Kaplan and David P. Norton, "The Balanced Scorecard – Measures That Drive Performance," *Harvard Business Review* (January–February 1992): 71–79.

Index